North American B-25 Mitchell

Other titles in the Crowood Aviation Series

North American
B-25 Mitchell

Jerry Scutts

The Crowood Press

First published in 2001 by
The Crowood Press Ltd
Ramsbury, Marlborough
Wiltshire SN8 2HR

British Library Cataloguing-in-Publication Data
A catalogue record for this book is available from
the British Library.

ISBN 1 86126 394 5

Acknowledgements

A book such as this draws upon many sources and calls for the assistance of numerous individuals and organizations. My principal thanks must go to Norman L. Avery for photographs and ever-helpful data on all things B-25; M/Sgt David A. Byrd, USAF of the US National Archives, who kindly supplied a copy of the recently declassified accident report on the crash of the NA-40; Ian Carter; Jim Crow; Clarence Fu; Dan Hagedorn; Jim Halley; Jack Lambert; Howerd Levy; Nicholas R. Loveless; Frank F. Smith; John Stanaway and Geoffrey J. Thomas for very full data on RAF PR operations in the Far East. The Imperial War Museum, North American Aviation and the United States Air Force, Navy and Marines also helped immeasurably with the all-important photographs. Some data is quoted from the newsletters of the 57th Bomb Wing Association, with kind permission. My thanks to everyone.

Typefaces used: Goudy (text),
Cheltenham (headings).

Typeset and designed by
D & N Publishing
Baydon, Marlborough, Wiltshire.

Printed and bound in Great Britain by
Bookcraft, Bath.

Contents

Introduction

Of all the combat aircraft that fought on the Allied side in World War II, the North American B-25 Mitchell was one of the best and most well known. One of two medium bombers fielded by the United States, the B-25 gained lasting fame early in its combat career by flying the April 1942 carrier raid on Tokyo, an operation it has been linked with ever since.

The aircraft was named after Gen William C. 'Billy' Mitchell, the Assistant Chief of the US Air Service, whose outspoken views on the poor state of American airpower led to his court martial and resignation in 1925. Just over a decade later Mitchell's foresight could be put into context: the need for a new generation of military aircraft was becoming acute. In service by the time the US went to war, the B-25 was in the forefront of those modern combat aircraft that would serve America and her allies so well in history's greatest conflict.

Even before the famous Tokyo raid of April 1942 the B-25 was at war, fighting a rearguard action against the Japanese in the Pacific. When it first came to Europe to equip groups in the Western Desert opposing the Afrika Korps, the B-25 proved a reliable aircraft against heavy opposition. In time, B-25 units spread their wings over the battlefields of Italy, China, Burma, New Guinea and innumerable Pacific islands, their crews carving an enviable place in the annals of American airpower. Supplied to Britain, the Mitchell served the RAF well in the days when the war in Europe was anything but an assured victory for the Allies. In Australian, Dutch and Russian hands B-25s also fought the Germans, while Marine Corps pilots developed the art of close air support for their 'Leathernecks' in the bitter fight for the Philippines.

Along the way, a docile medium bomber was turned into the most heavily armed ground strafer in the word. Equipped even with an aerial field gun, North American's flying artillery cut a swathe of destruction through Axis forces over all the major battlefronts until final victory was achieved.

As the most numerous bomber to survive into peacetime, the B-25 enjoyed a civilian career, became a film star, and restored pride to far-flung air forces, and finally emerged as a prized warbird, the star of numerous air shows around the world. Museums have preserved B-25s in some numbers, so future generations may appreciate what the aircraft meant to the US war effort during the most terrible conflict in history.

This book is respectfully and admiringly dedicated to all those who returned safely, and particularly to those who made the supreme sacrifice while flying in B-25s.

Jeremy C. Scutts
London, autumn 2000

CHAPTER ONE

Ambitious Project

As part of the massive and exceedingly rapid expansion of the US aviation industry in the early years of the 1940s, North American Aviation of Inglewood, California, gave its own forces and those of the country's allies two of the best military concerns that were bought and incorporated into it, NAA developed more or less in parallel with the rest of the US aeronautics industry, to the point where, when massive expansion of the US air forces was called for, the industry rose to the challenge.

James H. 'Dutch' Kindelberger (left) and Lee Atwood, the two men who principally guided North American Aviation through its wartime years. via NAA

aircraft in the world: the B-25 Mitchell and the P-51 Mustang. This was a quite remarkable achievement by a company with modest resources that was only a little over a decade old when war broke out in Europe in 1939, and which, shortly before that date, had built nothing much larger than trainers. Formed in 1928 from a not untypical amalgam of smaller

Yet in the early 1930s the industry remained small, and orders from the US government were numbered in tens rather than hundreds. Expansion, with the express aim of modernizing military forces, was slow, even though it was generally agreed to be important at home. Military budgets remained modest as the nation finally emerged from the horrors of the

depression years – but business was picking up: in aviation, American companies were exploring numerous innovations, and foreign governments, particularly those representing European countries, looked with interest at what was then being built on the other side of the Atlantic. Considering the worrying rise of dictatorships in Germany and Italy, their need to acquire aircraft were perceived to be even greater than Australia, South America and Scandinavia, which similarly saw America as a source of supply for a whole range of aircraft, both military and civil. Japan's war with China in 1937 and the civil war in Spain which had begun the previous year, only served to point up the real threat that some areas of the world were beginning to face. These, and other 'localized' conflicts of the late 1930s, were soon demonstrating the significant part that airpower had to play in modern war.

An indication of the urgent need to re-equip national air arms with modern aeroplanes was demonstrated most forcibly by France, which went shopping for various types to replace its woefully inadequate military aircraft. American aircraft would eventually supplement indigenous new designs being produced under a nationalized industrial system initiated in 1936 that was proving to be inefficient and agonizingly slow in meeting delivery schedules. Despite outside help, France would ultimately suffer the trauma of military defeat, the consequence of rearming with 'too little, too late'.

Although it had its own well-established aircraft industry, Britain also placed orders with American firms, primarily for types that would save on somewhat limited production resources. A 1938 order for 200 North American Harvard trainers for the RAF was, from the American standpoint, unprecedentedly huge. It contrasted sharply with the delivery of sixty BC-1 trainers and O-47 observation aircraft to the US Army Air Corps in August 1938 – the largest order yet placed with a single US company since World War I.

NA-21 3-4-37
LEFT SIDE VIEW

(Above) The NA-21, seen in early 1937, was NAA's first tentative venture into the medium bomber market. via NAA

Joe Barton (left) and Ed Virgin were responsible for much of the B-25 prototype flying and flight testing throughout its production span. via NAA

B-25 Forebear

For the first half decade or so of its existence, NAA had not ventured into the design of aircraft larger than those powered by a single engine, and had generally restricted its activities to building trainers. The NA-16 of 1935 was the forerunner of the BT-9, BC-1 and AT-6 Texan/Harvard line that included some of the most successful aircraft of all time. The GA-43 ten-seat passenger liner of 1933 had been considerably larger than a military trainer, but was still powered by a single engine. Five GA-43s were built before the government decreed that for safety reasons, airliners would in future be required to be powered by at least two engines.

Metal was cut on something more ambitious in 1937 when the NA-21 Dragon took shape. With the Army Air Corps designation XB-21, this twin-engined bomber was fitted with superchargers for high altitude flight, it featured power-operated turret armament, a tailwheel landing gear,

(Top) **The NA-40 in 'unpolished' finish and displaying some of the features that, with changes, would make the B-25 an outstanding success.** via NAA

(Above) **When the polishers had finished the NA-40 (X14221) gleamed. It went to Wright Field for early Army tests looking much as it does here.** via NAA

and single fin and rudder configuration. With regard to the superchargers for its Pratt & Whitney, R-2180-1 Hornet engines, the XB-21 was the first aircraft of its size – it spanned 95ft (29m) and was 61ft 9in (18.8m) long – to have these fitted. With five 0.3in machine guns, it was also considered (at least numerically) well armed for its day.

Although it was a well proportioned design with a superficial resemblance to the slightly smaller Douglas B-18, the XB-21 did not possess a particularly outstanding performance and was not ordered into production. Budgetary restraints were a factor in the decision to order the B-18 rather than the XB-21, as Douglas was able to offer the former under series production contract terms at a unit price of $63,977, whereas NAA quoted $122,600 for each XB-21, even on quantities of more than fifty.

In addition, such designs were victims of circumstance, and of official indecisiveness over exactly what types of aircraft were required to equip the Air Corps. At the time that the XB-21 appeared, there was much deliberation as to the merits of the four-engined as opposed to the twin-engined bomber: funding could not then stretch to great numbers of both, but there was a clear need for the smaller attack aircraft and/or medium bomber.

Having learned much from the XB-21 exercise, NAA turned its attention to a second bomber design: this would appear later in 1937 as the NA-40. It was another twin intended to meet the requirements for aircraft in the only vaguely defined 'medium' class: it had a tricycle undercarriage and raised tandem cockpit, it provided bomb stowage in the fuselage, and it offered a good, rather than outstanding, performance. Choosing a twin vertical tail-fin layout was a departure from previous NAA practice, while the underslung engine nacelles allowed for some flexibility in engine installation. The NA-40 was impressive enough as an engineering exercise, and it had promising development potential.

There was every sign that modern bombers would soon be required by the Air Corps in very large numbers. Events on the world stage moved so swiftly in the last half decade of the 1930s that the aeronautical industries of the world had an immense task keeping abreast of modernization, particularly in aerial weapons. In the US these events were closely monitored. Gen Henry H. Arnold, the recently appointed Chief of the Army Air Corps, wrote of the German takeover of Czechoslovakia in 1938:

> ... the nation with the greatest navy in the world (Britain) ... in alliance with the nation having the most powerful army in the world (France) ... capitulated without a struggle to Germany's newly created airpower.

While it was true enough that Hitler's Luftwaffe was flaunted as a superior weapon in a world still very much locked into the trench warfare mentality of World War I, and into the belief in Maginot Line-type fixed fortifications, the propaganda emanating from Berlin was not backed by much real substance. In terms of 100 per cent government backing for her industry, a seemingly sound organization, and practical experience through a successful deployment in Spain as the Condor Legion, the Luftwaffe appeared to possess a real edge over her European – and indeed American – rivals. And the bold words of carefully manipulated facts, both broadcast and written, worked wonderfully well for the embryo Third Reich, buying it valuable time.

Unfortunately, few independent individuals were in a position to check the facts and figures. Had the true picture been known it would have been obvious that the German bombers of the late 1930s – all of them in the medium class – were in many respects technically inferior to those on the drawing boards in Britain and the US; only the later Ju 88 could be considered of real quality. Hap Arnold sent Charles Lindberg on a comprehensive fact-finding tour of Germany, and the famous Atlantic solo flyer did his best to be objective. Given a warm welcome by the Nazi hierarchy, he reported back as best he could.

In Lindberg's opinion the Germans did appear to have a substantial lead, particularly in dive bombing, which the US – and to a far lesser extent Britain and France – had pursued. The US Navy particularly favoured the dive bomber as a means to attack shipping targets accurately, and had brought the SBD Dauntless into service before the war. In Japan, even better dive bombers were being developed for the Imperial Navy, though evidently it was even harder for Western nations to substantiate the quality of such machines.

The US Army, having included single-engined dive bombers in its inventory for some years, gradually moved towards larger machines with two or four engines, able to deliver bombs in conventional 'straight and level' flight over considerable ranges. In terms of deploying dive bombers from land bases, the US Army was largely unable, try as it might, to broaden out the undoubtedly successful use of such by the Navy and the Marine Corps. Incidentally, it was NAA that would later give the US Army its one and only (and last) successful wartime dive bomber in the shape of the A-36 Invader, the career of which was curtailed only by a limited production run.

With war in Europe an increasingly real possibility, Franklin Roosevelt moved to

Specification – NA-40 (figures in parentheses for NA-40B)	
Type:	Attack bomber with crew of five
Powerplant:	Two 1,100hp 14-cylinder Pratt & Whitney R-1830-S6C3-G Twin Wasp engines each providing 1,100hp for take-off (Two 1,350hp 14-cylinder Wright Cyclone GR-2600-A71 engines each providing 1,600hp for take-off)
Weights:	Empty 13,000lb/5,896kg (13,960lb/6,330kg); loaded 19,500lb/8,845kg (21,000lb/9,530kg)
Dimensions:	Wingspan 66ft (20.10m); length 47ft 10in (14.58m); height 12ft 2in (3.70m); wing area 599sq ft (55.6sq m)
Performance:	Maximum speed 268mph/431km/h (287mph/462km/h) Range 1,200 miles (1,930km) Service ceiling 26,000ft/7,900m (25,000ft/7,600m)
Armament:	Four fixed 0.3in machine guns in outboard wing panels (installed only on NA-40B); three 0.3in MGs in nose, dorsal and ventral tunnel positions; normal bomb load of 1,200lb (544kg)
Number built:	1

expand the US armed forces to unprecedented size. The president was extremely worried at the inflated figures he was being given on the strength of the Luftwaffe, as was Hap Arnold, who apparently believed them implicitly. On 28 September 1938, FDR proposed an expansion plan which was honed by Arnold and presented to Congress in January 1939. That April the Air Corps was authorized to expand from the then-current level of 2,300 aircraft to 5,500 aircraft in twenty-four groups by June 1941.

Mitchell Forerunner

During the remaining months of peace in Europe, NAA – then under the guiding hand of president James 'Dutch' Kindelberger – completed and began taxiing tests on the NA-40 in preparation for the first flight. This historic event occurred on 29 January 1939, with company pilot Paul B. Balfour and engineer Frank H. Lyons at the controls. Unfortunately they soon experienced problems, in that the aircraft developed severe tail buffeting which got worse as the speed increased, and fluctuating oil and cylinder-head temperatures could not be stabilized by various cowl flap settings; however, they managed to land without mishap. Close scrutiny revealed that the engine exhaust system was inadequate, and this was revised by fitting 'elbow' pipe sections and long tailpipes to the exhaust stacks. The trailing edges of the nacelle were also modified by adding square fairings.

Further flights showed that these 'fixes' overcame the problems only partially, NAA determining that the real fault lay with the NA-40's engines themselves. In addition, the slow feathering of the Curtiss propellers meant that single-engined flight was out of the question. These troubles meant that the speed of the NA-40 was increased only gradually over a period of time: in fourteen flights – a total time of 5hr 20min in the air – the top recorded speed was 265mph (426km/h). This was not far short of the company's performance estimate of a maximum 280mph (450km/h) at 5,000ft (1,500m).

Despite its modest performance, the NA-40 had a number of admirable features, including a tricycle undercarriage, a shoulder wing, and underslung engine nacelles which were considered to be aerodynamically efficient and with easy access for maintenance. A low fuselage frontal area was achieved by seating the pilot and co-

pilot in tandem under a raised 'greenhouse' cockpit canopy. A crew of five was envisaged for a projected production variant, the two-pilot flight deck complement being completed by a bombardier/navigator, a radio operator/gunner and a second gunner.

The original NA-40 powerplants were two Pratt & Whitney R-1830-S6C3-G radials of 1,100hp each, although the engine manufacturer confirmed that either of its planned R-2130 and R-2800 models would fit the prototype's nacelles without difficulty. A design that enabled the easy installing of alternative engines had long been sound aeronautical engineering practice; moreover NAA did not overlook the possibility of selling a bomber similar to the NA-40 to foreign customers, so important to the company to date. Therefore, specifications were prepared for an export version which could have been powered by British Bristol Pegasus engines.

By 1 March 1939 the NA-40's engines had been changed: Wright GR-2600-A71-3 engines were fitted, these providing 1,600hp each for take-off, and in this form the aircraft was re-designated the NA-40B (with the civil registration X14221). More-streamlined nacelles were fitted, as were larger diameter cowlings with less taper at the front as compared with the originals. Exhaust collector rings replaced the over-wing-type exhaust used with the P. & W. engines, the carburettor air scoops being moved slightly further aft. The original intention was to fit Hamilton Standard propellers which had a faster, fully feathering capability as compared with the Curtiss electric type, but these were not available; storage batteries were therefore fitted to provide a temporary power boost.

Better Results

Balfour, Lyons and Bill Wheeler, another NAA engineer, took the NA-40B up for about an hour on 1 March. This flight was much more satisfactory than the very first had been, and simulated single engine tests were completed without any signs of vibration or overheating. On the down side it was found that the spark plug of no. 9 cylinder of both engines suffered excessive fouling, and this persisted, although a temporary remedy was to rig substitute ignition harnesses from friction tape. But despite these technical faults, it should be emphasized that the NA-40 was a very important prototype for North American:

not only did it furnish the company's engineers with much valuable flight data for aircraft in this class, but it also impressed USAAC officials at Wright Field when it was flown there for its military demonstration beginning on 12 March. Accompanied by North American technical representative Rudolph 'Rudy' Stolz, Balfour and Lyons flew the NA-40B to Ohio, with en-route stops at Albuquerque, New Mexico and Kansas City, Kansas where it was refuelled and inspected.

By 1939, Air Corps' procurement of new aircraft followed an established pattern: when a requirement had been determined, a set of specifications was issued; these included performance requirements, and also the date and time when the physical article had to be at Wright Field for bid opening and competition with other entries. Thus in response to Proposal 38-385, NAA put forward the NA-40, Martin submitted the Model 167, and Douglas the DB-7B. Both Stearman's Model X-100 and Bell's Model 9 were withdrawn early on, and the DB-7B was destroyed in a crash on 23 January 1939.

To judge the entries, a trial board was appointed consisting of AAC pilots who would award 'quality' points as the aircraft '... performed necessary tests to determine (its) tactical efficiency'. Consequently, Major Younger A. Pitts, temporarily assigned as test pilot to the NA-40 project, undertook the programme. Over the course of about a month, flight tests proceeded well, with the NA-40 making a good impression on the trial board and accumulating more points than the other entries. In deference to the slow-feathering propellers, no single engine tests (with the engine shut down and the propeller fully feathered) were conducted. A one-engine shutdown was simulated by alternately idling the engines with the prop in fully fine pitch, and trimming the aircraft to approximate 'hands off' flight. North American had specifically requested that no dead engine/fully feathering test flights be attempted from Wright Field until all company tests had been completed to the satisfaction of its own trial board.

This request was apparently complied with until 11 April, when a further flight was arranged with 1st Lt George F. McGuire at the controls. Pitts occupied the co-pilot's seat, and 2nd Lt James W. Anderson, a member of the Air Reserve based at March Field, acted as gunner in the aft fuselage position. McGuire, a member of the utility board who was also usually based at March Field, had been ordered to take up the NA-40B on this occasion specifically to check the instrument flight characteristics and single engine performance sections of the test programme. Some aerial gunnery practice was also scheduled, with a P-26 fighter acting as an interceptor.

The 'single engine' phase of the NA-40B programme still posed a problem for NAA. For Air Corps testing, while pilots evaluated all aspects of performance against government specifications, the aircraft was technically owned by the government, and no company employees were allowed aboard; only when the tests had been completed did the prototype revert to company control. Regarding the single-engine trial that McGuire had requested, NAA promised to arrange this after the Wright Field evaluation had finished. Stolz was therefore very surprised to be told that McGuire had obtained permission from the head of the board to have him along for this flight. The NA-40 was, McGuire stated, to be taken up for a routine cross-country flight lasting three and a half hours – but it appears that he had been briefed for, and fully intended to complete, the single-engine test. But just as the flight taxied out, Younger Pitts arrived in a Jeep, stating that he was replacing Stolz. McGuire, having assured Stolz that he would not fly the aircraft on one engine without him being on board, took off.

For a few minutes all appeared to go well, but then the startled North American personnel watching from the ground saw their aircraft approach the field at about 500mph (800km/h) – with one engine shut down and the propeller feathered.

Few of the watchers were very surprised at what happened during the next few seconds. Put into a turn, the NA-40B lost a little altitude and went into a gentle, flat spin, striking a hill with one wing when it was some two miles away from the airfield; this absorbed most of the impact shock. Sliding down the hill, the aircraft spun round on its axis, shedding its tailplane after contact with a tree, and finally came to rest with its starboard wing high. Fortunately no fire was immediately apparent, and the fire engine reached the scene to find all the crew safely out of the wreck – in fact, as the fire took hold, the three men were already en route back to Wright Field in two civilian cars that had stopped near the scene of the crash.

Then McGuire and Anderson, sharing seats in one of the cars, apparently remem-

bered that the stabilizer of the Air Corps bombsight may have been aboard the NA-40B, and so promptly returned to the crash scene; but here, a Wright Field ambulance took them to the dispensary for any necessary medical treatment. Pitts was already in the dispensary when they arrived.

As for the NA-40B, it had hit the ground in a shallow, skidding turn and now lay forlornly, 'wrapped up' under the impact; the tail section had broken away, but the wing remained virtually intact apart from a sheared-off section on the starboard tip. The starboard engine and propeller was also relatively undamaged, though the front fuselage had severed a few feet in front of the wing. When the ruptured tanks ignited, a typical fuel fire, with towering clouds of boiling smoke, consumed most of the fuselage. The wreckage 'settled back' after the fire had been smothered, the wings then being nearly parallel with the ground.

Although the board of enquiry at Wright Field could do little other than cite technical failure as the cause of the crash of the NA-40, the findings did not take into account North American's warnings regarding the risk of single engine operation. These had clearly been overlooked, even though McGuire had been repeatedly made aware of its implications. For the record, the board's outline parameters were to determine the cause of the crash within '... the contractual obligations of NAA and the Government to determine if the procedure followed in the performance testing complied with all specific agreements and War Department regulations.'

The board heard witness statements, and concluded that the inability of the Hamilton hydraulic propeller to be unfeathered in the air was the primary cause of the crash: with one engine out at low altitude, McGuire had had very little chance to save the aircraft. There were, however, conflicting eye-witness and crew reports as to exactly what happened on the NA-40's final flight – and it has to be said, a hint of a cover-up so as to avoid any charge of youthful exuberance on the part of the pilot. Kindelberger told Stolz to make himself scarce for a few days so as not to cause the Air Corps (the company's customer) any embarrassment by making a conflicting statement on the events. That seems to have worked, as the report was written and filed – and the fact that the behaviour of the NA-40 on the final flight was not entirely resolved, was all but forgotten.[1]

Privately NAA laid the responsibility for the crash squarely on McGuire, strongly suspecting that he had ignored the company's advice on single engine flying. In the US in those days, young pilots – even those with the responsibility of test-flying new aircraft – were notorious for letting exuberance overrule prudence, particularly when they were asked to fly the new 'hot ships' coming along at that time; it appears that many of them took one look at the performance charts and promptly went out to prove them to the hilt – and more than one came unstuck in the process. And this would not be the last time that NAA came up against this over-confident approach.

While the loss of the NA-40 was an undoubted setback to NAA, Dutch Kindelberger appeared unruffled – and merely thankful that the test crew had survived the crash. The amount of data that the aircraft had previously accumulated was adequate proof to the Air Corps that the basic design was sound, and it was estimated that building a similar aircraft was well within the company's engineering and production capacity. However, there was no Air Corps production contract for the NA-40 – and in fact no manufacturer was judged to have won the attack bomber competition. As the North American and Douglas designs had crashed, and the Bell and Stearman submissions were rejected, Martin's 167 was the natural winner; but the Air Corps refused it a production contract. Having studied reports on the medium bombers then in service in Europe, the USAAC urged manufacturers to 'build better': for example, it was strongly believed that new US light bombers should be capable of higher speeds – up to 300 to 345mph (480 to 550km/h).

This important requirement was reflected in Air Corps proposal No. 39-640 for a new medium bomber, issued on 11 March 1939: it stated that the winning aircraft should be able to carry a bomb load of 3,000lb (1,360kg) over a range of 2,000 miles (3,200km) at a top speed of more than 300mph (480km/h). Its deployment was to include operating at altitudes between 8,000 and 14,000ft (2,400 and 4,250m), undertaking the primary role of supporting ground forces, and attacking a range of tactical targets. In response, NAA prepared the NA-62, with Douglas submitting the B-23, and Martin the Model 179. The AAC wanted an initial 385 examples of the winning design delivered within two years.

War Impetus

Even when war broke out in Europe in September 1939, US aircraft manufacturers had time to adapt their designs to incorporate features that were essential to survival under actual combat conditions. Consequently, self-sealing fuel tanks, armour protection and improved armament were incorporated into the NA-62 design, with further refinements (particularly in armament) being made before most US aircraft saw action.

As far as configuration went, the most modern American aircraft were comfortably in advance of what then passed for medium bombers in Europe. Tricycle landing gear, for example, would soon no longer be an innovation, but an industry standard, not only for twin-engined bombers but for all categories of aircraft. By contrast, the indigenous types equipping America's allies – as well as the Axis powers – were almost universally traditional 'tail-draggers', a configuration also

chosen for the Martin 167 and Stearman XA-21. The term was actually unknown in those days, not being coined until the 1950s when most new aircraft were of tricycle landing gear configuration.

The American situation was less encouraging with regard to powerplants, as the choice of those suitable for the winners of the medium bomber competition was limited. Although the mainstream engine manufacturers then had ambitious R&D programmes, relatively few units had been

(Above) Unarmed for an early test flight, the NA-62 Mitchell prototype has the 'production' vertical tail surfaces retouched in on this print, which was actually taken on the ground at Muroc when the aircraft had the original square fins. Companies regularly did this to save cash, retouching charges being much cheaper than a flight to get new PR pictures! via NAA

(Below) In its final configuration, the NA-62 retained some of the main features of the NA-40 including the continuous dihedral wings, tricycle landing gear and twin fins and rudders, the latter shown here in final 'triangular' form. via NAA

(Above) **From head on, the fuselage cross-section of the NA-62 was more in proportion compared to the NA-40.** via NAA

In a remarkably trouble-free test programme the first NA-62 performed very well. This, the only mishap during the test programme, was the result of an inflight engine fire. The aircraft was quickly repaired. via NAA

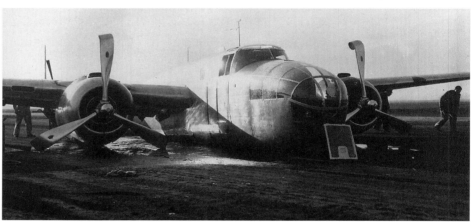

tested, or had entered production by the spring of 1939. North American noted that there were no suitable liquid-cooled engines, and the choice of a power source for its design submission to the proposal fell more or less naturally on the air-cooled P. & W. R-2800, or the Wright R-2600 or R-3350 – and of these, only the R-2600 had actually been built and test-run. Wisely, the company opted for an engine that was proven, if a little down on power, rather than something potentially better, but as yet awaiting the results of tests.

Having drawn up a whole series of engineering options around the specification for the NA-40, the company was well placed to submit these as part of its NA-62 design for Proposal 39-640. In effect, NAA gave the customer free rein

to opt for the configuration required; during its short existence the NA-40 had enabled the company, through practical feedback from flight tests, to refine such areas as the vertical tail design, engine cooling and propeller feathering, which undoubtedly saved valuable time. In total, NAA offered eighty-three design options on the NA-62.

A system whereby the customer in effect chose what was required from paper designs, saved the industry the time and cost of building prototypes that might have turned out to be a complete waste of effort: by narrowing down the design parameters before any construction work was done, the need for a prototype (which may itself have required considerable modification) was eliminated. The AAC selected a win-

ning design by awarding quality points for the merits of each submission.

Putting NAA's rivals for a bomber contract into context, Douglas had flown the Model DB-7B, the A-20 forerunner, on 26 October 1938. The NA-40 had come next, in January 1939, and the Martin Model 167 (the XA-22 forerunner of the Maryland) in February 1939. The Douglas B-23 first flew on 27 July 1939; the date of the Stearman X-100's first flight – a single example ordered by the AAC as the XA-21 – is not known, though it was delivered in the autumn of 1939. These were the immediate contemporaries of the NA-62; it was some twenty months before the Martin Model 179, which became the B-26 Marauder, made its first flight, on 25 November 1940.

Army Choice

The winner of Proposal 39-640 was the B-26 with 813.6 quality points; the NA-62 scored 673.6 for second place, and the B-23 was third with 610.3. But for limited capacity the entire contract might have gone to the Marauder, but Martin could only guarantee to deliver 201 aircraft of the Army order in the time allowed. NAA consequently picked up a contract for the balance to 385, namely 184 B-25s.

Within the Army Air Corps expansion plans, the two principal medium bomber types would eventually be confirmed as the B-25 and B-26. Broadly speaking, these would attack tactical targets from medium (10,000–15,000ft (3,000–4,500m)) altitudes, while the two four-engined heavies, the B-17 and B-24, would undertake a strategic role; where, when and how these operations would be carried out, awaited future events.

In the Army's 'attack' category the A-20 would be a lasting success, with less fortune attending the A-24 dive bomber. Ordered virtually straight off the Navy production lines, initially as the SBD-3A (the suffix letter indicating 'Army') in June 1941, the Dauntless was to prove less than successful in service. Nor would the final single-engined type ordered in this category, the Curtiss A-25 Shrike, find a USAAF role.

This meant that, in the early years of combat, the Army would rely on one attack bomber, two mediums and two heavy bombers; what could not be envisaged was the virtual amalgam of the attack aircraft's role into that of the medium bomber, and a major slice of the medium bomber's *raison d'être* being absorbed by the fighter bomber. Late in the war the Army redressed the balance by bringing the A-26 Invader into service to exemplify the final, and arguably the best, example of the piston-engined attack bomber.

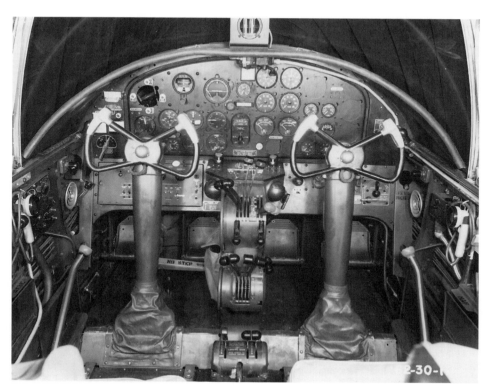

(Above) The flightdeck of the B-25A was well laid out, with the controls falling easily to hand. *via NAA*

(Below) The first production Mitchell served the company as a transport until 1944, and later had its camouflage paint removed in line with AAF practice. *via NAA*

CHAPTER TWO

The B-25

Industry response to the proposal for a new Air Corps medium bomber was generally poor, many concerns feeling such aircraft to be way beyond their capacity, despite the attraction of lucrative government contracts. Apart from the two winning submissions chosen by the Design Review Board, the Douglas B-23 – an improved B-18 – was awarded a production run that extended to only thirty-eight aircraft.

In choosing the B-26 for development and series production, the Air Corps accepted that this was a very advanced aircraft, one that would stretch resources, especially as it was designed to be powered by engines as yet unproven. In contrast, the B-25 looked a more sedate design exercise, well within current, highly advanced

(Top) Early production B-25s had 'clean' cowlings with half-ring exhausts, 'kidney'-shaped waist hatches and an 'open' tail bumper. via NAA

(Above) From the rear quarter the B-25's elaborate tail defence, which was an unpowered single-gun cupola, clearly added excess weight. It was deleted in the **B-25B.** via NAA

US industry standards: the NA-62, the board concluded, would be economical to build in quantity, easy to maintain under field conditions, and would not require much modification of the crew training programme, as was indicated by the high performance and more demanding B-26.

Germany had invaded and all but subjugated Poland by the time North American Aviation received the initial contract for 184 B-25s. Approved on 20 September 1939 – a week before the opening campaign of World War II ended in a German victory – the contract was worth $11,771,000, an enormous sum representing a huge challenge to fulfil. Due to the lateness of the re-equipment programme and the situation in Europe, the Air Corps had decided that it could dispense with company prototypes (as outlined above) – awaiting the completion and flight trials of prototypes, as per traditional practice, could take up to three years, and that time was no longer available.

Fortunately the US aero industry had already broadened its production facilities to absorb large-scale contracts, initially from European customers. NAA had built a new plant at Mines Field, Los Angeles, which could if necessary be expanded: the airfield was of adequate size, and the plant had been designed specifically to build military aircraft. The Inglewood/El Segundo area in which Mines Field was located also enjoyed a favourable 'year round' climate, ideal for flying.

Under the able direction of Lee Atwood, NAA vice president and chief engineer, the NA-62 project proceeded with all speed. Having pioneered the technique of splitting airframes into a number of sub-assemblies with the BT-9 trainer, the company was able to complete new aircraft with a minimum of delay: breaking down each type into convenient sections enabled work to be concurrently undertaken at other locations with the maximum number of people employed, thus reducing costs. And when the aircraft entered service, the same approach speeded up the process of repair, damaged sections being removed and new ones 'spliced' into the airframe.

Although NAA's engineers had explored scores of detail changes in configuring the new bomber, it had been decided to retain a number of NA-40 design features, including the twin fin and rudders, a tricycle landing gear, and the general shape of the underslung engine cowlings. A similar wing area (although this was lowered to a mid-fuselage position) also showed that NAA had achieved excellent proportions with the NA-40, with good weight distribution.

The NA-62 was a larger aircraft overall than the NA-40 – some 6ft (2m) longer in the fuselage – and capable of lifting a greater payload; it also promised to have a better speed and range. The inevitable weight penalty of design 'add-ons' pushed the NA-40's 20,000lb (9,000kg) gross weight up, to top out at a gross of 28,000lb (12,700kg) for the NA-62.

It was in the fuselage, and particularly the flightcrew compartment, that the NA-62 made the greatest departure from the NA-40. The original raised tandem canopy gave way to side-by-side seating for the pilot and co-pilot, the cockpit itself being incorporated as a fuselage step forward of the wing. The longer nose area, with clear panels for a bombardier station, was more streamlined, with an access crawl-way incorporated below the flight-deck. Despite its lower wing, the NA-62's fuselage profile was slimmer, the new design having lost the somewhat cumbersome, 'belly-scraping-the-ground' look of the NA-40.

North American opted to fit a modestly tapered wing of continuous dihedral to the NA-62, this carrying the nacelles that in turn would accommodate the Wright R-2600 engines. These were not the preferred powerplant, company engineers favouring the Pratt & Whitney R-2800 which promised 2,000hp, 300hp more than the Wright engine and with slightly less frontal area and therefore offering less drag. But the Air Corps specified the Wright engine, primarily on the grounds that it was proven.

Although in comparison with the Martin B-26 the NA-62 appeared a more boxy, less streamlined design, this was not to be a limiting factor: NAA reduced the bomber's frontal area by limiting the fuselage width to 56.5in (143.5cm), which enabled the installation of a comfortable cockpit, a roomy enough glazed bombardier's station, and a bomb-bay area aft of the flightdeck of reasonable size. The curves on the aircraft, though subtle, were certainly there, even if not to the same extent as on the Marauder. NAA's seemingly more traditional, perhaps cautious approach in designing the NA-62 was reflected elsewhere in the industry, as it was well known that not only were curved airframe sections harder to machine at the close tolerances required, they could be significantly more costly.

Specification – North American B-25	
Type:	Medium bomber with crew of five
Powerplant:	Two 1,700hp 14-cylinder Wright Cyclone R-2600-9 engines each providing 1,350hp at 13,000ft (4,000m)
Weights:	Empty 17,258lb (7,827kg); loaded 28,557lb (12,951kg)
Dimensions:	Wingspan 67ft 6in (20.59m); length 54ft 1in (16.50m); height 15ft 9in (4.80m); wing area 610sq ft (56.7sq m)
Performance:	Maximum speed 322mph at 15,000ft (518km/h at 4,600m); Range 2,000 miles (3,200km); service ceiling 30,000ft (9,000m)
Armament:	Three 0.3in guns in nose, waist and ventral positions; one 0.5in machine gun in tail cone; bomb load of 3,000lb (1,360kg)
Number built:	Twenty-four (AAF serial numbers 40-2165 to 40-2188)

NB First production aircraft (believed nine) fitted with constant dihedral wing; most retrofitted with standard gull wing.

Early Armament

Due consideration was given to armament for the B-25 which, by 1939 Air Corps standards, still centred mainly on the light 0.3in machine gun. A power turret was not part of the original design, there being instead up to five flexible (hand-held) guns in nose, rear fuselage ventral and dorsal and waist positions. A departure from the usual 'peashooter' 0.3in guns was the single 0.5in machine gun which could be mounted in the extreme tail and operated from a plexiglass clamshell cupola. Of these guns, the nose position had three alternative sockets. This armament would prove to be less than adequate in combat – although to be fair, few designers anywhere

Slight nose-wheel oleo weakness was evident on wartime bombers with a tricycle landing gear, leading to this type of incident. NAA largely cured any such weakness before the B-25 saw combat. via NAA

in the world then realized the capacity for medium bombers to carry at least double the number of machine guns – even a battery of cannon – than had originally been allowed for.

With the initial NA-62 contract confirmed, NAA built a 1:9 scale B-25 for testing in the wind tunnel at the California Institute of Technology. These tests confirmed the soundness of the design, and work proceeded on a full-scale mockup for official scrutiny. This was completed by 9 November 1939 when members of the Air Corps Mock-Up Board visited the plant. A static test airframe was also built and was ready for shipping to Wright Field on 4 July 1940, around 156,000 engineering man hours having produced 8,500 drawings to finalize the design.

The building and assembly of the first B-25 (40-2165) was all but completed by the summer of 1940 when the first ground and taxiing tests took place. Some nosewheel shimmy (and actual failure) was apparent during taxi tests, necessitating the fitting of an improved, redesigned damper. A not

uncommon problem with tricycle-gear aircraft in general (the early B-26s suffered numerous such failures), any inherent nosewheel oleo weakness in the B-25 was cured early in the development programme – although it is true to state that a nosewheel oleo represented a classic aeronautical compromise because it had to be light but also immensely strong, capable of rough treatment under field conditions without breaking.

First Flight

On 19 August 1940, while the Battle of Britain raged on the other side of the Atlantic and the fate of America's greatest wartime ally hung in the balance, the first B-25 flew. That day, German airmen flying bombers not too dissimilar to the B-25 and trying to ward off RAF fighter attacks with machine guns of similar light calibre specified to defend it, were even then pointing the way to important changes in Allied medium bomber armament.

Vance Breese and NAA engineer Roy Ferren enjoyed a successful maiden flight, although subsequent time in the air gave Ferren some cause for concern. He detected a tendency for the B-25 to enter a severe roll-yaw condition. Breese, one of a group of independent test pilots hired by NAA for the B-25 test programme, appeared to be less concerned, and did not specifically cite any adverse handling qualities.

Ferren's doubts about the B-25 under all flight regimes was soon confirmed. The wing was cited as the cause – although it is rather ironic that aircraft with continuous wing dihedral are actually extremely stable, and in the case of the B-25, it was this very stability that affected its accuracy as a bomber: any small trim corrections made by the pilot on a practice bombing run were amplified on the pilot's direction indicator (PDI) linked to the Norden bombsight. Correcting with the rudders to centre the PDI needle would invariably bank the aircraft just enough to throw the bomb off to one side if the automatic release was used.

Early production examples of the B-25 ran to nine aircraft, all originally fitted with continuous wing dihedral and the 'square' fin and rudder configuration. After the first flight of the B-25 (no suffix was applied to these early machines), numerous detail changes were introduced.

Ferren also reported that the aircraft exhibited notable overstability in certain flight attitudes through the phenomenon known as Dutch roll, and this was traced to the continuous wing dihedral. Pre-service testing at Wright Field more or less confirmed the manufacturer's findings in this respect. The first production B-25 (40-2165) was retained by NAA; ships numbers two and three (40-2166 and 40-2167) passed to Wright Field, the latter being used as a static 'test-to-destruction' vehicle. The first aircraft suffered a crash landing during its early test phase: fitted with the second modification of the vertical tail fins, it came down after an inflight fire caused by the rupture of a right engine fuel line. Pilot Vance Breese took immediate action and made a well-controlled landing on the grass between the Mines Field runways, and NAA's fire department minimized any further damage; the aircraft was quickly repaired.

Tail Refinement

For eleven weeks after the B-25's first flight, NAA's Engineering and Wing and Tail Surface Production departments gave much attention to the tail surfaces of the new bomber. Putting in time around the clock, engineers added sections to the top and bottom of the fins and rudders, ready for Vance Breese to test-fly the revision the following morning. Gradually the familiar 'pear-shaped' vertical tail surfaces of the B-25 evolved, a definite move away from the original square configuration of the NA-40 and the NA-62. Ships 40-2177 and 40-2178 were despatched to Chanute and Lowry Fields respectively for additional Army testing.

Ed Virgin and Louis Waite flew the first B-25 to be fitted with the new gull wing on 25 February 1941. The distinctive wing configuration – which Breese succinctly called the 'shot duck look'! – was apparently fitted to the B-25 after the tenth production example, with the first aircraft being returned to the factory to have the modification carried out. All succeeding B-25s had the revised wing, in which the

dihedral of the sections outboard of the nacelles was all but eliminated. From directly ahead these sections appeared to be horizontal, but there was actually a small degree of negative dihedral ending in upswept tips.

It was about this time that Lee Atwood came up with the name 'Mitchell' for the new bomber. No immediate decision was taken on this, but when nobody came up with anything better, Mitchell it became. Most people agreed that perpetuating the name of one of America's leading advocates of a strong national defence in this way was highly appropriate. Interestingly, the national emergency engendered by Pearl Harbor brought about an edict for AAC personnel to drop numerical designations for 'security reasons' and use aircraft names instead. This only partially caught on.

Built To Last

The first B-25 led a long and useful life in company service. It was retained as a corporate transport to ferry NAA president Dutch Kindelberger around the North American plants and to many meetings during the war years. With its interior stripped – incidentally without the aid of any engineering drawings, but accomplished easily enough by skilled engineers employing time-honoured 'hand-waving' methods – the aircraft had its military interior altered to make for better comfort as befitted an executive transport. Built with a standard bombardier nose, the original B-25 – named 'Whiskey Express' – acquired a 'solid' nose during the course of its company career, and was often flown by NAA corporate pilot Edgar 'Ed' Stewart, who may ultimately have claimed a record for the number of hours he spent at the controls of any B-25.

The 'Express' lasted until 8 January 1945, when a loss of hydraulic pressure obliged Stewart to belly the aircraft in at Mines Field. There were no crew injuries, but the resulting damage placed it beyond repair and fit only for scrapping. Other executive B-25s based on the early military models were to follow – about which more later.

First In Service

While NAA introduced the revised wing onto the production line, the first straight wing examples of the B-25 were accepted by the Air Corps in February 1941. During

that month, 40-2168 and 40-2169 (completed on 27 February) the fourth and fifth production examples respectively, were delivered to the 17th Bomb Group (Light) at McChord Field, Washington. The first of these went to the group's Headquarters Squadron, while the component 34th BS took 40-2169. In total, nineteen of the twenty-four B-25s built were delivered to the 17th BG for initial service evaluation. These camouflaged aircraft carried the tail markings in vogue at the time: no serial numbers were presented, but each was given a plane-in-group number in the range 36–49, although these were not entirely inclusive as tail number 45 was allocated to a B-18. No distinction was made between early straight- and gull-wing B-25s received by the 17th, the numerical sequence incorporating both.

After completing the two dozen B-25s, the company turned its attention to an improved version, the B-25A. One of the most important changes made in the B-25A was the fitting of self-sealing fuel cells in the forward section of the wings. Seen to be vital to the safety of aircraft in combat, these nevertheless imposed the problem of increasing gross weight to 27,000lb (12,250kg), and as a consequence reducing range (to 1,350 miles/2,170km), a conflicting but hardly unforeseen challenge that was overcome in the B-25C. The internal fuel capacity of the A model was 692 gallons (3,146l) as compared to 916gal (4,164l) for the B-25 – although this could be increased to 1,112gal (5,055l) by fitting a 420gal (1,909l) tank in the bomb-bay; this was jettisonable in an emergency. Armour protection of ⅜in (9mm) thickness was also added, to compound the weight/performance challenge. Armour protection, another essential item for the modern warplane, was provided for the pilots, bombardier, waist gunner and tail gunner.

Engines for the B-25A were the same Wright R-2600-9s as fitted in the B-25, which gave a maximum speed of 315mph (506.8km/h) at 30,000ft (4,000m) and a service ceiling of 27,000ft (8,230m). Performance did fall short of that of the B-25 but not by much, top speed being reduced by some 7mph (11km/h) at 15,000ft (2,000m) altitude.

Ed Virgin flew the first B-25A (40-2189) on 25 February 1941, NAA wasting no time in producing this improved series of aircraft under contract W535-ac-13258, which covered all early examples prior to the B-25C. Forty B-25A models (40-2189

Production of B-25As getting into its stride at Inglewood in 1941. Note the masking for the propeller warning stripe of the nearest aircraft, and the application of the national insignia to other airframes prior to camouflaging. via NAA

Specification – B-25A	
Type:	Medium bomber with crew of five
Powerplant:	Two 1,700hp 14-cylinder Wright Cyclone R-2600-9 engines each providing 1,350hp at 13,000ft (4,000m)
Weights:	Empty 17,870lb (8,106kg); loaded 27,100lb (12,290kg)
Dimensions:	Wingspan 67ft 7in (20.60m); length 54ft 1in (16.50m); height 15ft 9in (4.80m); wing area 610sq ft (56.7sq m)
Performance:	Maximum speed 315mph at 30,000ft (507km/h at 4,000m); Range 1,350 miles (2,170km); Service ceiling 27,000ft (8,230m)
Armament:	As for B-25
Number built:	40 (AAF serial numbers 40-2189 to 40-2228)

to 40-2228) were built, and whereas the two dozen B-25s had been allocated almost exclusively for testing, the new model became the first to enter AAF service as a combat-ready type.

In the late spring of 1941 the 17th Bomb Group, led by Lt Col Walter R. Peck from March 1941, took delivery of sixteen B-25As: this brought its total acceptances of Mitchells to date to thirty-five aircraft. Other early recipients of the B-25A were the following units, each of which are understood to have received six aircraft: the 30th BG based at New Orleans, Louisiana; the 39th BG (Spokane, Washington); the 43rd BG (Bangor, Maine); and the 44th BG, then based at McDill, Florida. A single example of the B-25A remained at Wright Field pending the delivery of the next production model; this may subsequently have been delivered to a group, as the above total makes forty-one aircraft – thus one more than NAA actually built!

(Above) The elegant lines of the B-25A with the original straight wing. Provision of a dorsal hatch for a single machine gun was an early step towards arming the aircraft adequately for combat. via NAA

At the waist positions, mounting and stowage points were provided for a pair of 0.3in machine guns. via NAA

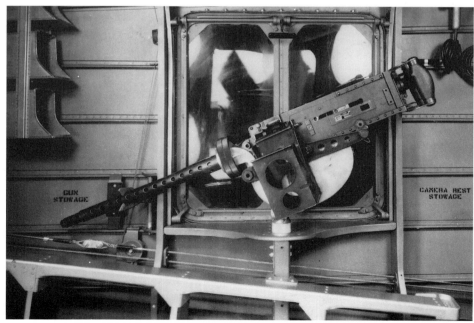

Of these early recipient units, only the 17th was destined to take the B-25 into action, and then only briefly. The rest mainly converted to B-24s, although the 30th Group's 38th and 819th Squadrons (the latter beginning life as the 3rd Anti-submarine Squadron), the 39th's 402nd Squadron (which was the 12th Recon Sqn prior to April 1942), and the 43rd Group's 63rd and 65th Squadrons retained it for a longer period during 1941–42.[2]

A similar arrangement was provided for a dorsal hatch gun, although the prominent mounting plinth intruded into the available rear fuselage space. via NAA

It should be borne in mind that the composition of the AAF in 1941–42 was undergoing not only expansion but revision, too, with a considerable degree of unit redesignation and reassignment. For example, B-25s issued in small numbers to groups which were engaged on sea search operations during the first few months of the Pacific war did not necessarily retain Mitchells when they were reassigned.

The B-25B

The passage of time and the loss of company records has unfortunately failed to preserve the exact first flight date of the B-25B. Suffice to say that it took place in the early part of 1941, probably with Paul Balfour or Ed Virgin at the controls. The relatively few changes (other than the introduction of gun turrets) found to be necessary enabled production of the B-25B to be initiated quickly and for deliveries to commence during the early summer of 1941, fourteen having been accepted by the AAF that August. A few weeks previously, on 20 June, the old Air Corps had become the new Army Air Forces.

The smooth flow of B-25B model deliveries was temporarily broken by the fifteenth example (40-2243) which was destroyed, and was therefore struck from the initial order for 120. Output thereafter continued smoothly, and NAA had delivered the balance of 119 aircraft by the time of Pearl Harbor. This delivery completed the first contract for 184 B-25s.

Turrets Added

The most significant differences as compared to previous B-25s was that the B model introduced a Bendix Type 'L' dorsal turret mounting two Colt-Browning M-2 model 0.5in machine guns. This conventional, clear-view turret was complemented by an unglazed Bendix Type 'K' ventral turret, made retractable to reduce drag, and remotely sighted and fired via a system of periscopic (prismatic) mirrors. By retaining only a single 0.3in MG socket in the bombardier's nose station, NAA generally

Specification – B-25B	
Type:	Medium bomber with crew of five
Powerplant:	Two R-2600-9 Wright Cyclone engines
Weights:	Empty 20,000lb (9,072kg); loaded 28,460lb (12,909kg)
Dimensions:	As for B-25A
Performance:	Maximum speed 300mph (483km/h); Range 1,300 miles (2,092km); 23,500ft (7,160m)
Armament:	One 0.3in MG in nose; two 0.5in MG in Bendix Type N dorsal turret, and two 0.5in MG in Bendix Type K ventral turret with remote sighting; bomb load of 3,000lb (1,360kg)
Number built:	120 (AAF serial numbers 40-2229 to 40-2348)

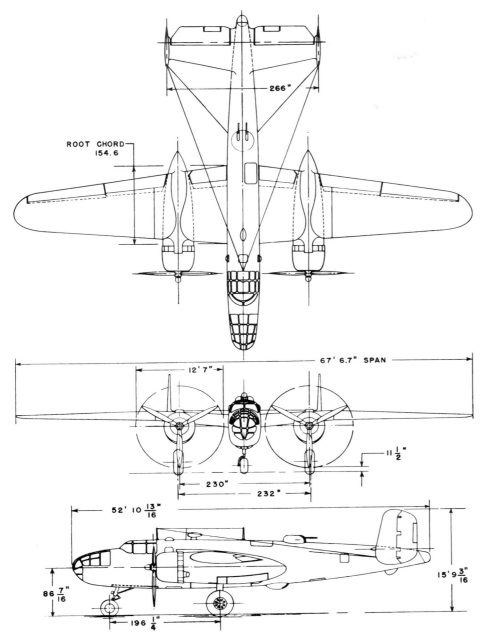

ammunition boxes and other equipment had been installed.

Some weight to counteract that imposed by the two turrets was saved through not having to provide armour protection for the early manned (prone) position in the extreme tail, a clear-vision tail-cone now covering the end of the fuselage. Overall weight inevitably rose, however, to 20,000lb (9,072kg) empty, about 3,750lb (1,700kg) more than the B-25 – although in loaded condition the B-25B was only marginally heavier than both previous models. This was fortunate, since the turret armament became the standard (and very necessary) basic defence of the aircraft. The Bendix unit, with a beautifully streamlined and virtually frameless cupola, typified the excellent design of most US aircraft gun turrets which, with some minor changes, would continue to grace all B-25s from then onwards.

All did not, however, go well with the early B-25 turrets. For months the dorsal turret proved only partially reliable, the main fault being traced to the electrical system incorporated by Bendix. In 1940 it was standard practice for the Armament Laboratory at Wright Field to allocate turret development to various specialist manufacturers. These then developed the most ideal turret defence based on the configuration of the aircraft, crew numbers, available fields of fire, and so forth. Bendix apparently experienced numerous difficulties during its early turret development. Among the problems B-25 gunners experienced was having to allow for a 'dead' spot in azimuth travel, just where the cupola moved past its neutral position. This made smooth tracking of a target next to impossible, and added to the gunners' already high workload. Neither were stoppages completely unknown, the guns in some individual turret mountings refusing to fire as a pair; this was a problem that persisted for some time.

Neither was the retractable lower turret the most outstanding feat of wartime engineering: at 600lb (270kg) it was heavy, and it was slow, taking 55 seconds to reach the fully lowered position, and requiring eleven separate functions to fire the guns. These included lowering the device, charging the guns, and obtaining sight alignment via the aiming mirrors, which often caused optical distortion, making accurate tracking and firing at a moving target extremely difficult. This particular aircraft turret had a relatively short life in American service; it was dropped during production of the B-25G-5,

Three-view drawing of the B-25B showing the overall dimensions. Only the fuselage length was to change, starting with the B-25G. via NAA

'cleaned up' the interior of the B-25B as regards guns. Installation points for waist guns designed for use from small aft fuselage windows (which gave a limited field of fire) were deleted, although these positions were subsequently utilized in combat areas on some of the later model B-25s. Also dropped were the optional ball and socket locations for guns to fire from the side panels in the bombardier nose – but again, photographic

evidence shows that some combat units reinstated these mounts.

It was soon realized that nose defence of the B-25 could be adequately covered by guns firing more or less 'straight ahead'. This was far more preferable to the bombardier manoeuvring a heavy and bulky machine gun to fire from alternate sides in what was a very limited space once a bombsight, bomb-release gear, a seat,

NAA provided the B-25 nose gunner with a single 0.3in machine gun in the early models. It was soon evident that this was not nearly heavy enough. Real Photos

Part of the progressive increase in B-25 defensive armament was a dorsal turret from the B model onwards, seen here under factory test. Early turrets were to give considerable trouble in service, probably because they were a war expedient and not part of the original NA-62 design. via NAA

as from aircraft 42-65001. In any event, the Mitchell's lower turret was often removed from those earlier aircraft already in US service where a weight-saving of several hundred pounds could be better utilized, usually by an additional fuel tank. On the other hand, non-US Mitchell operators, in particular the RAF, mastered the complex lower turret and made it an integral part of the aircraft's defence when flying in tight formations.

With an otherwise similar specification to the B-25A, the B model was slightly slower as a result of the weight and drag of the turrets – but 300mph (480km/h) at 15,000ft (4,570m) was still very respectable, and a testimony to the integrity of the design, which proved able to accommodate additional weight with little adverse effect on performance. It did, however, become a truism that the B-25's least positive quality was its ability to climb very fast. And although NAA probably attempted some rudimentary sound-proofing, the aircraft remained very noisy in the cockpit once the engines had been started, though crews got used to it. Besides, such a thing was of minor importance to young crews flying what was considered to be 'the hottest ship in the Air Corps' at the time.

Early Problem

The B-25s of the 17th Bomb Group were due to participate in the massive Army manoeuvres held in Louisiana and North Carolina between September and November 1941: these involved some 850 Army, Navy and Marine Corps aircraft flying about 4,000 sorties. In its first simulated combat test the new medium bomber was part of the Red Army defending against the Blue Army. Red crosses on white circular fields were applied in washable paint to the fuselage and wings of each participating B-25. All went well for the B-25 element until 6 November 1941, when disaster struck: taking off at Daniel Field in Georgia, a B-25A had just got airborne when it suddenly crashed and blew up, killing the crew of four. Examination of the wreckage and checks on other B-25s eventually determined that a self-sealing compound in the fuel hoses had ruptured on the inside, blistered, and as a result had almost closed off the flow of fuel: there had been just enough coming through to enable run-up and a brief full power check, but not enough to sustain flow at maximum engine

(Right) Taken on 19 May 1942, this factory view of the turret installation shows the central position on the sight and some of the gun operating mechanism to advantage. via NAA

At the same time as the dorsal turret was installed, NAA provided the B-25 with ventral defence in the form of a remotely sighted Bendix turret, the internal controls of which can be seen in this interior view of the turret fully retracted. Note the scanning window at right. via NAA

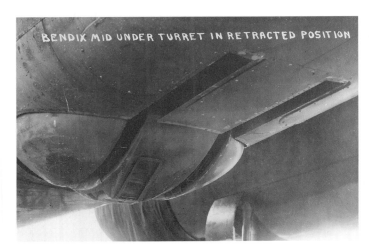

Externally, the twin ventral turret gun barrels stowed neatly, cutting drag to a minimum, although the installation was often removed to save weight. via NAA

In the fully down position the turret was ready for use if the gunner could obtain a good 'lock on' using the mirror sighting system. via NAA

revolutions. Improved tanks and hoses were fitted to cure the problem, which was found in most of those already fitted in B-25s.

Within days of the end of the 'war games', conflict became a reality for the US when the Japanese attacked Pearl Harbor. On 7 December 1941 the immediate US declaration of war on Japan was followed by that on Germany on the 11th. Initially thrown into some confusion when a second Japanese strike on the US mainland seemed

false alarms. One such was on 24 December when the crew of Lt Everett W. Holstrom (subsequently assigned B-25B 40-2282 for the Tokyo raid) of the 95th BS, 17th Group, reported that they had sighted and sunk an IJN submarine off the mouth of the Columbia River. Later examined by joint USN-British Admiralty committees which were set up to assess sinkings and damage to enemy submarines, 'Brick' Holstrom's claim could not be substantiated.

observation), let alone sink submarines; not until 31 December 1941 was a U-boat officially reported.

B-25Bs of the regular bomb squadrons were nevertheless welcome participants on anti-submarine patrols, which required as many aircraft as possible. Although few US aircraft then boasted radar, the U-boat skippers were not to know that and, as regards hostile air patrols, it was prudent simply to avoid them whenever possible.

B-25Bs by the dozen as Inglewood hums to meet production schedule. Mass output of Mitchells was underway just as the AAF faced burgeoning war commitments around the world. via NAA

likely, the military and the country collectively breathed easier when this failed to materialize. Air defence and shipping patrols were stepped up, and the 'pioneer' 17th and other early recipients of the B-25, which had trained hard to bring crews up to the required standard of efficiency, were now confronted with the urgency of war.

Offshore patrols by Army bombers helped the Navy maintain a watch on the Pacific sea lanes, but next to no surface traffic was identified as Japanese, despite some

With Germany recognized as the primary Axis adversary, anti-submarine patrols off the Atlantic seaboard were also initiated by AAF aircraft. Almost anything that could fly any distance was sent off over the ocean: B-25s, B-26s, B-17s, B-18s, B-24s and B-34s joined in the optimistic hunt for an almost totally elusive adversary. Directed by First Bomber Command at the behest of the US Navy, these patrols were mainly undertaken by aircraft ill-equipped to find (apart from crew

As 1941 waned, units equipped with the B-25 – including the 5th and 6th Anti-Submarine Squadrons (the former then in its original guise as the 41st Bomb Squadron based at Orlando), and the 17th Group which had moved to Lexington County Airport in South Carolina – continued to amass flying hours on ocean patrols. It was tedious work, but at the very least the young crews got to know their aircraft thoroughly and built up experience that would serve them well in combat.

CHAPTER THREE

Developing the Range

Fine inflight view of a B-25C-NA on factory test flight shows the generally similar configuration of the early models (with detail differences) up to the B-25G. via NAA

The B-25C

Having completed 119 B-25Bs (out of the 120 ordered as 40-2229 to 40-2348), NAA incorporated further changes and improvements to produce the B-25C. Externally similar to its immediate predecessor, this became the first true combat model of the Mitchell to be mass-produced; it was built in seven sub-types (*see* specification box). Several contracts cov-

ered the production of 1,625 B-25Cs, all of which were completed at Inglewood. Ed Virgin took up the initial example of the new model (41-12434) for its first flight, on 9 November 1941. Further proof that, as before, NAA could quickly incorporate changes on an established production line without appreciable delay in delivery schedules, was reflected in the fact that the USAAF accepted its first B-25C in December.

Although externally similar to the B-25B, the new model Mitchell had numerous changes 'under the skin'. Power was provided by Wright R-2600-13 engines, with Holley carburettors that replaced the Bendix Stromberg type.

Aircraft ordered by the Dutch government under the model number NA-90 were among the first B-25Cs built, these having their engines fitted with 'finger' exhausts that protruded aft of the cowl

Specification – B-25C

Type:	Medium bomber with crew of five
Powerplant:	Two 1,700hp 14-cylinder R-2600-13 Wright Cyclone engines
Weights:	Empty 20,300lb (9,210kg); loaded 34,000lb (15,420kg)
Dimensions:	As for B-25B
Performance:	Maximum speed 284mph (457km/h) Range 1,500 miles (2,400km) 21,200ft (6,460m)
Armament:	As for B-25B
Number built:	605 (AAF serial numbers 41-12434 to 41-13038)

NB From 41-12817 fuel capacity increase and scanning window added to navigator's compartment on starboard side; standard provision for Norden, Estoppey or Sperry bombsight; camera provision.

B-25C-1

Specification as for B-25C except for addition of wing racks and ventral torpedo release gear

Number built: 258 (AAF serial numbers: 41-13039 to 41-13296)

B-25C-5

Specification as for B-25C-1 except for substitution of 0.3in nose gun with 0.5in MG; finger-type exhausts; winterization provision

Number built: 162 (AAF serial numbers 42-53332 to 42-53493)

B-25C-10

Specification as for B-25C-5 except for addition of AM reading compass; improved cabin heating and improved scanning lens in fuselage adjacent to lower gun turret; 42-32281 became XB-25E with heated wing and 42-32372 became B-25H prototype

Number built: 150 (AAF serial numbers 42-32233 to 42-32382)

B-25C-15

Specification as for B-25C-10 except for Clayton 'S'-type flame damping exhaust stacks on each individual cylinder and provision for emergency hydraulic landing gear lowering

Number built: 150 (AAF serial numbers 42-32383 to 42-32532)

NB Five aircraft (42-32384 to 42-32388) modified as B-25G-1s

B25-C-20

Specification as for B-25C-15

Number built: 200 (AAF serial numbers 42-64502 to 42-64701)

B-25C-25

Specification as for B-25C-20 except for provision of 'clear view' windscreen; 215 US gal bomb-bay fuel cell and 335gal (1,523l) metal bomb-bay tank on every second aircraft

Number built: 100 (AAF serial numbers 42-64702 to 42-64801)

flaps. It was found, however, that although these provided a degree of flame damping, they were prone to cracking, and the majority of B-25Cs were instead fitted with a collector ring; these terminated in a shorter exhaust pipe than on earlier B-25 engines, and gave off an impressive glow visible over a considerable distance, particularly at night. At that point not too much night flying was envisaged for the B-25, so this drawback was not immediately addressed.

Despite its uprated engines, the B-25C could not quite equal the 300mph (483km/h) top speed of the B model, managing only 284mph (457km/h) at 15,000ft (4,570m). Service ceiling was also lower than before, at 23,500ft (7,160m). An extra 200 miles (320km) range was nevertheless achieved by fitting six auxiliary wing cells (three on each side) holding a total of 152gal (691 litres) per side. In addition, provision was made for two ferry tanks to fit in the waist compartment, these holding 62.5gal (284l) each. With the fixed bomb-bay tank (215gal/977l) plus a droppable bay tank (335gal/1,523l) holding a total of 550gal (2,500l), the B-25C could also be fitted with a ferry tank. De-icing equipment was also introduced.

The outer wing structure was strengthened pending the fitting of up to four bomb racks on the B-25C-1, from aircraft 41-13039 onwards. The internal bomb racks were also revised and provided with A-2 electric release gear. To aim the bombs, the B-25C was wired to take three different sights: the Norden M series, the Estoppey D-8 or the British Sperry Mk IX. The sight

Before they got into combat, B-25 crews learnt their trade at the controls of Mitchell trainers. Many of these soon took on a 'beat-up' look, like this turretless D-5 model photographed over Sacramento in southern California when assigned to one of the Western Training Command bases. via NAA

support bracket was changed or fitted with an adaptor depending on the type of sight fitted.

A change was made in the type of dorsal turret fitted to the B-25C, the Bendix Model 'N' being of the amplidyne type which meant that it was powered by two motor generators, one for rotating the turret in azimuth, and one for elevating the guns. The standard armament chosen for the B-25 in medium bomber configuration remained the same as earlier models until on the B-25C-5 batch (42-53332 to 42-53493) a 0.5in machine gun was introduced to replace the 0.3in weapon in the nose position. At the same time a single fixed 0.5in MG was installed in the lower starboard side of the nose for operation from the cockpit.

The B-25C-5 also reintroduced the 'finger' flame-damping exhaust collector; however, this was still not as satisfactory as the more efficient Clayton 'S'-type flame dampers provided for each individual cylinder. Introduced on the B-25C-15 (42-32383), these distinctive exhausts appeared as two rows of seven small fairings in a 'staggered' pattern around the exterior of each engine cowling, a feature that was to remain on all subsequent wartime Mitchells.

Among the other changes introduced towards the end of B-25C production, in the early spring of 1943, was some cleaning

(Above) NAA's house journal *North American Skyline* published many stories about the B-25, an aircraft the wartime workforce was very enthusiastic about building. In this view a B-25B awaits its typical load of 500lb bombs. via NAA

Some cockpit layout changes were evident as B-25 development proceeded. Full dual controls were fitted to most models, as in this view. via NAA

up of the cockpit to improve the view from the flightdeck. Provision was also made for hydraulic lowering of the landing gear in an emergency, cabin heating was improved, and on the B-25C-25, the final variant of this series, a 335gal (1,523l) metal bomb-bay tank was installed in every second aircraft built.

New Kansas Plant

Paul Balfour flew the first example of the B-25D (41-29648) on 3 January 1942, by which time NAA had established a second production facility in Texas to handle burgeoning orders for P-51s. To do the same for B-25s, a third plant had been opened in Kansas during December 1941. Production of B-25Ds began before the year was out, the first three aircraft being delivered to the AAF during February 1942.

The Kansas City plant was established under a programme instigated by William Knudsen, who later became director general of the US Office of Production Management. Under the Knudsen Plan, existing aircraft manufacturers were to operate

Among the many trials carried out on Mitchells was an investigation into the benefits of four-bladed propellers. The first was B-25C-15 (42-32383), which was also fitted with new carburation. Four blades were never adopted for production aircraft. NAA via N. Avery

As well as tests to improve engine efficiency, NAA expended much effort on boosting the B-25's armament. Twin package gun sets and enclosed, heavily framed waist windows were tried out on this B-25D-10, which also had blast plates rivetted in front of the fuselage gun barrels. via NAA

new plants under generous subsidies, and the automobile industry would gear up to produce not cars, but aircraft components. As far as the Kansas plant was concerned, the government built it, and NAA operated it for the government, with General Motors' Fisher Body Division building B-25 sub-assemblies.

The B-25D

Externally similar and fitted with much the same equipment as before, the early B-25Ds paralleled their B-25C counterparts from Inglewood, although progressive refinements and changes were introduced during production to result in a total of nine sub-variants (see specification box) from Kansas, two more than the B-25C. Detail differences in equipment between the two models resulted in a run of numerical designators in blocks of five to identify the changes. Among these was the provision of armour plate behind the co-pilot's seat, the introduction of a portable oxygen system and self-sealing oil tanks, and the installation of another fixed, forward-firing 0.5in gun in the starboard side of the plexiglass nose. Deliveries of the B-25C and D to the Army overlapped, with the final Kansas City-built B-25D being accepted in March 1944.

Boosted Gunnery

Data compiled on Axis fighter interception of Allied bombers during World War II invariably recorded numerous attacks from directly aft. Any bomber without extreme tail defence was deemed to be that little bit more vulnerable to fighters, and in the case of the B-25, a number of C and D models had their armament increased by the installation of a single 'stinger' gun in place of the plexiglas tail-cone. In addition, enclosed waist windows were often located just aft of the wing, forward of the dorsal turret (which was retained), and a raised cockpit was provided for the tail gunner.

None of the early B-25C/D models was built with extreme tail defence, and it was left to service depots, forward maintenance units operated by Air Service Command, and workshops run by the combat groups, to carry out the modifications. All such units played a vital part in maintaining the flow of new and repaired combat aircraft to the operational squadrons, and all were capable

Specification – B-25D	
Type:	Medium bomber with crew of five
Powerplant:	Two R-2600-13 engines with Holley 1685 carburettors
Weights:	Empty 20,000lb (9,000kg); loaded 36,500lb (16,560kg)
Dimensions:	As for B-25C
Performance:	Maximum speed 284mph (457km/h) Range 1,500 miles (2,400km) Service ceiling 21,200ft (6,460m)
Armament:	As for B-25C
Number built:	200 (AAF serial numbers 41-29648 to 41-29847)

B-25D-1
Specification as for B-25D except for addition of external wing bomb racks; self-sealing fuel cells in outboard wing centre section; carburettor air filters; self-sealing oil tanks; torpedo rack; navigator's scanning window and Bendix Amplidyne turrets; finger-type exhaust collector

Number built: 100 (AAF serial numbers 41-29848 to 41-29947)

B-25D-5
Specification as for B-25D-1 except for substitution of 0.3in nose machine gun with 0.5in flexible gun and two fixed 0.5in MGs; improved scanning lens; 585gal droppable bomb-bay fuel tank on every third aircraft. Added provision for additional cabin heating from 41-30057 onwards

Number built: 225 (AAF serial numbers 41-29948 to 41-30172)

B-25D-10
Specification as for B-25C-5 except for provision for additional winterization equipment; installation of remote reading compass; emergency hydraulic landing gear lowering and elimination of conduit shielding box

Number built: 180 (AAF serial numbers 41-30173 to 41-30352)

B-25D-15
Specification as for B-25D-10 except for replacement of finger-type exhausts by Clayton 'S'-type exhaust stacks and additionally on second batch (from 41-30533) installation of clear vision windscreen; armour plate behind co-pilot; 230gal (1,045l) self-sealing bomb-bay fuel tank, and 325gal (1,480l) bomb-bay tank on every second aircraft

Number built: 180 plus 315 (total 495) (AAF serial numbers 41-30353 to 41-30532
and 41-30533 to 41-30847)

B-25D-20
Specification as for B-25D-15

Number built: 25 (AAF serial numbers 42-87113 to 42-87137)

B-25D-25
Specification as for B-25D-20 except for provision of portable oxygen system

Number built: 315 (AAF serial numbers 42-87138 to 42-87452)

B-25D-30
Specification as for B-25D-25, except for winterization changes and heated air windscreen defrosting panel

Number built: 160 plus 340 (total 500) (AAF serial numbers 42-87453 to 42-87612
and 43-3280 to 43-3619)

B-25D-35
Specification as for B-25D-30

Number built: 250 (AAF serial numbers 43-3620 to 43-3869)

NAA had dropped tail armament in the B-25B, but the troops wanted it back on the B-25C and D. This is the company's design for a twin gun installation in place of the tail observation dome, although there were many single-gun modifications to Mitchells 'in the field'. NAA via N. Avery

of carrying out field modifications. In the case of the B-25 they were often concerned with armament changes. The tapered tail of the B-25C/D left little space for the breech of a 0.5in machine gun, and installing a machine gun usually meant chopping back the fuselage plates flush with the trailing edge of the tailplane to create the maximum possible space and improve the field of fire – which was, in any event, limited to a few degrees in azimuth, elevation and depression. To operate the gun from his 'open' position, the gunner had originally to lie prone. The installation of a cockpit over the tailplane allowed space for a seat, enabling him to sit upright, which was a considerable improvement.

Internally the B-25 could accommodate most AAF bomb weights up to 2,000lb, although this larger capacity bomb carriage was abandoned on late model B-25Hs and Js. via NAA

As well as bombs, the internal bay of the B-25 could hold four depth charges. NAA via N. Avery

(Above) Wing racks to take bombs or depth charges were a welcome boost to the offensive capability of the B-25C/D series. Dummy depth charges are 'hooked up' in this view, the 'one-two' combination being standard for both types of weapon. NAA via N. Avery

Minor revisions were made to the cockpit throughout the B-25's production span, although most of those configured as medium bombers had a flightdeck that looked much like this. The aircraft in this photo, dated 11 May 1944, is identified as an RB-25. via NAA

No identifying model number is known to have been allocated to these hybrid B-25s – or indeed the total of aircraft involved – despite them being numerous, although the RAF did identify those machines it received as the Mitchell IIa. When the larger waist windows were installed, individual aircraft also sported external bracing struts attached to the fuselage longerons as an added safety measure. Each window and its gimbal gun mount weighed several hundred pounds, and some crusty engineers doubtless felt that it was best to be safe rather than sorry.

The other uprating of B-25 armament was the Fifth Air Force-pioneered, twin-fuselage package guns. Initially consisting of a pair of Brownings enclosed by a single fairing, NAA developed individual fuselage fairings to enclose the breech of up to four 'fifties, from the B-25H onwards.

The foregoing 'package' of gunnery changes did not necessarily follow any particular pattern; frontline B-25s were seen with many variations, and the degree of modification tended to be dictated by the conditions prevailing in the theatre. Towards the end of the war, when fighter interception in some areas was rare, the process could go the other way, with the removal of dorsal turrets on B-25Js being fairly common.

Camera Provision

As production of the B-25C/D proceeded, reports from the war fronts indicated the need for more specialized combat roles. Although medium bombers were not always the aircraft most suited to meet these, the B-25 made an important contribution to photographic reconnaissance, one of the most significant developments in military aviation in World War II. The result was the F-10.

Not to be confused with standard B-25s, most of which were delivered from the factories with the ability to take aerial photographs of bomb strikes with a range of ventrally mounted cameras, the specialized F-10 was otherwise a B-25D. The 'F' prefix followed regular AAF practice for identifying photo-recon variants of the leading bombers and fighters. Ordered primarily for conducting large-scale photomapping, all forty-five F-10 conversions were from new B-25Ds built between late 1942 and early 1943. The necessary modifications were carried out at facilities adjacent to NAA's Kansas City plant.

By stripping out all armament, armour plate and bombing equipment, about 1,000lb (450kg) in weight was saved before a fairing designed to take three cameras was installed in the forward section of the bombardier's nose compartment. This tri-metrogen arrangement consisted of three K-17 or T-5 6in (15cm) cameras arranged to view directly down and at oblique angles via 'bug-eye' apertures on the left and right sides. These cameras provided excellent panoramic photographs, and in tests, the 'trimet' showed that a single F-10 flying at 20,000ft (6,100m) and maintaining an ASI of 200mph (320km/h), could photograph 20,000sq miles (51,800sq km) of territory in four hours. Unprecedented horizon-to-horizon visual coverage was backed by a drafting device which translated the oblique photographs onto an accurate flat map scale that matched the vertical prints. Actually entering AAF service some time before the designation was officially confirmed on 18 August 1943, the F-10 was initially issued to the 311th Photo Wing and the 1st Photo Charting Group.

From bases around the world, these units carried out large-scale aerial mapping operations which were particularly useful for updating existing military charts, and confirming all aspects of overseas ferry routes from the US. They also opened up various remote parts of the globe to the

A surviving B-25D, one of the F-10 tri-metrogen camera conversions, fortunately still existed in 1980 when the Air Force Museum wanted a 'B-25B' exhibit to commemorate the Doolittle raid on Tokyo. It was stripped, altered and repainted for that purpose to good effect. via NAA

camera lens, so that areas of wilderness dangerous to downed aircraft could be accurately charted, some for the first time.

The F-10 was not, however, used in combat zones, the Photographic Requirements Section of the USAAF Air Staff having concluded, on 13 May 1943, that '... tactically it was not possible to use these ships in the combat theaters'. This referred specifically to the relatively poor performance of the B-25, particularly at altitude, in direct relation to solo penetrations of heavily defended areas; a similar view was taken of the F-9, the photo model of the B-17. These comments were entirely justified in contested war zones where fighter-type performance was increasingly necessary for sheer survival and the ability to return home safely with the necessary photographs.

But despite the official view, the value of the F-10's 'trimet' camera system was appreciated, and examples were integrated into the inventories of some combat units operating over areas relatively free from enemy interference. Progressive Allied successes

made some skies increasingly safe, particularly in the China-Burma-India (CBI) and Mediterranean Theatre of Operations (MTO), and some regions of the Pacific. Consequently from mid-1943, the 18th Combat Mapping Squadron was based in New Caledonia and the New Hebrides to fly sorties over the South Pacific. In addition, the 19th Reconnaissance Sqn operated over the Middle East and Africa.

A contemporary listing of wartime AAF PR/mapping units includes fourteen with B-25s as part of their wartime complement of aircraft in overseas combat zones; of these, five also had some F-10s.[1] It should be borne in mind that such units regularly operated a mix of types, one or two Mitchells without any special modifications being quite capable of flying useful reconnaissance sorties; but in general they should not be assumed to be F-10s unless specifically identified as such.

Notwithstanding any restrictions placed on the F-10, the standard B-25s that equipped the combat units assembled one of the most impressive 'portfolios' of combat images taken anywhere during the war. A single automatic camera, most commonly a Fairchild K-17 (12in/30cm lens) or K-24 (7in/18cm lens) was mounted aft of the bomb-bay in all B-25 production models, and the images obtained during combat missions provided AAF intelligence sections with thousands of prints of enemy installations – particularly in the Pacific, where low-level strafing and bombing runs enabled cameras to record with a clarity of detail that at times was little short of incredible. Thus the B-25 may not have been the ideal specialized PR aircraft – but in standard form it excelled in the ability to bring home combat photos second to none.

Not Wanted On Voyage…

In the transitional pre-/early war period in which aircraft such as the B-25 were developed for the US air forces, some items of equipment were specified that did not find much use in combat. One was the aerial torpedo, the release and carrying gear for which was developed rapidly soon after Pearl Harbor and introduced on the B-25C-1. Tests with B-25B 40-2274 performed in the spring of 1942 revealed that the drag of a torpedo, suspended on a bomb-bay rack and semi-enclosed by the partially shut bay doors, reduced cruise speed by 14mph (22.5km/h) – though otherwise no adverse effects were found in the way the B-25 handled.

The aerial torpedo was a weapon much used by some air forces and hardly at all by others, and one which had long been considered the ideal anti-shipping weapon; this belief persisted for some time, even after other forms of ordnance had proved equally, if not more effective. In the US, opinion was divided. Even the Navy had to appreciate the equal status of bombs as effective weapons against ships, particularly in the light of the appalling record of the early American torpedoes used by submarines and surface vessels.

As far as Army medium bombers were concerned, aerial torpedos were dropped in anger by B-26s; but after an initial and ineffectual flurry of activity by the Marauders at Midway in June 1942, little further operational use was made of them, by this or any other type. Torpedo release gear nevertheless remained on the B-25 through to the J model, and the early disappointing results did not mean the end of the North American medium's association with similar weapons, as B-25Js of the 41st BG did fly some late war sorties with a specially developed version. Otherwise most B-25s

---

Orphan in the Eighth

A standard B-25 became the sole representative of the North American medium in the Eighth Air Force when B-25C-5 (42-53357) arrived at Honington, Suffolk, from the 2nd Base Air Depot at Burtonwood, Lancashire. Believed to have been an aircraft originally assigned to the 310th Group, the B-25 ostensibly served as the nucleus of an intended combat group in the Eighth's 3rd Bomb Wing. When plans to operate both B-25s and B-26s were changed (Mitchells being dropped in favour of an all-B-26 force), this orphan was seconded to Eighth AF HQ as a communications aircraft: it was named 'Miss Nashville'. It passed to the 7th Photo Group at Mount Farm in September 1943 where it was used as a hack, and for some dual instruction training of F-5 Lightning pilots. Lt Gen James Doolittle, Eighth AF commanding general, flew it briefly, probably pleasantly surprised to find a 'Tokyo raider' in the middle of Oxfordshire!

Painted black, and with AEAF stripes added on 5 June 1944, the aircraft flew thirteen night photo missions to V-1 launching sites in August in the hands of the 25th Bomb Group. Then pressed into service as a courier aircraft, it carried photographs to UK bases and the US Twelfth Army HQ in France.

Its usefulness was prematurely curtailed: on a run to Hamm, a small forward airfield near Luxembourg on 26 October, 'Miss Nashville' was flown by Lt Bob Kraft. The intelligence material delivered, Kraft took off to return to England – but the B-25 was mistakenly fired on by American AA near Chalon-sur-Seine airfield. It caught fire, and although Kraft managed to land at Chalon, the aircraft skidded off the runway and hit a tree, killing him and the flight engineer and badly injuring the co-pilot.

Sea-search radar with Yagi antennae was first fitted to US Army B-25C/Ds when they were called upon to assist the Navy in searching for submarines off the US coast. In September 1943, this formation from the 77th Bomb Squadron, 28th Composite Group, was a little further afield – off Attu in the Aleutians. USAF

(Above) **The famous PBJ-1D (BuAer 35094) named 'Jonah' tested radar and weaponry for the Marine Mitchells. The radome for the APS-3 set, similar to installations in Army B-25s, was mounted in place of the ventral gun turret. The external torpedo was the standard Navy type for use by aircraft.**
Smithsonian Institution

Boosting the armament of the B-25C/D in medium bomber configuration was begun by adding a flexible 'fifty' in the nose and a fixed gun of similar calibre for use by the pilot. IWM

simply remained capable of carrying a single Mk 13 aerial torpedo, 22.5in (57cm) in diameter, and shortened in overall length to 13.4ft (4m) for aircraft use, as compared with the standard naval types.[2]

Experimentation with what later became known as 'stand-off' weapons for medium bombers continued, however, and the B-25 was used to test a number of types which attempted to overcome the lack of an internal guidance system. The wartime solution was often to attach small, vertical and horizontal aerodynamic surfaces to stabilize a body section containing the warhead, such as in the GB-13 which was developed both as a glide bomb and a glide torpedo, the latter being designated as the GT-1 for training purposes. These weapons were made to 'fly' into the target by means of either pre-set gyros or, in later versions, by utilizing radio signal guidance.

In operation, the torpedo was released from the parent aircraft, and while in the glide, a paravane was released on the end of a cord which trailed about 20ft (6m) below it. The other end of the cord was fastened to detonators on the airframe. When the paravane struck the water it filled, the weight of water exerting enough pull on the detonators to discharge them, thus blowing off the wings, tail and horizontal supports and freeing the torpedo to make its run. The tail-mounted mechanism was pre-set to enable the torpedo to zig-zag or travel in circles to avoid detection.

One version of the GB-13 tested on the B-25 had a rudimentary seeker head developed by Ratron Marine and built into a bulky wooden nose that also enclosed the warhead. Other experimental models tested infra-red, flares, radar and TV camera guidance.

The primary target for this and similar weapons was shipping, but such innovations were rarely found to be as effective as attacks with conventional ordnance – which undeniably carried significant risk to the aircrew, as the bomber invariably had to fly over the target ship and be exposed to its defensive fire. That was one of the main reasons why stand-off weapons appeared so attractive. Testing with B-25 carrier aircraft continued throughout most of the war, to lead eventually to an entirely new family of postwar anti-shipping weapons.

CHAPTER FOUR

Gearing Up to Fight

After the US declaration of war, the USAAF clearly needed to put as many combat groups as possible into the field to fight the Axis powers; having agreed that the defeat of Germany took first priority, the call on groups for service in Europe would be high. But the country could hardly ignore the Japanese, an enemy virtually on its doorstep, and the Army therefore had to husband its resources carefully. Air bases had to be found in remaining areas of the Pacific that were still secure from Japanese occupation, yet within range of bombers if any kind of offensive action was to be hard enough to hurt the enemy. There seemed to be precious few of these bases, however, since possible locations from which the Army could counter-attack were threatened and then engulfed by the Japanese in the weeks after the devastation of the fleet at Pearl. Within days of their undeclared war the Japanese had secured Guam, and occupied Tarawa and Makin in the Gilberts – although they did suffer a costly rebuff when attempting to invade Wake Island. But that setback was only temporary, and by 25 December the enemy tide had engulfed

bases in China and the port of Hong Kong. Imperial Navy bombers based on Formosa were soon able attack the northern Philippines, the islands deemed to be vital as a base for any decisive US riposte in the northern Pacific.

Pre-war American planning had emphasized that the loss of bases in the Philippines would be little short of disastrous, but that unpalatable situation unfolded almost hourly during that fateful winter. The systematic destruction of the Far East Air Forces at Clark, Iba, Nichols and other airfields took place at almost the same time as the carrier force struck Hawaii, owing to the different time zones prevailing in these locations, albeit some 5,000 miles (8,000km) apart. With little opposition the Japanese landed in Manila Bay and Lamon Bay on 22–24 December; Douglas MacArthur evacuated and fell back to the Bataan peninsular. Manila was in enemy hands by 2 January 1942, and by February Bataan was under siege; this was not lifted until Allied surrender, after MacArthur's departure on 11 March. In the meantime Japanese forces had landed

on the southern Philippine island of Mindanao as well as the Visayen islands in the centre of the archipelago.

During the first months of 1942 the grim catalogue of Allied losses continued, causing increasing gloom amongst the Allied leaders. The fall of Singapore on 15 February meant that, having secured strategic points in Malaya, there was little to prevent the Japanese from taking Burma and the entire Dutch East Indies.

It was in this atmosphere of uncertainty as to where any kind of Allied front line could eventually be drawn that plans were made to strike back with a rebuilt Far East Air Force: this force would be centred on Australia. Having returned home, MacArthur had established an HQ at Brisbane and, notwithstanding the threat of a Japanese invasion of Australia, had initiated a slow build-up of bomber forces in that country.

In terms of US medium bombers, the first in the theatre were the B-26 Marauders of the 22nd Bomb Group, several of which had arrived on 25 March. The RAAF had already struck back at the Japanese as best it could, but its small numbers, not to mention marauding enemy fighters, had prevented attacks from being very effective. At this time North American was in the process of meeting early orders for overseas customers, principally the Netherlands – an initial allocation of 162 aircraft (under contract 7131L/NA placed on 30 June 1941) for the Dutch was being completed even as that country's position in the East Indies grew increasingly precarious. These Mitchells (with type number NA-90) were originally scheduled for delivery over four months, from November 1942 to February 1943, but the Dutch requested the US government to effect earlier delivery, and it was accordingly agreed to release sixty B-25Cs from USAAF Contract AC-16070. Signed on 1 October 1940, the latter covered 863 aircraft (B-25Cs and C-1s) with serial numbers 41-12434 to 41-13296.

This seemingly sound arrangement became confused because of the developing

First combat group to get the Mitchell was the 17th Bomb Group at McChord Field, Washington. No. 43 was 40-2180, one of the nineteen B-25s delivered to the unit. via NAA

war situation, and resulted in an accounting and administrative nightmare for the Dutch who had already paid, in cash, for their 162 original aircraft. And time was fast running out for any retaliatory action in the Dutch East Indies.

A ferry route was established to get Allied combat aircraft, initially the Dutch Mitchells, to Australia with all speed. This route originated at Hamilton Field near San Francisco, went via Hawaii and out across the Pacific to Fiji, and thence to Brisbane. It was first used by B-25s on 2 March, the day before Japanese forces landed at Sourabaya in Java. From then on, each day brought news of Allied setbacks in Java, until on the 8th the island

was formally surrendered by the Dutch C-in-C. This put future prosecution of the war under a joint US, Australian and British command, which included the Netherlands and New Zealand.

With a starting date of 1 April, the US undertook responsibility for combat operations throughout the Pacific, extending this to include China, Australia and New Zealand, with the British undertaking the defence of India, the Indian Ocean and Sumatra. As the South-West Pacific Area (SWPA), MacArthur's command was vast: in practical, operational terms it generally

(Right) **The Inglewood factory apron held many interesting aircraft in 1941, among them B-25Cs painted in basic 'customer colours'. This line-up includes examples for Russia, the Netherlands (41-12462/N5-126), Britain and the AAF. At far left is a second Mitchell with RAF roundels, a B-25C (41-12446) that was not delivered to the UK.** via NAA

Many Mitchells were flown to their overseas combat theatres, while others were shipped. In this view a line of C/D models awaits loading for North Africa at a US port; the aircraft are tied down in the usual way. IWM

Dutch Mitchells would have been the first to go into action over Java, had the island held out against the Japanese. As it was, several of the early Dutch machines made the type's combat debut in the hands of USAAF and RAF pilots. This line-up shows B-25Cs which served at the Royal Netherlands Military Flying School at Jackson, Mississippi. via NAA

meant all air operations by army, navy and marine units using land bases. Carrier operations came under the control of the Pacific Ocean Area (POA) commanded by Admiral Chester W. Nimitz.

Part of the build-up of personnel and aircraft in Australia was the arrival of Lt Col John H. Davies of the 3rd Attack Group, and Jack Fox, senior North American Aviation Field Service Representative in the SWPA. Responsible for company liaison with the Dutch in respect of their B-25 order, Fox was one of a small army of highly qualified aircraft technicians – popularly known as 'plane doctors' – who spent six months to a year with the combat groups. The field representatives made a vitally important contribution to the Allied war effort by trouble-shooting a catalogue of problems with individual aircraft types. NAA eventually had about a hundred of these civilian technicians on all the war fronts, primarily to look after the B-25 and P-51. Jack Fox was to spend some forty-four months with the Fifth Air Force, during which time the Mitchell underwent its metamorphosis from medium bomber to strafer.

Another character to swell the cast list in the early saga of the B-25 was Paul 'Pappy' Gunn. An ex-Navy and Philippine Airlines pilot, Gunn knew the islands intimately, and he willingly became an unofficial adviser to an ad hoc reincarnation of the '3rd Attack'. Lacking time or facilities for formal induction into the USAAF, Gunn was given the honorary rank of captain.

The 3rd had arrived in Australia during February, along with some members of the 38th Bomb Group, without aircraft. As the southern Philippines were still holding out against the Japanese, it was decided to mount a retaliatory heavy and medium bomber raid on some of the main bases so recently vacated by Allied forces and now in enemy hands. 'Big Jim' Davies looked to the now-idle Dutch B-25s as the only source of medium bombers for his group. With the Indies lost, the Dutch crews had little immediate operational use for their bombers, although a training programme was initiated under the guiding hand of Jack Fox. The B-25s had been at Brisbane for two weeks when Davies suggested that the 3rd use these aircraft to get into action. A conference on 22 March between Dutch and US officials confirmed that twelve aircraft would be transferred to the USAAF.

With parts of the Philippines still in friendly hands, retaliatory attacks could be made on enemy-occupied air and naval bases by mediums if they staged through the airfields that remained under Allied control. A direct attack was out of the question as Australia lay beyond the maximum range of the B-25. But the Australian garrison at Port Moresby in Papua New Guinea was the longer-term answer: if the bombers could use the airfields on that peninsula, raids on the Philippines were still a practical possibility. Mediums were favoured because although B-17s had already bombed enemy ships and other targets from high altitude, these had proved largely ineffective.

Hostile Land

The fact that the Allies and the Japanese could occupy airfields on the same land mass gives an idea of the sheer size of New Guinea. At that time a largely unexplored territory, it was far from ideal for air operations. Inhabited by primitive tribes and almost totally covered in dense rainforest, the country had the Owen Stanley mountain range bisecting it like a central spine. Weather over the area was – to put it kindly – unpredictable and very often extremely dangerous, with low-hanging cloud and mist often shrouding the mountain peaks.

It goes without saying that New Guinea was as far removed from an ideal place to fight a ground war as it was possible to get – but when the US broke the Japanese naval code, it was revealed that the enemy indeed intended to invade Port Moresby by an initial landing at Milne Bay. But forewarned of Japanese intentions, a suitable Allied response could be prepared. If the invasion could be repelled and Port Moresby and its ring of airfields held, Japanese plans could be thwarted – harassed by Allied troops on the ground, pounded from the air and blockaded by naval forces, it was estimated that a military campaign in New Guinea by the Japanese Army could be made all but unsustainable.

Deploying its fighters effectively, the JNAF fought to gain air superiority to cover future amphibious landings. Held by the Australians, both Moresby and Milne Bay lay on the opposite side of the Owen Stanley range, and for the time being the only war to speak of in the SWPA was between the respective air forces.

Positive moves to get the first B-25s into action were made on 27 March when orders indicating that John Davies had legitimate claim on the Dutch B-25s were cut by Gen Eugene Eubank, SWPA Director of Plans. Having confirmed that the twenty-four B-25s were at Batchelor Field, Davies flew down to FEAF ADVON headquarters at Brisbane to suggest he commandeer them. There was some protest at first, Eubank fearing a diplomatic incident if the Americans simply flew the Mitchells away. But realizing that time was short, Davies persuaded his superior that as other B-25s were on the way (which was true enough), surely the Dutch could replace their aircraft from American supplies. Eubank finally agreed, and signed the necessary orders.

Davies flew to Charters Towers, rounded up twenty-four pilots from the 13th and 90th Bomb Squadrons, and took off in a C-47 for the 900-mile (1,500km) flight to

(Above) John 'Big Jim' Davies and his crew back from the Royce mission to the Philippines, the first B-25 mission in World War II. All aircraft returned safely to Australia, Davies' having picked up a few holes from enemy flak. via NAA

Port Moresby's airfields gave the Allies a foothold in New Guinea for flying medium bomber missions to enemy targets located further north. Occasionally, damaged aircraft had to get down fast, and this B-25C (41-12898) came to rest at 'Fourteen-Mile Drome', one of the strips surrounding the port. USAF

Batchelor Field. It arrived at 1700hr, and having reassured an American officer that his men had come specifically to pick up the aircraft, Davies and his group climbed aboard the B-25s and began taking off at 1830hr. Thirty minutes later the last Mitchell had left.

While Davies and his formation were in the air, the lines of communication between various official bodies became very busy: the upshot was that when the B-25s put down at Archer Field outside Brisbane to refuel, offi-

cialdom stepped in, backed up by MPs, and told Davies that he could not leave until his orders could be verified. But Gen Eubank could not be contacted, and with more talk of the urgency of hitting back at the enemy, Davies, supported by Pappy Gunn, won the day. The major who commanded Archer Field could hardly refuse — a written order superseded any verbal order he had from elsewhere. He waved the MPs away and the B-25s took off again. FEAF's message to hold them back arrived too late.

The above confusion probably came about because there was not enough time to inform everyone who 'needed to know' about the previously agreed transfer of the Dutch Mitchells. It has passed into the annals of B-25 history that the 3rd spirited or simply whisked the aircraft away, but this was far from the truth. However, it is perhaps understandable that those not privy to the details of the agreement questioned Davies' orders, as they had — as they saw it — a perfect right to do so.

The Dutch B-25s touched down at Charters Towers in the dark, their pilots being guided in by runway lights. Willing hands from the 3rd Attack helped get them into revetments and away from inquisitive eyes. But the official signals continued to fly, and by the 28th the confusion continued to the extent that the Archer Field commander was placed under arrest, pending court martial, for allowing twelve aircraft to be removed without proper authority. Fortunately Gen Eubank was finally located, and FEAF commander Gen George Brett called him. The conversation was brief, Brett concurring with the need to get the US into the war in New Guinea without wasting any more time.

The popularized version of this saga usually rounds out with Pappy Gunn flying back to Batchelor Field to request the bombsights which had apparently been removed from the appropriated B-25s. Rumour has it that these were taken from the Dutch stores at gunpoint – but it is just another example of 'need to know' principles not being widely applied, because in fact the Dutch B-25s had been configured to take the Estoppey D-8 sight. Factory installation of the support bracket mounting for this particular sight probably included a removable adaptor, and it may be that Gunn saw this installation and mistakenly believed it to be for a Sperry sight, quantities of which he further understood to have been stored by the Dutch. In fact Sperry sights were never delivered with these early aircraft because they had not been ordered.

Advanced bombsights or not, having obtained a dozen B-25Cs, the 3rd Attack was operational. Meanwhile, the 89th BS was awaiting the arrival of A-20s, and went to work servicing the B-17s belonging to the 19th BG, while the 8th BS equipped with A-24 dive bombers as a temporary expedient. Personnel of the 38th Bomb Group (Medium) had also undertaken assembly and maintenance work while awaiting B-25s. The only other bomb group almost ready to move to the Pacific at that time was the 22nd, with B-26s.

By early April 1942 the SWPA command, very much a joint US–Australian organization, had become more firmly established. Among the American officers appointed to occupy senior staff positions was Brig Gen Ralph Royce, fresh from a fact-finding tour in England. Royce set about planning – and leading – the combat debut of the B-25C in the hands of the 3rd Attack Group.

By the 11th, a force of ten Mitchells had been assembled. John Davies flew the leading aircraft, the B-25s in their turn following three B-17s (led by Royce) which undertook navigation. One B-25 crew had

When the 38th Bomb Group arrived in the south-west Pacific, it brought much needed muscle to FEAF. Based for a time at Borona, the unit's early Mitchells included 'Ole Cappy', seen in a typical open-air servicing area. USAF

to stay behind in Darwin, their aircraft having suffered a torn mainwheel tyre. The rest took off from Darwin and set course for Mindanao, skirting enemy-held islands and towering storm clouds en route. The force became dispersed, each crew being obliged to make their landing approach independently; thus Robert Strickland's flight of five B-25s put down at Del Monte with the three B-17s, and Herman Lowery's flight landed at Valentia, a dispersal strip 40 miles (65km) away. When night fell, Filipino groundcrews removed the long-range tanks and bombed up the aircraft.

But time was now getting short if much further Allied retaliation was to originate in the Philippines: on 9 April the Japanese had captured Bataan, which resulted in a hurried evacuation of American and Filipino personnel from Corregidor. While Mindanao remained in Allied hands it was possible to ferry people out (including some AAF groundcrews), although suitable transport aircraft were in very short supply. And so this limited retaliation began, with just six battered P-40s representing a token escort force to pin down the enemy air units based at Davao and protect the bombers should they be attacked during take-off and landing.

Combat Debut

At dawn on 12 April the B-25 made its Pacific war debut by attacking Cebu City and Davao about 100 miles (160km) to the north of Del Monte, while the B-17s bombed Nichols Field on Luzon. On return, Lowery's B-25s returned to Valentia, while Strickland's flight landed at Maramag, another grass dispersal strip near Del Monte. Two P-40s got airborne to cover the refuelling and rearming of the bombers for a repeat raid in the afternoon. On 13 April the B-25s attacked again, one raid being made on Cebu and two on Davao, their primary target being the dock area. The P-40 escort was not called upon, and despite groundfire being described as 'intense', no Mitchells were lost. Stung into action, the Japanese bombed Del Monte and badly damaged one of the B-17s.

Ten B-25s and two remaining B-17s landed at Del Monte at dusk on the 13th. With fuel and bomb stocks low, it was time to return to Australia. Toiling through the night once again, the loyal groundcrews prepared the bombers, realizing as they did so that their own future was uncertain, to say the least. Around midnight the Royce force took off and set course, each machine laden down with passengers. Only nine B-25s left,

'Scat', a B-25C of the 38th Bomb Group, gets some detail attention at Garbutt airfield near Townsville, Australia, on 11 November 1942. USAF

however, as Gunn's aircraft needed a replacement for a long-range tank that had been destroyed when the enemy bombed Del Monte. In fact it took another two days for Gunn to locate and fit two tanks salvaged from a B-18. He finally arrived in Australia on 16 April.

None of the B-25s had been located by the Japanese, and in total the small force managed at least twenty sorties before the Royce mission returned to Australia. In their first war sorties the B-25s had suffered no crew casualties and no aircraft losses in return for the claimed sinking of a Japanese freighter, the possible sinking of two more, and the downing of three enemy aircraft. As regards damage, Col Davies' aircraft (B-25C 41-12483) had

picked up a few holes from enemy ground-fire. The 3rd BG was awarded a DUC for this daring series of raids, while Davies received a well earned DSC.

The ten B-25Cs (with former Dutch serials where known) that flew the World War II debut mission, with their pilots and co-pilots, were as follows:

41-12441 (?) (13th BS) Capt Herman Lowery*; Lt Lee Walker
41-12442 (?) (13th BS) Lt Gus Heiss*; Lt Ed Townsend*;
41-12443 (N5-123) (13th BS) Lt J.R. Smith*; Lt Peter Talley*;
41-12455 (N5-124) (90th BS) Lt Wilson; Lt J.J. Keeter
41-12466 (N5-125) (13th BS) Lt Feltham; Lt Linn;
41-12472 (?) (13th BS) Lt Malcolm Peterson; Lt Harry Mangan*;
41-12480 (N5-128) (HQ 3rd BG) Capt Robert Strickland; Maj Hipps
41-12483 (N5-129) (HQ 3rd BG) Col John H. Davies*; Lt James McAfee*;
41-12485 (?) (90th BS) Capt Paul I. Gunn; Lt Frank Bender*;
41-12511 (N5-127) (13th BS) Lt Maull; Lt Howie West.

NB: Gunn's aircraft has also been identified as 41-12498 (N5-130)
* ex-27th BG

For the time being the 3rd BG remained in Australia, and enough B-25s arrived for crews of the 13th and 90th Squadrons to fly an increasing number of combat missions. If anything, it was A-20s that were in short supply for the 3rd, the 8th BS of which continued to fly the A-24 Dauntless.[1]

Precious B-25s were lost as the 3rd maintained the pressure on the enemy garrisons at Lae, Gasmata, Salamaua and Buna during April. Then on 5 May, Lt Lee Walker's B-25 came home with the electrifying news that a Japanese fleet was heading for Moresby. In fact it did not materialize because the Navy stepped in, and the Battle of the Coral Sea caused the enemy to withdraw.

American bomber crews were not alone in lacking sufficient aircraft during this desperately difficult period, as RAAF squadrons were also in need of US aircraft to add more strength to their own operations. A modest RAF presence in the SWPA also became directly associated with early B-25 operations, again by utilizing some of the Dutch aircraft, albeit in the more passive role of photographic reconnaissance.

Many early model B-25s gave sterling service, and finished their combat days on more peaceful courier duties. A two-star general used this B-25C-20 (42-64530) pictured here at Whenuapi, near Auckland, New Zealand, circa 1945. P.A. Harrison

CHAPTER FIVE

Not as Briefed

Following the raid on Pearl Harbor, American citizens suffered extreme frustration and a burning national desire to retaliate against Japan. The armed forces chiefs conferred long and hard to find a way for America to strike back, but it was far from easy. One of the reasons was that the joint US-British Arcadia Conference of late 1941–42 had confirmed an intention merely to contain the Japanese so as to concentrate first and foremost on the defeat of Nazi Germany, and the AAC was in the throes of introducing a whole new generation of aircraft into service. If flung into combat with ill-trained crews and unproven equipment, losses would be high against an enemy who was clearly far better equipped militarily than anyone in the West had imagined. The modest despatch of bombers to Australia was unlikely to produce spectacular results immediately: something more positive was required.

As with many great ideas, the concept of a carrier strike came about indirectly. During the early planning for an initial landing by US forces in the European war zone – which became Operation *Torch* in November 1942 – a way was sought to transfer AAF bombers and fighters to front line bases quickly and with minimum risk. Both carriers and aircraft would be vulnerable to attack if they attempted to enter ports still contested by the enemy. Hap Arnold consulted the Chief of Naval Operations, Admiral Ernest King, and Capt Francis Low, a submariner on the CNO's staff. When the idea of flying Army fighters from carriers was put forward the Navy confirmed that this could be done without difficulty. It was then a short step for Francis Low to develop the idea into a carrier strike on Japan with Army bombers.

Capt Duncan, King's air officer, agreed that after the raid the bombers would have to not turn back, but fly on to land in the nearest friendly territory, which was then in China. Duncan presented his findings to Arnold, who in turn brought in Lt Col James Doolittle. As Arnold's special projects officer, Doolittle was well qualified to examine the plan and confirm that it was feasible. A 'Tokyo Project' was formed in great secrecy, and the carrier *Hornet* was chosen to ferry the bombers as near to the coast of Japan as was possible.

Negotiations with China confirmed that airfields at Chuchow, Kweilin, Kian, Lishui and Yushan would be expecting the B-25s. Of these, Yushan was the nearest to Japan and Kweilin the furthest; the use of Chuchow, although it was closest to the eastern coast of China, remained in some doubt until the last minute, as Chinese premier Chaing Kai Shek feared possible Japanese retaliation in an area hitherto unoccupied by the loathed enemy. His fears were far from groundless.

Doolittle and Duncan had few illusions as to the limitations of the idea. They realized that taking the *Hornet* close enough to Japan as part of a conventional Navy carrier strike would be highly dangerous for the ships involved, and probably very limited in terms of the high explosive it could deliver. But if the *Hornet* could ferry and launch twenty B-25s, Doolittle would command a force with a punch heavy enough to cause some damage to the target. Above all, a small number of warships should have an even chance of taking the enemy completely by surprise – and the psychological impact of that would be enormous.

Once a 'long-range' carrier attack was deemed to be feasible, the detail planning got underway. Of the three medium/light bombers then in AAC service, it was eventually realized that the B-25 was the only real choice for such a demanding operation. Of the alternatives, Doolittle himself quickly ruled out the B-17 – although a heavy bomber would have been preferred had it been possible to use one – and the Douglas B-23. This medium bomber was ruled out early because its 92ft (28m) wingspan would not have cleared the *Hornet*'s island.

Out too went the B-26: the Marauder was not only in short supply, but was more bulky in terms of deck parking space, and it needed about 1,000ft (300m) to take off safely – and the *Hornet* had an overall flightdeck length of 809ft (247m). The A-20 was not really considered because Doolittle had stipulated that to make the raid worthwhile, each participating aircraft would have to carry 2,000lb (609kg) of bombs and be capable of a maximum range of 2,400 miles (3,860km). Early A-20s had too little range, hardly any space for extra fuel, and only half the required bomb capacity. The B-25 it would be.

When the project team got down to making some measurements it was seen that successfully launching a force of B-25s from the deck of the *Hornet* would still take some doing. The wingspan of the largest Navy carrier bomber of the day was that of the TBD Devastator, at 50ft (15m). The B-25B spanned 67ft 7in (20.6m), and although that extra 17ft (5m) or so could be accommodated on a carrier flightdeck, the Mitchell's tricycle gear and high, twin-tail configuration meant that it had to be considered as occupying a large 'box' of space. The beam of the *Hornet* was 83ft 3in (25.4m), and even the Navy's 'tail-dragger' bombers and fighters had to be bunched closely together, almost interlocking if necessary, in order to pack a substantial number of them on the flightdeck for ferrying purposes. Furthermore, smaller aircraft could be moved around the flightdeck – but that would be far from easy with a medium bomber the size of the B-25. Therefore, pretake-off marshalling of the Mitchells had to be kept to the very minimum.

Hanger storage of the Army bombers was ruled out at an early stage. Each B-25 would have to ride across the Pacific secured to the deck of the *Hornet*, and it was found that, rather than parking the bombers nose to tail, more could be fitted on if they were parked off the deck centreline in what amounted to a tight 'V' formation.

Although the raid was originally planned around twenty B-25s, that number was reduced to eighteen. Then, considering the available area of the flightdeck, it was seen that a maximum of sixteen B-25s fitted comfortably without crowding, which might have proved dangerous during taxiing and take-off. And both Army and Navy chiefs were agreed that that was still a sizable enough force.

Each B-25B would carry a bombload of 2,000lb (900kg), making a total of 32,000lb (14,500kg) to deliver on specified targets in Tokyo, Kobe and Nagoya. If the Doolittle force achieved any sort of bomb concentration, then some damage could be done – certainly enough to shake up the Japanese and achieve the object of the raid. But the most important consideration for the B-25B was range and fuel load. It proved possible to increase the basic tankage of the aircraft to 1,150gal (5,230l), which gave a theoretical range of 2,250 miles (3,620km) at a speed of 170mph (270km/h). Fuel consumption in lean cruise condition was brought down to as little as 80gal (360l) per hour. Space for a 50gal (230l) tank – exactly the amount required for engine run-up and take-off – was found by removing the B-25's remotely controlled ventral turret, which also saved 450lb (200kg) in weight. Tanks of 160 and 230gal (730 and 1,050l) were located in the bombardier's crawl-way and over the top of the bomb-bay, which allowed space for four 500lb (230kg) demolition bombs and a cluster of incendiaries.

As for aiming the bombs, the AAF was unwilling to risk even one Sperry or Norden bombsight falling into enemy hands, let alone up to sixteen of them, and it was decided that an alternative method would have to be found. This problem actually solved itself: quite apart from the fact that the Norden's capabilities were still jealously guarded, it was designed to function at conventional bomber altitudes. At the low, below 1,000ft (300m), height that the Tokyo force would maintain, it would have been of little use anyway.

Ross Greening addressed himself to the problem, and came up with a remarkably simple solution: the '20 cent' sight, so called because it cost about that much to manufacture! Greening reasoned that providing each B-25 bombardier could transfer his sighting and drift allowance skills with a real sight to a far simpler device, the basic principles would still apply. And so it was to prove.

Taking the lead-line depth gauge used on the old Mississippi River boats as his first principle, Greening was able to concoct a device consisting of little more than an angled sighting bar fixed to a backplate marked off in degrees. It was made to fix into the Norden linkages, thus enabling the bombardiers to pass turn information to the pilot through the PDI – pilot direction indicator – instrument. This dispensed with any need for verbal communication. By simply computing the dropping angle of the bombs and setting that figure on the 'Mark Twain' sight, each of Doolittle's bombardiers could release his load as the target became aligned with the sighting bar. The Raiders consequently flew their mission with a bombsight costing next to nothing – a Norden sight carried a price tag of about $10,000.

Greening also thought up some extra 'armament' to deter any Japanese fighters that might happen to intercept the force. Even though each B-25B had two ball-and-socket nose positions for a single 'fifty, no forward guns were carried; and owing to very tight weight limits, only the top turret in each aircraft was armed. It was fervently hoped that Tokyo would be so completely taken by surprise by the sudden appearance of the Army bombers that no enemy fighters would have time to intervene. But just in case, Greening devised dummy 'broomhandle' guns: two of these were located in the extreme end of each B-25B fuselage, which in standard form had only a small plexiglass cone for observation purposes.

Doolittle considered that twenty-four B-25Bs should be reserved for the mission; this figure allowed for ample 'wastage', hopefully ensuring that at least fifteen would be available. There was little disagreement as to the source of crews for the raid, as the B-25B had then entered service with only the 17th BG and the attached 89th RS. Then based at Pendleton in Oregon, most group personnel responded when they were asked to volunteer for a special mission. Doolittle's unit was therefore a cross-section of crews from the 34th, 37th, 95th and 89th Squadrons, and those chosen to go on the operation also 'donated' their aircraft; in Doolittle's opinion it was important to keep together crews who knew each other and functioned well during operational flights. After moving to Eglin Field, Florida, the three squadron commanders drew up rosters of the twenty-four crews, who were to begin special training without delay.

Maj John Hilger, Doolittle's second-in-command, shouldered the ultimate responsibility for seeing that these regular combat crews could soon make ultra-short take-offs in their sleep. Early on, Hilger enlisted the practical help of Lt Henry Miller, USN, flying instructor at Pensacola Naval Air Station; he would assist the crews in carrier-style operation using fully laden Army bombers. It was decided that the full twenty-four crews would not only be trained, but would also actually embark on the *Hornet*, even though some of them would inevitably not be required for the raid itself; then if any crew member dropped out at the last minute, or fell sick, they could be replaced immediately. Also, if every man who knew even the slightest detail of the raid was aboard the carrier, nobody would be in a position inadvertently to tell what he knew, thus avoiding even the remotest possibility of a disgruntled, non-participating individual talking. In such an operation total secrecy was paramount, as Doolittle constantly stressed throughout the weeks beforehand.

While the training programme took place on land, Doolittle wanted some practical figures from a real carrier launch. Two B-25s were therefore loaded aboard the *Hornet* at Norfolk, Virginia, and on 2 February she sailed for a point off the Atlantic seaboard, far from prying eyes. Once they were beyond the sight of land, the project's naval co-ordinator Capt Donald Duncan watched Lts John Fitzgerald and James McCarthy (neither of whom flew the actual mission) carry out the first carrier launches associated with the special project. As the first B-25 was spotted for take-off, Fitzgerald ran up the engines to maximum revolutions. And when the launching officer made the 'go' signal, the Army crew was surprised at how quickly their aircraft lifted off, significantly short of the end of the flightdeck. Both B-25s joined up and turned for home, having set a small record – the *Hornet*'s crew had just witnessed the launch of the largest-ever aircraft from the deck of a US carrier. More importantly for the success of the special mission, it was now certain that a loaded B-25B could make a carrier launch without difficulty.

Doolittle, meanwhile, had a far from easy time in ensuring that his B-25s were prepared for the unusual mission, even though he enjoyed a direct line to Hap Arnold. It was Doolittle's responsibility to closely monitor the modification work, undertaken at McClellan Field by the Sacramento Air Depot. Each aircraft needed new propellers, hydraulic valves for the dorsal turrets, and back-type parachutes to replace the standard seat type. One of the most important additions was to install a 160gal (730l) Mareng flexible fuel cell in the bombardier's crawl-way in each aircraft, a lightweight, synthetic rubber cell designed by Martin Aircraft to fit any available space, which could be rolled up and stored when it had been emptied. Another, 60gal (270l) fuel tank, was located in the space for the ventral turret. Other modifications included the removal of the liaison radio sets, and the replacement of plexiglass windows adjacent to the navigator's position with a new type.

All these changes had to be completed in a matter of weeks by civilian contractors, and it was fortunate that the 17th BG crews were able to remain with their aircraft for most of the time. As diplomatically as possible, they dissuaded the maintenance crews from being too heavy-handed. Carburettor settings were particularly critical to fuel consumption, and Doolittle himself was incensed on one occasion when clouds of black smoke and backfiring told him a mechanic could not start an engine of one of his B-25Bs. More smoke and grinding metal was too much for Doolittle, who jumped into the bomber and shouldered the hapless mechanic away from the controls – and his consternation was justified when he found that the carburettor settings, which had been carefully adjusted and which by intention did not conform to 'the book', had all been changed!

It was this sort of attitude that frustrated everyone concerned with the project. Civilian employees of the depot failed to

appreciate the sense of urgency that inspired the military personnel – and of course Doolittle could not tell them why this handful of standard Army bombers needed such extra care. Later, malfunctions experienced by some crews on the actual raid revealed that not all instructions had been followed 'to the letter'.

At last all the B-25s were flown from Sacramento to NAS Alameda – even

though some still lacked all the specified modifications, including the new navigators' windows. After a thorough inspection, the sixteen Mitchells selected for the mission were parked on the wharf next to the *Hornet*. Each bomber was drained of fuel, linked via the nose-wheel towbar to a navy 'donkey', and moved to the pier. Cranes then hoisted the B-25s bodily onto the *Hornet*'s deck, without any airframe

(Above) Doolittle and his crews await the take-off time aboard the carrier. Obvious delight at knowing the target shows on many faces. via NAA

Lashed down firmly to prevent collisions as the *Hornet* rolled her way across the Pacific, Army and Navy crewmen chew the fat. At right is the B-25B flown by the crew of Edward York and Robert Emmens. US Navy

disassembly being necessary. The Army crews filed up the gangplank. With fifteen Mitchells aboard his ship, Capt Marc A. Mitscher thought there was room for one more, and Doolittle was happy with that: he wanted a full complement, as he planned to have the last aircraft fly off the carrier a short distance out of port and return home. He thought that a practical demonstration of how a B-25 could take off from a carrier would give the crews extra confidence that such a feat was not only possible, but easier than it might have seemed. This demonstration flight was subsequently cancelled, however, because it was decided that all sixteen aircraft should travel to Tokyo.

Hornet slipped her moorings on the morning of 2 April, passed under the Golden Gate Bridge, and headed out of San Francisco Bay into the Pacific. Accompanying the carrier were the cruisers *Nashville* and *Vincennes*, four ships of Destroyer Division 22, and the tanker *Cimarron*. Shortly after she set sail, the *Hornet* was visited by a Navy airship: the 'blimp' crew lowered two boxes of navigator's windows for those B-25s that had not yet had them fitted.

On 8 April, Vice Admiral Halsey sailed from Pearl Harbor with the carrier *Enterprise*, the cruisers *Northampton* and *Salt Lake City*, plus four destroyers and the tanker *Sabine*. Five days later the two groups joined up about 1,000 miles

(Above) Navy men view the B-25s, perhaps wondering if the Army pilots can take off successfully. As the days passed the deck looked increasingly small to the Mitchell crews. At right foreground is the aircraft of crew No. 7, captained by Ted Lawson. US Navy

A good view of the tethering method used to restrain the Mitchells on *Hornet*'s deck against the pull of the ocean swell. Several aircraft including Ross Greening's 'Hari Carrier' had nose art before they were loaded, and this was left on for the Tokyo raid. US Navy

(1,600km) east of Midway Island, to become Task Force 16. In the afternoon of 2 April, Mitscher decided not to keep the sailors in suspense any longer, and announced over the ship's loudspeaker: 'This force is bound for Tokyo!' The reaction throughout the *Hornet* was immediate – and deafening. Halsey heard a similar response from the *Enterprise* crew, while semaphore signallers informed the rest of the task force.

As her own deck was full of B-25s, the *Hornet* could not provide her own combat air patrol in the event of attack, and this duty was handed to the naval flyers of the 'Big E'. If the Japanese had attacked the US task force, either the B-25s would have been flown off, their crews taking their chance either to find land or to ditch, or they would have been pushed over the side to clear the flightdeck and enable *Hornet's* air group to defend the ship.

All went smoothly until the 18th, when TF 16 suspected that it had been detected. Japanese picket boats stationed 700 miles (1,130km) east of the home islands were sighted, and *Enterprise* launched elements

sage confirming the presence of the American force (which was indeed the case). Not taking any chances on that possibility, Halsey and Doolittle elected to launch the B-25s. *Hornet* was then 668 nautical miles (620 st miles/1,000km) off Inuboe Saki, the nearest point of Japan: in other

the Mitchells had to be launched was a mile less fuel for the bombers to reach China after the raid – but that could not be helped in the circumstances. Furthermore the weather conditions were far from favourable: a 40-knot gale was blowing, and waves with 30ft (9m) crests pitched the *Hornet* violently, her deck dropping and rising in the swell. Her escorting destroyers had departed earlier due to the weather, only the carrier and the cruisers proceeding towards the intended launch point.

'Vulture's Row' view of the largest 'air group' the *Hornet* had carried into action. The aircraft flown by Everett Holstrom's crew shows to advantage the dummy 'broom-handle' tail guns. US Navy

'Get 'Em in the Air!'

Shortly before 08.00hr, Doolittle's crew settled themselves aboard; one of America's most experienced flyers, he eased the B-25 forward, and at a signal from the *Hornet's* LSO, brought the engines to full revolutions. The bomber eased forwards on the spray-lashed deck, gathered speed, and lifted off at exactly 08.20hr. Seeing Doolittle's Mitchell safely away – and helped no doubt by the prayers of every pilot on the carrier – the rest prepared to follow. They took off in a pre-determined numerical order, after Doolittle in number one. In deference to the weather a launching plan was prepared based on the intervals between swells: thus every time the carrier deck rose, a Mitchell would be flown off, the pilot timing his launch as the deck returned to the horizontal.

Flap position was believed to be critical for a good take-off, as Travis Hoover was to discover: Hoover followed Doolittle's B-25s, but he deployed too much flap, and the nose of the aircraft rose a little too high – so a large board with the chalked message 'Stabilizer Neutral' was displayed to the remaining pilots from the island of the *Hornet*. Ted Lawson, who later wrote a graphic personal account of the raid[1], forgot his flaps entirely, but his lift-off was so smooth that few of the crew felt a thing.

All Army crewmen were very conscious that each B-25's right wingtip cleared the bulk of the *Hornet's* island by just 8ft (2.4m) during the short take-off roll, and the last pilot, the luckless William Farrow, had a slightly more eventful launch than the rest when his aircraft sideslipped enough to risk a collision with the bridge. Farrow corrected, but meanwhile a member of the deck-handling party lost his footing and stumbled into the arc of one of the B-25's spinning propellers. He subsequently had his arm amputated.

of VF-6's Wildcats towards the *Nitto Maru*, the nearest of the boats. This was eventually sunk (by prolonged gunfire from the *Nashville*), but it had to be assumed that the enemy had transmitted a radio mes-

words, the bombers would have to fly 150 miles (240km) further than they had planned in order to bomb their targets.

Doolittle had always known that every mile further off the Japanese mainland that

(Above) Regular engine runs were made as *Hornet* and her escort – including the cruiser *Nashville* seen in the background – headed for the Tokyo raid launching point. US Navy

Discovered by Japanese picket boats, the raid had to launch early, Doolittle's Mitchell making the first take-off, followed by fifteen others. There was but one mishap, when a rating lost an arm to a spinning propeller. via NAA

The crew of the *Hornet* were tense as each B-25 ran up to full power and raced down the flightdeck; the ship was practically defenceless until all the bombers had departed, and a take-off crash did not bear thinking about. Luckily no such incident occurred, and by 09.20 the last B-25 felt air under its wheels.

The revised, early take-off was a disappointment, but the Americans were right to be prudent because the enemy picket-boat messages had indeed forewarned Adm

Nagumo's First Carrier Fleet, which was at sea returning to Japan after raiding Ceylon. It comprised five carriers, four battleships, three cruisers and nine destroyers. Picking

up the message, this force did make an attempt to pursue TF 16, though abandoned the chase on 22 April. There were also thirteen IJN submarines at sea at the time which could have posed a threat, although this never materialized. In view of this potentially dangerous situation, Halsey wasted no time in speeding back to Pearl Harbor.

With their crews watching the B-25s until they disappeared, the American ships withdrew. Doolittle meanwhile set course and led his small unit to Japan. The main force of thirteen aircraft had been briefed to attack Tokyo, while two went to Nagoya and one to Kobe. Having joined up, the Mitchell force encountered clearer weather as it approached the Japanese mainland. In five three-plane flights, with Doolittle's ship leading, the formation opened out to give the impression that there were more aircraft approaching – just in case the Japanese defences were plotting their progress. But as they raced over the outlying districts of the city, it was clear to the crews that their approach had not been recognized for what it was, because anyone glancing up assumed the B-25s to be Japanese, and waved.

Lt Travis Hoover of the 37th BS dropped his bombs in the northern part of Tokyo, while Capt David Jones of the 95th BS, leading the second flight, released his over the city centre. In the third flight, Capt York of the 95th BS selected points on the south side and Tokyo Bay area. Ross Greening of the 89th RS led the fourth flight which dropped its bombs on Yoko-hama and the Yokosuka naval base; and finally the three bombers of Maj John Hilger's fifth flight swept over Nagoya and Kobe. Doolittle himself made landfall about 80 miles (130km) north of Tokyo. Some 10 miles (16km) north of the Japan-ese capital he encountered enemy fighters, which made no attempt to engage. There was considerable air activity, and over half the crews reported seeing airborne fighters, numerous trainers, and a number of busy airfields. AA fire was observed by all but three crews, including Hoover, who sepa-rated from Doolittle to bomb. Fire was described as between light and heavy, although whether the Japanese gunners were getting more into the spirit of the realistic air defence exercise being held over Tokyo that day, or were making seri-ous attempts to destroy the intruders, remains a moot point. Crews did report being bracketed by shells, however.

Using his camera from the cockpit win-dows of ship No. 13, Lt Richard A. Knobloch, co-pilot to Lt Edgar E. McElroy, exposed vital photographic evidence of the

The *Hornet* had little choice but to launch the B-25s into the teeth of a 40-knot gale. via NAA

While pilot Edgar McElroy held the aircraft steady, Lt Richard Knobloch snapped a few photos from the right-hand seat – the only visual record taken of the raid in progress. This was how the Yokosuka dock area looked as the B-25 swept over dozens of potential targets. US Navy

raid – even though the fact that none of the bombers was likely to return, thereby reducing the chances that his film would ever reach safe hands. But part of it *did* sur-vive, and at least two prints were widely published to reveal potential target areas in the Japanese capital for the first time. Some

AA fire followed the racing B-25s, and enemy fighters were spotted by the Ameri-can crews. One aircraft was hit by flak, but flew on, while Lt Joyce's crew blazed away at fighters that attacked them, apparently with some success for the American turret gunner, who claimed several as destroyed.

A suitable decal applied to B-25C-1 (42-13133) perpetuated Ted Lawson's personal insignia, to mark his part in the Tokyo raid for the 1944 film *Thirty Seconds over Tokyo*, which was based on his book. Note the nose of the NAA XB-28 at left. via NAA

Only one B-25, that flown by Lt Everett Holstrom of the 95th BS, failed to bomb anything more concrete than water: harassed by Japanese fighters, Holstrom jettisoned his bombload into the sea while making good his escape. Most of the citizens of Tokyo naturally assumed that the bombers were flown by their own Army or Navy pilots conducting a highly realistic exercise: that they could belong to anyone else was unthinkable. Only when the bombs actually exploded did some of them realize the awful truth – but in general the full implications of the raid only sunk in later.

Halsey himself had picked up part of the reaction to the raid: tuned into a broadcast from Tokyo, the admiral heard the air-raid sirens sound even as the announcer was speaking. With undisguised satisfaction he realized that Doolittle's bombers had arrived.

Escape

With their bombs gone, the Doolittle force faced arguably the toughest part of the flight as they headed south over the Sea of Japan to a landfall on mainland China. During the sea crossing, Ross Greening saw, photographed and shot up a trawler. Due to the longer-than-expected flight after leaving the *Hornet*, daylight was fading as the bombers approached China, and rather than trying to find airfields in unfamiliar terrain in pitch darkness, most crews elected either to ditch off the coast, or to bail out over land. In total, fifty men took to their 'chutes, and only one was killed making the jump. Those crews who rode their aircraft down to ditch or crash-land suffered the most casualties – and in the case of eight men, capture by the Japanese.

Down in Russia

As the raiders left the enemy mainland behind, one B-25 broke off from the rest: Edward 'Ski' York of the 95th BS, flying 40-2242, realized that his engines were burning fuel much too fast, a fault attributable to improper setting of his carburettors at Sacramento. Deciding that he would never make any of the Chinese bases, York changed course and flew almost due north, more or less following the coast of China until a peninsula of mountainous land put the lone B-25 off the coast of Russia. Executing a 180-degree turn, York flew back along the coast, the crew looking for a likely landing point. Nobody wanted to fly directly over Vladivostok, which was almost certain to be defended, so York turned inland and flew into Siberia: a landing on Russian soil was preferable to ditching.

York then spotted a small airport which turned out to be in Primorskkrai, some 40 miles (64km) north of Vladivostock, and elected to land; and everyone aboard the Mitchell was greatly relieved when he put the aircraft down safely at 17.45. It had been a long day.

Relief turned to frustration, however, when the York crew were interned by the 'friendly' Russians. The five Americans were held captive for over a year, mainly because the Soviets prevented any news of their presence in the country being revealed outside a small circle of officials. As the only bomber to survive the Tokyo raid and land intact, B-25B 40-2242 was presumably evaluated by the Russians – although they had already done this to some extent in the US. The ultimate fate of the aircraft is unknown.

Eight B-25s had bombed their primary targets, and five others had hit secondaries. Those that inadvertently overshot their targets and bombed what were predominantly residential districts inevitably caused some civilian casualties. These deaths, publicly condemned by a regime that had already butchered thousands, were made the excuse for executing three B-25 crew members in October 1942. A fourth man died of maltreatment in December 1943.

As the world learned soon enough, the daring and courageous raid on Tokyo was hailed as a great success, and served as an immense morale-booster to the American people. It caused consternation throughout the Japanese government, who considered its implications to be of a seriousness that far outweighed the amount of damage actually inflicted. As a result, the defences of the Tokyo area, both in terms of AA guns and fighter units, were increased, and most importantly, they were never substantially reduced – even when Japanese air forces in the field were crying out for reinforcements, and long before Tokyo was faced with a much greater threat from B-29 attacks at the end of the war, the imperial planners would not relax the city's fighter defence.

Of the sixteen B-25Bs participating in the raid, fifteen were destroyed in crashes on land, or ditchings. The largest number, including that flown by Doolittle, went down in China after their crews bailed out. His crew abandoned their aircraft near Tien Mu Shen, about 70 miles (110km) north of Chuchow, whilst Doolittle himself came down a short distance from the wreck.

Thoroughly depressed, he examined the remains of the B-25 and was photographed sitting on one of the shattered wings.

Convinced that the raid had been a failure, Doolittle returned home via Chungking in mid-May to learn that at least in propaganda terms, his small force had provided a much-needed boost to the Allied cause. Subsequent analysis of the raid also showed that most of the bombs had landed in the right place, and had damaged some of the industrial areas of the Japanese capital and dock installations at the Yokosuka naval base. Back home the press clamoured for details of the raid, but for security reasons Roosevelt maintained the secret of the involvement of a carrier for twelve months; he added to the mystery of how the B-25s had managed to get so close to Japan by announcing that they had come from 'Shangri-la'. This mythical area of Tibet invented by author James Hilton for his book *Lost Horizon* served to hide the *Hornet*'s identity until it was officially divulged.

In catching the imagination of the American public, the Tokyo raid also earned the B-25 a lasting place in aviation history. However, although the general public linked that single operation of April 1942 indelibly with the Mitchell, neither its first association with carriers nor its attacks on Japan remained unique, as will be described later.

Return to Combat

The majority of the Tokyo raid crews were re-assigned when they returned home, among them B-25 pilot Ross Greening. Subsequently shot down on a B-26 mission on 17 July 1943, he became a prisoner and ended up at Stalag Luft 1 at Barth, Germany. Greening was a trained artist and a writer, and it was he who perpetuated the phrase 'Not as Briefed' when he later published a book on the Tokyo raid under that title. It contained his artwork, much of it done within the confines of German barbed wire.

The indomitable bravery of Chinese civilians in helping the downed US crews evade the clutches of the Japanese became a major part of the aftermath of the raid. Militarily the loss of Chuchow, Lishui and Yushan airfields was felt when the enemy swept into eastern China to conduct an orgy of reprisals, extreme in its brutality even by Japanese standards. Airfields were systematically ploughed up, to such an

extent that it was easier to build new ones than to try to repair them.

Claire Chennault, then commanding the American Volunteer Group in China, was chagrined that because of security he had not been told of the raid, and publicly stated that had he been so informed he could undoubtedly have saved the bombers by using his early warning network to guide them to safe landings. A ready-made force of B-25s would also have been invaluable to Chennault at a time when bombers were worth their weight in gold in the CBI. And he had been promised a force of bombers for some time.

Japanese reaction to the raid was quite strange: it was said that they perpetuated a particularly deep hatred for the B-25, the aircraft that had first violated their airspace. Mitchells could not be sent over the home islands for more than two years after the Doolittle raid – though the US also bore in mind the propaganda value of the medium bombers returning. When that day came in July 1945 it proved to the Japanese without a shadow of doubt that if the home islands were within range of twin-engined aircraft, then their military position was little short of dire.

Medal of Honor (I)

Of the three B-25 pilots decorated with America's supreme award for gallantry, James Harold Doolittle was the first. The medal was awarded for leading the April 1942 Tokyo raid, one of the most inspired and daring military air actions of the war. Afterwards, fame followed Doolittle throughout his career, the raid often being directly linked with his name in print.

At the time, Doolittle himself was unsure as to the success of the raid – he was pictured sitting dejectedly on the wing of his B-25B (40-2344), wrecked on a Chinese hillside, and felt very unlike a hero, shunning medals. Having returned home, saddened by the loss of his entire force, he was nevertheless persuaded as to the morale-boosting value of the nation's highest honour going to the survivor of a particularly hazardous action. It indeed inspired great faith in the B-25 and the Army Air Forces.

'Jimmy' Doolittle had an outstanding World War II career subsequent to the Tokyo raid. He commanded the Twelfth, Fifteenth and Eighth Air Forces, rising progressively in rank to lieutenant general. Retiring from the Air Force in 1946, he enjoyed a successful business career as an oil company executive; he took full retirement in 1959. At Castle AFB in 1980 he was able to take the controls of a Mitchell 'one more time'. This aircraft, a B-25D/F-10, was restored to convincing B-25B configuration before the USAF presented it to the Air Force Museum. Doolittle passed away on 27 September 1993, aged ninety-seven.

Big Gun Mitchell

North American produced the B-25A and B under the manufacturer's identification number NA-62, and the B-25C as the NA-82, 90, 93, 94 and 96; the number changes identified aircraft intended for overseas customers as well as for the AAF. As the flow of Mitchells increased, a network of modification centres was organized to back up company facilities in making limited changes to the airframe, and in completing the installation of equipment. The airlines were brought into this important programme, NAA eventually using Northwest, TWA and Mid Continent to speed the process of making ready B-25s for combat operations. During 1942, 110 B-25s passed through modification centres, the figure rising to 271 for 1943.

A significant adaptation of the original airframe was the B-25G – though the company made no change to the original identification NA-96. Based on the B-25C, it was the first Mitchell version able to accommodate a 75mm cannon in the forward fuselage. One of the few practical results of a widespread pre-war research programme – and one by no means restricted to the US – into airborne use of heavy calibre cannon, the B-25G was the first of two Mitchell versions that NAA would build, and which would see combat. As events transpired, the B-25 was the only American aircraft to use cannon in a calibre larger than 37mm in combat during World War II.

Cannon Background

Experiments to mount large-calibre aircraft cannon seem to have originated in France as early as 1910, when Gabriel Voisin mounted a 37mm Hotchkiss in one of his biplanes. Development lagged in the 1920s, but work was done in the US, primarily to adapt French 37mm guns to improve muzzle velocity, rate of fire and reliability. The results obtained by John Browning, hired by the Colt Patent Firearms Company to further develop the French gun, created

some interest, although aircraft structures strong enough to mount such large weapons hardly existed.

When metal airframes appeared in the 1930s, much heavier weapons became more practical and Browning's work was taken up by the US Ordnance Department. Encouraging results led to a proposal to include 37mm and 75mm cannon in the armament options for a number of new attack aircraft. A 75mm cannon was fitted for air-firing testing in a Douglas B-18 in 1938, and the results appeared to confirm that a stream of heavy calibre shells would pulverize many types of ground target. The inherent drawbacks of cannon – primarily heavy weight, a slow rate of fire and limited storage space for the bulky ammunition, all of which had some detrimental effect on aircraft performance – had to be accepted in the overriding belief that such weapons had a worthwhile military application.

The size and weight of the weapon ruled out anything but a fuselage mounting, positively indicating a twin-engined aircraft. Further experimental firings at Eglin Field in 1940 resulted in the Army circulating proposals to industry.

Even before the new role of 'strafer' had been defined, the Air Corps reasoned that fitting a heavy calibre cannon in a specialized 'destroyer'-type aircraft would make

---

Specification – B-25G-1

Type:	Attack bomber with crew of five
Powerplant:	Two Wright R-2600-13s
Weights:	Empty 19,200lb (8,700kg); loaded 35,000lb (15,900kg)
Dimensions:	Wingspan 67ft 6in (20.57m); length 51ft (15.50m); height 15ft 9in (4.80m); wing area 610sq ft (56sq m)
Performance:	Maximum speed 280mph (451km/h) Range 1,560 miles (2,510km) Service ceiling 24,300ft (7,400m)
Armament:	One 75mm M-4 cannon with 21rpg, plus two 0.5in MG in shortened nose; two 0.5in MG in dorsal turret; two 0.5in MG in ventral turret; 3,000lb (1,360kg) of bombs in fuselage bay
Number built:	5; AAF serial numbers 42-32384 to 42-32388 (modified B-25C-15s)

NB First Mitchell fitted with 75mm cannon in short, 'solid' nose; contoured armour plate in port side windscreen and forward fuselage plate on pilot's side, behind pilots, forward of cannoneer's station, at bulkhead aft of turrets and around 75mm ammunition rack; crew complement: pilot and co-pilot, navigator/cannoneer and two gunners.

B-25G-5

Specification as for B-25G-1 except for deletion of ventral turret from aircraft 42-65001

Number built:	100 plus 200, total 300 (AAF serial numbers 42-64802 to 42-64901, and 42-64902 to 42-65101)

B-25G-10

Specification as for B-25G-5

Number built:	100 (AAF serial numbers 42-65102 to 42-65201)

The M-4 75mm cannon that turned the B-25G into a 'flying field gun'. Apart from the steel flatbed, the entire gun and carriage assembly were bolted to the floor of the aircraft in the space previously provided as a crawl-way for the bombardier. via NAA

(Right) In situ, this early 75mm cannon installation includes the four-segment 'petal' intended to prevent ingress of dust into the barrel. It was dispensed with after revealing a tendency to jam. via NAA

ground strafing safer. Undoubtedly borrowing the idea – and the name – from the German *Zerstörer* concept, the Army envisaged an aircraft able to use a gun capable of firing large calibre, explosive shells; it would expend fewer rounds than machine guns to destroy targets, with consequently less time spent over those targets. Repeat passes, which often proved so deadly when enemy ground gunners found the range, would be greatly reduced. Development time for a completely new aircraft suitable for this role would have been at least a year, but the Army wanted something practical more quickly, if possible. The B-25 was the answer.

In adapting the B-25C to take a 75mm cannon, North American utilized the crawl-way provided for the bombardier; this enabled the breech of the weapon to be located without major airframe changes. Replacing the glass nose with a shorter, solid nose section also allowed the fitting of two 0.5in machine guns which could be used to 'range in' the cannon while providing some forward firepower

A hinged clamshell door allowed access to the top two 'fifties in the B-25G. The horizontal plate visible below the cover, and its telescopic struts, was provided for servicing purposes. via NAA

once the 21-round cannon ammunition supply had been expended.

An official go-ahead for a 75mm cannon installation in the B-25 was received by NAA early in 1942, and the company adapted B-25C 41-13296 for the first installation. Fitted with a Colt-designed M-4 cannon, this aircraft then became the sole XB-25G and the first Mitchell to bear an 'experimental' designation; it made its maiden flight in the hands of Ed Virgin on 22 October 1942.

Compensating for the additional weight of the cannon and armour protection for the gun mechanism by saving weight in other areas, NAA kept the newly configured Mitchell within a reasonable limit. The result was that the B-25G scaled out only 1,000lb (450kg) more than a standard B-25C, with a maximum loaded weight of 35,000lb (15,870kg). Otherwise configured as a production B-25C retaining the bombbay and dorsal turret, NAA had dropped the ventral turret as a weight-saving concession.

Ed Virgin made two flights in the XB-25G on 22 October, accompanied by test engineer Paul Brewer. These flights aimed to work out basic procedures for cannon loading and function using dummy rounds, the aircraft's performance being monitored in level flight, dive and climb. Stall characteristics were also verified, and in a dive the XB-25G reached an indicated 340mph (550km/h) without showing any adverse effects from the extra weight it carried. Pending the successful outcome of live firing tests, the Army had its 'destroyer'.

NAA wasted no time in finding out if the 'airborne field gun' worked. On 23 October, Virgin, Brewer and Col Horace Quinn, who had been instrumental in conducting the first 75mm cannon trials with the B-18 back in 1938, flew the XB-25G out over the Pacific. Using shells containing 50 per cent, then 75 per cent of the full propellant charge, the crew made a number of firing runs. They felt – and briefly saw – the shells as they shot away from the nose of the aircraft, although Virgin later reported that the jolt when the cannon was fired was no more severe than he had expected. One manifestation that nobody was prepared for was a fireball that appeared just ahead of the nose as unburned propellant powder ignited. The cause was partial combustion of the propellant within the barrel, the 'secondary' detonation out-

side the aircraft being accompanied by a sharp shockwave. Neither was present during the firing of live rounds using the full propellant charge.

This early model M-4 cannon had originally been fitted with a protective muzzle cover consisting of metal 'petals' that sprang open before use. These proved troublesome in that even a stronger spring would not always function correctly when the propellant charge for the shells exceeded 75 per cent. The cover was therefore abandoned.

On 31 October 1942 the XB-25G was flown to Kansas City to have bomb controls installed; it then returned to Inglewood for further tests. With ten hours' flight time completed it went to Eglin for Air Force trials. Shortly afterwards NAA received USAAF contract ac-27390 for 400 B-25Gs.

As production of the 75mm cannon-armed Mitchell – designated B-25G-1, G-5 and G-10 (see specification box) – proceeded, five additional standard B-25Cs were modified to similar configuration, as were fifty-eight B-25C-20s and C-25s. All 400 B-25Gs were delivered to the Army between May and August 1943, a small number being retained by the AAF School of Applied Tactics at Orlando, Florida.

Extensive tests were carried out to determine the suitability of the cannon in an anti-submarine role. It was found that the 75mm shells were quite capable of penetrating the hull of a submarine, and at least one B-25 crew later claimed to have sunk a Japanese boat using cannon fire. On those occasions when units could deploy the B-25G in line-abreast formation and open 'barrage' fire with as many shells as possible leaving the barrels in the shortest time, the effect was devastating, each shell weighing as much as seventy-eight 0.50cal bullets. Fifth Air Force crews were not alone in finding the cannon effective against bridges, not the easiest targets to destroy, whatever the ordnance used.

Into Service

Reaction to the 'big gun' Mitchell at operational level varied, depending very much where the recipient unit was based and what type of operation it had previously been conducting. Some field commanders reported that they could find no use for the B-25G largely because of its 'single pilot' cockpit, which inevitably posed restrictions in operation – and promptly returned them to depots, as did the 345th Bomb Group. The Air Apaches were adamant that their modified B-25C/D strafers were doing well enough with their devastating machine gun batteries: they had no use for a cannon-armed B-25 which was not as versatile an aircraft as the more conventional models. And although the Air Apaches did incorporate B-25Gs into group inventory later on, they were invariably modified to take extra machine guns in the cannon tunnel, the weapon itself being removed. Other Pacific-based groups carried out similar modifications, the cannon only being retained if targets that merited its use existed in some number.

A similar negative reaction to the cannon was found in the Middle East. Flying low and steady at low altitude to aim the cannon at potential German targets was not seen as a good insurance risk, and few B-25Gs saw widespread combat action with the Twelfth Air Force groups. The exception was the 310th and 321st Groups, which (as related elsewhere) had each converted one squadron and used that model in combat in the Mediterranean.

Burma and China were to see the greatest use of the B-25G in the hands of the Tenth and Fourteenth Air Force squadrons assigned to those areas where they enjoyed relatively little aerial opposition; examples were also operated by the Seventh and Thirteenth Air Forces in the Pacific. As inferred previously, however, a B-25G, easily recognized as such in service by its short 'solid' nose, was not necessarily a cannon-armed machine. Depots also modified a number of the G conversions of B-25Cs to take the eight-gun nose, and some aircraft also had zero-length, wing rocket launchers added.

The B-25H

North American meanwhile refined and developed the cannon-armed B-25, to the extent that a completely new model emerged in 1943. Known as the B-25H, it represented the initial example of a significant redesign of the Mitchell, with numerous improvements over all previous models. The AAF high command continued to show enthusiasm for attack aircraft armed with large calibre cannon, and so North American won approval for this Mitchell that was armed with a lighter, Oldsmobile-built T13E1 75mm cannon. In fact the gun was considerably revised as compared with the M4 in the B-25G with the same twenty-one-round magazine.

As the NA-98, the first B-25H was a modified C model, 42-32372, named 'Mortimer II' after the famous original Fifth Air Force strafer. For flight-test purposes an older M4 cannon was installed. Only a small jump or 'riding' seat was provided for the navigator/cannoneer, the provision for a co-pilot being dropped. This aircraft was first flown on 15 May 1943 by Ed Virgin, who along with Gus Pitcairn, Joe Barton and Bob Chilton, shared the subsequent flight-test programme. Also closely involved was Maj Tom Garrity of the 3rd Bomb Group. Successful tests with this modified C model led quickly to the completion of the first production B-25H (43-4105), which flew for the first time on 31 July 1943. The pilot on that occasion was Bob Chilton.

Externally the changes made to the B-25H were concentrated in the fuselage. Although the nose cross-section from the cockpit forward was identical to earlier models, aft of the wing the fuselage was gradually deepened by comparison with all earlier models, which tapered towards the tail. The Bendix dorsal turret was positioned well forward, occupying the location given over to the navigator's compartment in the B-25C, while the squared-off rear end of the fuselage incorporated a revised position with twin-'powered' guns. A distinctive 'fighter'-style sighting canopy, similar to the earlier B-25C/D hybrids but more smoothly contoured into the top of the rear fuselage,

Nose-on, a B-25G reveals baffle plates located in the cannon tunnel, the barrel rifling and a mooring/jacking point to the left of the cannon trough. The nose-wheel door is closing as the hydraulic pressure bleeds off. via NAA

Factory cutaway drawing of the B-25H showing all salient points plus propeller spinners, which were not fitted on production aircraft. via NAA

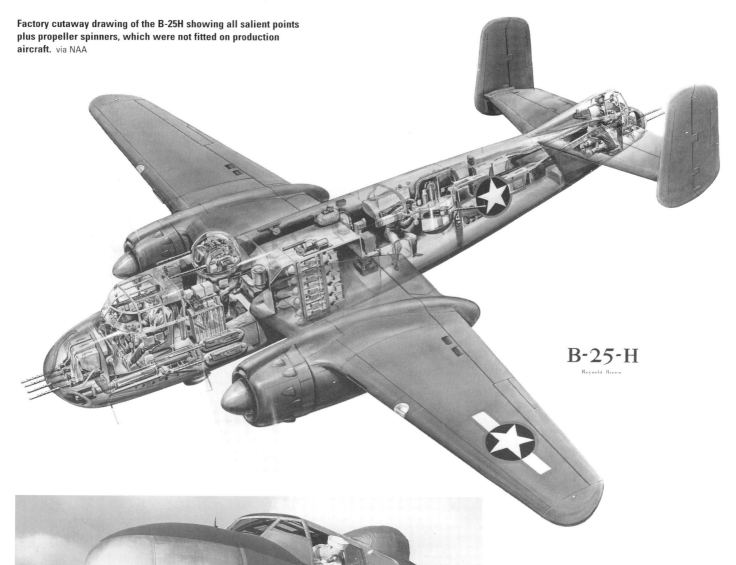

B-25-H

Reynold Brown

(Left) When NAA redesigned the B-25's fuselage, the 75mm cannon remained a weapon favoured by the Army, and 1,000 H models were built. Four guns were now available for 'ranging in' the cannon, and frontal firepower was boosted by four package guns for the H-5 model (one of which is shown) onwards. via NAA

completed the improvements for the rear gun position.

Waist gun defence was improved by fitting enclosed, convex windows in either side of the fuselage aft of the wing, and staggering them to provide more room for the gunners to work without getting in each other's way. The window on the port side was set further back from the wing trailing edge than that on the starboard side, which had its forward vertical frame a mere few inches away from the wing flaps. It would appear that NAA finalized the design of these windows some time before the B-25H appeared, as many were shipped to modification centres as conversion kits to uprate the armament of the B-25C/D. Each window had a cut-out for a gun mount in the lower rear corner. As described elsewhere, these hybrids became a regular sight in some squadrons, although the mid-fuselage position of the dorsal turret in the early model B-25s meant that the gunner's feet must have been close to the waist gunner's head at times. The B-25H's redesigned fuselage cured this, however.

At the tail, the B-25H's fuselage ended in a deeper section to accommodate a pair of 0.5in machine guns in a Bell M-7 hydraulic-electric turret. With the gunner seated close to his weapons, the turret had an excellent field of fire, with the occupant being protected by an angled, three-section armour-plate shield set directly in front of the gun triggers.

The offensive gunnery of the B-25H extended to factory-designed package fairings for a quartet of 'fifties, two per side low on the fuselage sides in line with the cockpit windows. Each gun breech was enclosed in a separate fairing with provision for 200 rounds per gun. The package guns, plus the four set in a horizontal line in the nose, were all operated by the pilot.

At first the fuselage package guns were restricted to the starboard (right) side of the B-25H, all 300 H-1 models being so configured. The 75mm cannon was positioned as on the B-25G, in the crawl-way provided for the aircraft's bombardier in conventional medium bombers. Operation of the cannon was also similar to that in the B-25G, with manual loading.

NAA's single Army contract (ac-30478) for the B-25H had been signed on 20 June 1942 and covered all 1,000 airframes in three sub-variants: H-1, H-5 and H-10 (see specification box). A proportion of these were not issued to combat units, but were retained as trainers in the US, and 248 were diverted to the Marines as the PBJ-1H. When delivered to service units in factory

With the bombardier gone, it seemed logical to save more weight in the B-25H by dropping the co-pilot. Used to configuring their B-25s to the way they wanted, the combat groups complained – it was not as easy to put the co-pilot's controls back as it was to substitute the big cannon for extra machine guns! via NAA

Specification – B-25H-1

Type:	Purpose-built attack bomber/strafer with crew of five
Powerplant:	Two R-2600-13
Weights:	Empty 19,600lb (8,900kg); loaded 35,000lb (15,870kg)
Dimensions:	Wingspan 67ft 1in (20.4m); length 51ft (15.5m); height 15ft 9in (4.8m); wing area 610sq ft (56.6sq m)
Performance:	Maximum speed 275mph (440km) at 13,000ft (4,000m) Range 1,350 miles (2,200km) Service ceiling 23,800ft (7,250m)
Armament:	One T13E1 75mm cannon with 21rpg plus four 0.5in MG in fuselage nose; four 0.5in MG in separate forward fuselage packages; two 0.5in MG in new forward dorsal turret; two 0.5in MG in waist positions and two 0.5in MG in Bell M-7 powered tail turret; 3,000lb (1,360kg) bomb load
Number built:	300 (AAF serial numbers 43-4105 to 43-4404)

NB No provision for co-pilot controls; first 100 aircraft (43-4105 to 43-4204) had package guns on starboard side only; armour protection for tail gunner. Crew complement: pilot; navigator/cannoneer; engineer/gunner; radio operator/gunner and tail gunner.

Specification – B-25H-5

Specification as for B-25H-1, apart from provision for four package guns on all aircraft; electric bomb controls and gunsight aim pointing camera

Number built: 300 (AAF serial numbers 43-4405 to 43-4704)

NB Deleted provision for carrying 2,000lb bomb from 43-4535.

Specification – B-25H-10

Specification as for B-25H-5 except for (from aircraft 43-4705) rearrangement of pilot's instruments; larger life-raft compartment and revision of brake system control cable

Number built: 400 (AAF serial numbers 43-4705 to 43-5104)

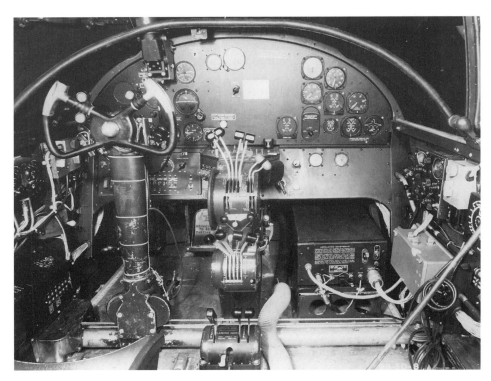

As part of the weight-saving exercise, NAA put a lighter 75mm cannon in the B-25H.
The whole installation was not excessively heavy, nor did the cannon
have much detrimental effect on aircraft performance.
NAA via N. Avery

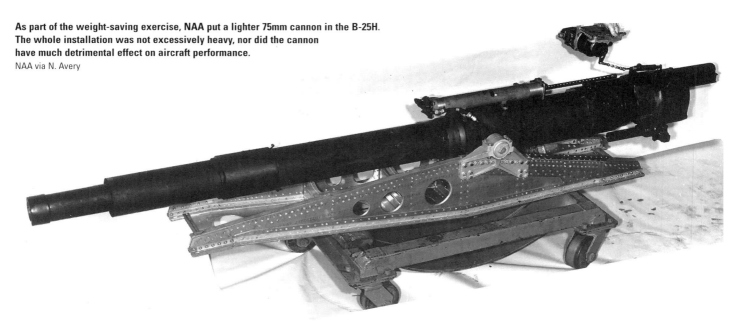

(Right) By deepening the fuselage of the H
model, the company was able to rejig the
armament. Moved right forward, aft of the
cockpit, the dorsal turret – one design of which
is pictured here – proved more efficient than
those of earlier models. via NAA

(Below) Each B-25H waist position was given
a convex 'bay window' complete with
protective glass and a heavy-duty gun-mount
cutout. via NAA

configuration, the B-25H faced similar restrictions as had applied to the B-25G: if there were few targets that needed the attention of a large cannon, then groups specified the bomber version, which was more easily converted to an alternative role, should the need arise.

What combat groups tended to do, as mentioned elsewhere, was to group the B-25G/Hs into one squadron – that way, any more specialized maintenance or modification could be carried out without any general disruption to operations. But whatever its configuration upon delivery, it was rare for a B-25 to stand idle for long; most combat units were always short of aircraft, and if a 75mm cannon did not seem the ideal weapon, it was easily removed and machine guns substituted. This practice created numerous hybrids, even to the point of a B-25G having what *looked* like a B-25H nose with four rather than two nose guns, plus one or two (two were favoured) mounted in the cannon tunnel.

(Above) Staggered just enough to give each gunner room to freely traverse his gun, the new waist positions in the B-25H proved more practical than before. via NAA

(Above) Inside the tail turret the guns were fired by the black, angled trigger grips visible at the top of the photo. The armour plate protection was highly appreciated in combat. via NAA

(Left) Bell, which also updated the Marauder's tail defence, designed an equally compact turret for the B-25H, the installation including a gunner's seat/kneeling pad for the first time. Note the zip fastening for the external dust boot over the gun breeches. via NAA

From above, the B-25H's tail turret reveals the armour plate, the sight mounting and part of the ammunition tracks. via NAA

(Below) Smoothly faired into the fuselage, the curvature of the B-25H's tail turret sighting cockpit was an improvement over the earlier depot- and field-rigged tail-gun positions on the C, D and G models. via NAA

Unit engineering sections, or personnel of the Air Service Command, carried out their own field modifications, which in the case of the cannon-armed aircraft, included adding nose vents to disperse 'gun gas' if this proved troublesome in combat. Additional armour plate was also added to the fuselage just forward of the package guns to minimize the 'popped rivet' blast effects – although it was quite common for front line units to remove package guns altogether, or to reduce them to one, rather than two per side; this was a common practice in the Twelfth Air Force groups. Such modifications remained 'local', and were sometimes restricted to a small number of B-25s. They were not necessarily incorporated on the production lines, although field representatives were aware of them and regularly submitted reports to the company.

Having made the strafer role synonymous with the B-25, NAA developed a prefabricated, superbly streamlined gun-nose to fit all models. This largely replaced the need for 'in the field' modification to turn a medium

bomber into a ground-attack aircraft, thus reducing the time that that individual aircraft spent on the ground. With eight Colt Browning guns, the strafer nose could bring an awesome weight of fire to bear, even without the four package guns and the top turret shooting directly ahead. The new nose enabled many B-25s to carry up to eighteen guns, it being possible for no less than fourteen of them to fire forward, an unprecedented figure and one that would have seemed incredible when the aircraft first entered service. In combat units the total number of guns was rarely used together, the four package weapons often being dispensed with to save weight.

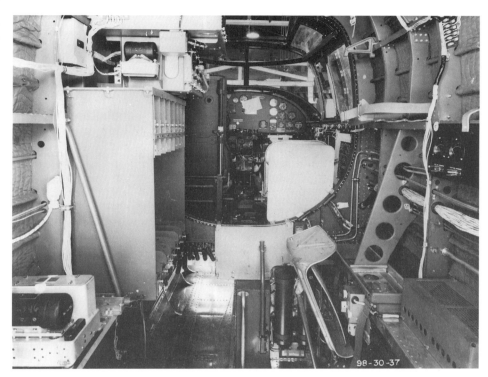

Looking forward, the interior of the B-25H shows the twenty-one-round magazine rack for the 75mm shells on the left. via NAA

(Below) **In addition to the four ranging guns which distinguished it from the G model, the B-25H's cockpit also had the armour plate panel in the pilot's windscreen first introduced on the B-25G.** via NAA

(Opposite page) With the machine-gun bay open for locating the ammunition feeds, a PBJ-1H exhibits the factory-supplied, full nose-gun fit of this model. Combat units would often make further changes to armament, however. via NAA

Factory cutaway of the B-25J configured as a standard medium bomber. via NAA

(Below) Single flexible and fixed machine guns were provided in early B-25Js, a second fixed gun being subsequently added. The bombsight mounting can be seen in its extreme forward position on the floor of the bombardier's compartment. via NAA

The B-25J

While the B-25H was on the drawing board, NAA married the existing bombardier nose section of the C/D models to the new, deeper fuselage of the B-25H to create a final wartime model, the NA-108. This, the B-25J, became the most widely produced Mitchell of them all

Joe Barton flew the first B-25J (43-3870) for the first time on 3 March 1943.[1] His 'no glitches' flight-test report enabled the company to move smoothly from building the older B-25s to producing the J model, initially to meet the first AAF order (ac-19341) for 235 aircraft, identified by the company as the B-25J-1. NAA eventually completed 4,318 B-25Js in eight sub-types (*see* specification box, page 64), more than any previous model.

The AAF accepted the last B-25D in March 1944. This did not, of course, mean an immediate changeover to the new model which was being delivered in quantity by December 1943: in most front-line units the B-25J supplemented, rather than replaced, earlier model Mitchells. Many of the latter completed scores of missions and became firm favourites with pilots.

Specification – B-25J-1

Type: Medium bomber with crew of six

Specification as for B-25H, except:

> Maximum speed 272mph at 13,000ft (438km/h at 4,000m)
> Service ceiling 24,200ft (8,420m)

Armament: One 0.5in flexible MG and one fixed 0.5in MG in bombardier nose; four 0.5in MG in fuselage packages; two 0.5in MG in dorsal turret; two 0.5in MG in waist positions, and two 0.5in MG in Bell turret. Internal provision for 3,000lb (1,360kg) of bombs, plus up to six 325lb (147kg) depth charges on four wing racks or equivalent weight of bombs; up to three 1,000lb bombs could be carried in fuselage bay rather than two as previously; two 1,600lb AP bombs could be accommodated.

Specification similar for previous blocks, except provision for carrying 2,000lb bomb deleted from 43-4019.

Number built: 235 plus 320 (total 555) (AAF serial numbers 43-3870 to 43-4104 and 43-27473 to 43-27792)

NB Essentially a B-25H fuselage with B-25C/D bombardier nose, the B-25J incorporated increased armour protection; restoration of full co-pilot controls with a revised instrument panel; electric bomb-bay doors and racks.

Crew complement: Pilot, co-pilot, bombardier/gunner, engineer/gunner, waist gunner and tail gunner.

B-25J-5
Specification as for B-25J-1 except for N-3C gunsight replacing N-3B sight and A-1 bombing head; flash suppressors available for top turret and package guns from aircraft 43-27793

Number built: 320 (AAF serial numbers 43-27793 to 43-28112

B-25J-10
Specification as for B-25J-5, except mounting lugs and controls for wing bombs and electric bomb doors from 43-35995

Number built: 410 (AAF serial numbers 43-28113 to 43-28222 and 43-35946 to 43-36245)

B-25J-15
Specification as for B-25J-10, except for N-8A optical sights on waist guns and provision for ring and bead sight for nose guns from 44-28711

Number built: 400 (AAF serial numbers 44-28711 to 44-29110

B-25J-20
Specification as for B-25J-15 except added second fixed 0.5in MG in nose (4in/10cm higher); hydraulic emergency brake system; added floor armour protection for bombardier; reinforced top turret canopy from 44-29111; Holley 1685 RB carburettors from 44-29340

Number built: 800 (AAF serial numbers 44-29111 to 44-29910)

B-25J-25
Specification as for B-25J-20 except new armoured seats for both pilots from 44-29911; additional armour plate deflectors for top turret guns during production run; provision for mounting chemical tank on wing racks from 44-30909

Number built: 1,000 (AAF serial numbers 44-29911 to 44-30910

B-25J-30
Specification as for B-25J-25 except for provision for chemical tank on wing bomb racks from 44-31111; C-6 electric bomb hoist from 44-31311; provision for T-64 zero-length wing rocket launchers from 44-31338; K-10 computing sight and M-8A gun mount in tail turret from 44-31491; glide bomb provision from 44-86692; N-9B bombsight from 44-86793; re-routed rudder control cables from 44-86799

Number built: 800 (AAF serial numbers 44-30911 to 44-31510 and 44-86692 to 44-86891

B-25J-35
Specification as for B-25J-30, except for provision for carriage of aerial mines from 44-86892.

Number built: 33 (105) (AAF serial numbers 44-86892 to 44-86897 and 45-8801 to 45-8818; 45-8820 to 45-8823; 45-8825 to 45-8828; 45-8832;
In addition, seventy-two B-25J-35s were completed to flying condition but not contractually taken on charge by USAAF:
45-8819; 45-8824; 45-8829 to 45-8831 and 45-8833 to 45-8899

GENERAL NOTES: Most models of B-25 had provision for a choice of at least ten different types of automatic aerial camera (including the hand-held K-20). Cameras were located in a standard fuselage location aft of the ventral turret well and linked to electrical operating equipment permanently attached to the aircraft. All types of photography were possible utilizing fuselage side windows and/or a dorsal hatch. Fairchild was a major wartime supplier of cameras to the AAF.

The changes noted are mainly those that in general affected the external appearance of aircraft; crew controls and so forth which are part and parcel of most series-built military aircraft, have not been included.

The changes made to the B-25J caused some adverse effect on performance – for example, the top speed dropped to 272mph at 13,000ft (438km/h at 4,000m), as compared to 280–284mph (450–457km/h) for the B-25D, a factor that was bound to be seen as a drawback by some combat crews. The somewhat different handling characteristics of the B-25J were quickly mastered, however, and as operational attrition took its inevitable toll on the inventory of B-25C/Ds, the Js gradually replaced them. It was common for groups to finish the war with a mix of early and late models.

Radar

The US Army and Navy followed more or less parallel tracks in equipping early model B-25s with radar, although while the Marines fitted virtually all their PBJs with sea-search sets, the Army's operational deployment of radar-equipped B-25s was limited. Operationally, PBJ-1Ds and AAF B-25Ds used the same sea-search set, which required nose- and wing-mounted yagi antennae; the 341st Bomb Group also utilized this radar for BTO – 'bombing through overcast' – in the Pacific during 1943–44. These early sets were replaced by centimetric, microwave radar which required only an enclosed fairing to protect the scanner.

Operationally the services diverged in regard to radar: the Marines flew combat

(Above) A beautifully streamlined 'solid' nose containing eight machine guns, compatible with all Mitchell models, met every requirement for the strafer role. A factory-fresh B-25J demonstrates the clean lines of the new nose. via NAA

(Below) Before deciding on eight fixed nose guns, NAA toyed with fitting the B-25J with a battery of four guns designed to elevate and depress for ground strafing. via NAA

overseas in PBJs with centimetric radar, whereas those Army B-25s with later-type radars saw service mainly on the 'home front', initially for ASW work but also to fulfil a valuable second role, training radar operators. In general, AAF B-25s had their radar scanners mounted ventrally in the centre fuselage location previously occupied

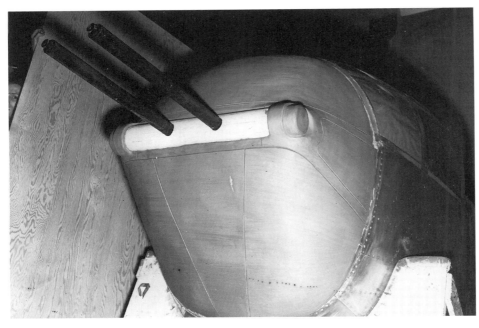

by the retractable gun turret. Early PBJ-1Ds were similar, although the Marine Mitchells soon changed to a centreline nose radome for the APS-3, and finally to a wing-tip mounted set on late production PBJ-1Js.

Army B-25s accommodated a number of different radar installations, the majority utilizing the ventral location for a 'thimble' or more bulbous radome not unlike the British H2S in design. Configuration depended on the type of radar fitted and its function; sets intended for mapping could be operated via parabolic antennae of smaller diameter in a thimble radome – some B-25s carried these in the extreme nose.

A number of civilian concerns bought surplus B-25s for postwar equipment evaluation work, Bendix being one example: it used B-25H 43-4106 (NX-5548N) for an extensive series of tests, including those for AN/FPS-46, an electronically steerable, long-range radar array associated with space technology. This particular Mitchell also tested the Bendix Doppler Radar System which was developed for commercial aircraft.

A variation on the wartime theme of radars that generally required bulky radomes for 'dish' scanners was the airfoil antennae of AN/APQ-7 Eagle. This high resolution radar was developed by the Radiation Laboratory of MIT in association with Bell Telephone, and was intended primarily for the blind bombing of land targets from high altitude. Part of the extensive evaluation programme called for AN/APQ-7 to be fitted to B-25J-25 44-30646, which had the 18ft- (5.5m-)span plywood airfoil located in a ventral position aft of the wing. Weighing 775lb (350kg), Eagle could also be used as a navigational aid. Operational deployment was restricted to B-24s and B-17s in Europe, and B-29s in the Pacific.

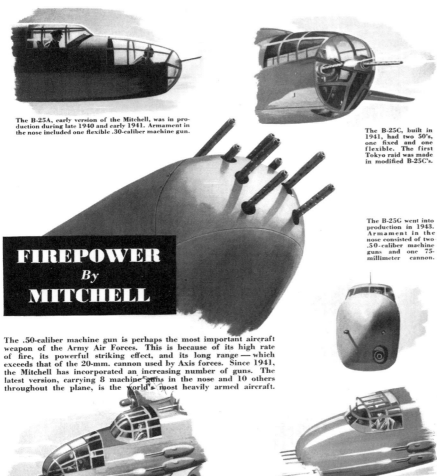

The B-25A, early version of the Mitchell, was in production during late 1940 and early 1941. Armament in the nose included one flexible .30-caliber machine gun.

The B-25C, built in 1941, had two 50's, one fixed and one flexible. The first Tokyo raid was made in modified B-25C's.

The B-25G went into production in 1943. Armament in the nose consisted of two .50-caliber machine guns and one 75-millimeter cannon.

FIREPOWER By MITCHELL

The .50-caliber machine gun is perhaps the most important aircraft weapon of the Army Air Forces. This is because of its high rate of fire, its powerful striking effect, and its long range — which exceeds that of the 20-mm. cannon used by Axis forces. Since 1941, the Mitchell has incorporated an increasing number of guns. The latest version, carrying 8 machine guns in the nose and 10 others throughout the plane, is the world's most heavily armed aircraft.

The B-25J, first built in 1943, mounts two 50's, one fixed and one flexible, in the bombardier's compartment, and two guns on each side of the fuselage.

The B-25H, also first built in 1943, carries a 75-mm. cannon and four .50-caliber machine guns in the nose, plus two package guns on either side of the fuselage.

B-25 'Super Strafer'

In line with a Wright Field Engineering Department request, NAA built the 302nd B-25H-5 (43-4406) as an improved or 'super' strafer. Fitted with Pratt & Whitney R-2800-51 engines, the NA-98X had, amongst numerous changes, new controls to reduce stick forces; and square, P-51 type wing-tips with balanced, 12in (30cm) longer ailerons plus propeller spinners. The package guns of the standard B-25H were removed, although the 75mm cannon was retained. The new engines gave some 3,000hp more than the standard Wright R-2600s, and at 2,700rpm enabled the NA-98X to attain a top speed of 340mph (547km/h) IAS. Test pilot Joe Barton first flew it on 31 March 1944, and everyone who had been involved agreed that this was what the B-25 could have been from the outset, had the R-2800 engines been made available to NAA.

It was unfortunate that the Army then assigned Maj Perry Ritchie to the flight-test programme. Ritchie was a very experienced test pilot who could be expected to get the best out of the new strafer – but he was a known 'hot shot'. To the horror of the NAA engineers, he tried out the B-25's strafing capabilities in no uncertain terms.

On 24 April 1944 Ritchie made another of his notorious low-level approaches to Mines Field, intending – as was his regular practice – to pull up in a climbing spiral before landing. At around 200ft (60m) both outer wing panels separated, and severed the entire tail assembly. Incredibly the aircraft banked and climbed another 300ft

(480m) or so, before it crashed east of Aviation Boulevard on the Mines Field approach. The wreckage was spread over a wide area, and both occupants were killed instantly.

Seemingly carried away with the undoubted exhilaration of flying a medium bomber like a fighter, Ritchie had misjudged things, having continually ignored NAA advice to avoid over-stressing the aircraft – and he certainly paid the price. Despite the crash being in no way attributable to any failure of the NA-98X, the Army thereafter lost interest in what would have been, by all accounts, a very promising development of the B-25.

(Below) **A B-25H with uprated engines, clipped wing-tips and propeller spinners, the NA-98X was the so-called 'super strafer'. Early flight tests showed an appreciable gain over standard models.** via NAA

(Bottom) **A foolhardy pilot, 'flat hatting' in the NA-98X, put paid to further super strafer development when he over-stressed the aircraft and killed himself. External changes from the standard H model can be appreciated in this view of the sole conversion made.** via NAA

CHAPTER SEVEN

Expansion in the Pacific

As the 3rd Bomb Group settled into a pattern of combat operations in the spring of 1942, Charters Towers in Queensland took on an increasing importance as a forward AAF operating base, with B-25 missions being staged through the New Guinea airfields surrounding Port Moresby. There were six main ones: Durand (Waigani), Schwimmer (Laloki), Berry (Bomana), Ward's, Jackson and Kila Kila. The last named was the nearest to the port on the shores of the Coral Sea and was known alternatively as 'Three Mile 'Drome', while Jackson became 'Seven Mile', the numbers referring to the distance they lay from the town. Furthest away was Thirty Mile, alias Rogers.

Reconnaissance was vital, and a typical mission duration for a B-25 could be about seventeen hours, as each crew had to fly from Australia to New Guinea, carry out their mission, and return to Moresby before undertaking the final leg back to Australia, usually at dusk. These missions held natural hazards aplenty, sometimes more lethal than any intervention by the Japanese. For example, on 24 April the 90th squadron CO, Capt R. D. Hubbard, was leading five B-25s to Moresby when they encountered a severe storm: three aircraft were forced to ditch, though fortunately just part of only one crew was lost.

More conventional opposition greeted Hubbard the following day when he made a solo attack on Lae: his bombing attack from 12,000ft (3,660m) was hotly challenged by one of the defending Japanese fighters, the contest lasting for thirty-five minutes. Hubbard got away with his daring exploit.

Lae's complement of A6M fighters of the Tainan Kokutai remained dangerous, but their efforts did not always result in US losses. On 30 April five Zekes attacked Lt Birnn's ship, but he escaped into cloud over the Owen Stanleys. Then on 4 May the same Lt Birnn spotted a Japanese invasion force heading for Moresby. Quickly all available aircraft of the 3rd BG were moved into the port airfields, poised to strike – though in the event they were not

needed, as the naval Battle of the Coral Sea thwarted Japanese plans.

As the spring of 1942 waned, so did Japan's military initiative in the Pacific, albeit almost imperceptibly at first. From the air the Allies continued to blast enemy installations, accepting the inevitable casualties as a result of combat, accidents and the weather. Targets such as Woodlark, Trobriand, Salamua, Cape Gloucester, Finschhafen and many more locations became a grimly repetitious litany of danger for the weary American crews.

In those days the enemy force opposing the AAF was still relatively small – as indeed was the number of American bombers available for combat. In percentage terms casualties were therefore correspondingly low, although there were occasions when the rate of loss leapt to disproportionate heights. One such was on 25 May, when the 3rd Group was hit hard by the A6M2s at Lae: these intercepted a force of eight B-25s, six from the 13th and two from the 90th Squadrons, briefed to attack the Japanese base.

As the B-25s swept in from seaward, their crews could see the Zekes taking off while they were still ten miles out. Fourteen Japanese fighters got airborne, one of them flown by the legendary Saburo Sakai, and by the time the B-25s were in range of their target, in the area known as Chinatown, they could hardly avoid the reception committee. They nevertheless bombed Lae's police barracks, wharf areas and aircraft dispersals, which meant that they also came under fire from the ground. Then the Japanese Navy pilots were on them.

The B-25 carrying Capt Herman F. Lowery, a Royce mission pilot and CO of the 13th BS, went down into the sea in flames, as did the ship flown by Lt Shearer, though Shearer and all the members of his crew survived, albeit with some severe wounds. The B-25s flown by Lts Wilson, Rulison and Hesselbarth were also lost. Lt Talley made it as far as Seven Mile drome at Moresby, but had to crash land. It was the worst day in a bad period for the '3rd

Attack': by the end of May they had flown 192 sorties, losing thirty-five men in combat and six more in accidents. In this particular incident the Lae Kokutai claimed all six B-25s shot down, all fourteen pilots having had a part in their destruction.

Being shot down over New Guinea could be a terrifying experience for young crews: many had only basic survival training, and little knowledge of either the local conditions or the primitive inhabitants who made the tropical rainforest their home. In fact these natives were often friendly to Allied airmen, and their assistance undoubtedly increased the number of those who survived from aircraft posted as missing. Downed crew members who evaded the Japanese were also helped to safety by local civilians and militias such as the New Guinea Volunteer Rifles. Flyers turned up days and weeks after going down, many with hair-raising tales to tell. Nevertheless their experiences were recorded so as to help others come to terms with jungle survival, and to improve the emergency rations and medical kits stowed in the aircraft. Such first-hand knowledge of jungle perils appeared in the AAF journal *Impact*, and was incorporated into training lectures to cadets.

June 1942

While Allied bombers kept the Japanese occupied on land, the US Navy sank four carriers at Midway, and by 6 June the Pacific war had fundamentally changed, with the Japanese all but stalemated. While that did not alter a pre-determined plan to capture Port Moresby, longer-term American strategy meanwhile centred on holding the Solomons, the outer perimeter of the Nipponese area of conquest. And further enemy consolidation in the Solomons left little room for Allied complacency: on 21 July 1942, 2,000 Japanese troops landed on the northern coast of New Guinea, between Lae and Salamua and the Australian garrison at Milne Bay.

Their goal was to march to Kokoda in the foothills of the Owen Stanleys, and drop down on Moresby. Having been prevented from invading the New Guinea port by the Coral Sea engagement, the Imperial Army gambled on a difficult, 100-mile overland route – and against all odds they reached Kokoda in eight days.

George Kenney's air units, which he officially headed as commander of Allied Forces in the South West Pacific Area from 4 August 1942, remained modest. Crews of the ninety or so medium and light bombers then on strength flew combat sorties to prevent the Imperial Army from taking Port Moresby and establishing more than a precarious foothold in New Guinea. They also reached out to bomb Rabaul, early raids often taking a toll of enemy aircraft parked on airfields which the Japanese imagined were all but immune from air attack.

By September 1942 the enemy's overland advance had been halted. Wear and tear meant that only a percentage of Kenney's bombers – ostensibly he had an additional sixty-two heavies at his disposal – were actually serviceable at any given time. In medium bomber terms, this soon came down to just thirty-seven B-25s and B-26s ready for immediate action. Kenney therefore had to find a way of making the aircraft he had more effective.

Birth of the Fifth

The above figures had not appreciably increased by the time Kenney's FEAF command became the Fifth Air Force on 3 September 1942. Located at the end of a very long and dangerous supply line, the Fifth continued to receive a trickle of replacement groups, aircraft and personnel, enough for it to maintain the offensive. Kenney could naturally have used more, but he was one of the first AAF commanders to realize that Washington's 'Germany first' policy would mean that largely he had to make do with the aircraft he was sent.

Kenney therefore needed to make sure that his medium bombers worked at maximum impact – a veritable thorn in the side of the Japanese – and he began with an A-20 mission on 31 August. That date recorded the first strafing attack by twin-engined AAF aircraft in the South West Pacific, and it was to have far-reaching effects. Pappy Gunn proposed to remove

all the bombardier's equipment in the nose, and to fill the space with forward-firing machine guns. This entailed substantial work because, when they arrived in the Pacific, all the NEIAF B-25Cs obtained by the 3rd Bomb Group were configured for the medium bombing role, with standard defensive armament.

Although the USAAF's 0.5in Browning machine gun had already proved its worth against Japanese targets, it weighed 64lb (29kg) without ammunition. Jack Fox gave the go-ahead for the 'strafer' installation, but had to ensure that the B-25 did not become overstressed by adding batteries of extra guns, and that the centre of gravity was not dangerously compromised. Tests aimed at boosting armament were run with both the B-25 and A-20, the field representatives keeping the manufacturers at home, and AAF headquarters in Australia, informed as to progress. George Kenney took a very keen interest, as he saw a paramount need for what he called 'commerce destroyers'. Even though Pappy Gunn and Jack Fox were the front-line team, NAA had previously considered various schemes to increase the firepower of the B-25.

It may have been a natural enough assumption that the place to fit extra guns in a B-25 was in the wings – if only to broaden the field of fire. Gunn had installed a single 0.3in machine gun in each landing-light bay of one B-25, and although these guns functioned well, NAA vetoed the installation on the grounds that undue vibration could overstress the main spar. Also dropped was a battery of 'thirties firing downwards from the bomb-bay: there was enough room for the guns, but ammunition storage would have been a problem.

It soon came apparent to US field commanders that to hit targets all but obscured by the thick canopy of jungle, Fifth Air Force bombers were not going to achieve much by attacking from anywhere near 'standard' medium (10–15,000ft/3–4,500m) altitudes. Therefore it followed that if the target approach was to be made as near to the ground as possible, the entire glass nose area of the B-25, including the bombardier's seat, his radio equipment, the bombsight and his flexible defensive gun, were superfluous. By removing everything in the nose, all the weight thus saved could be taken up by fitting extra fixed guns without disturbing the centre of gravity. This was quite critical on a B-25, particularly if the aircraft was already loaded with an extra fuel tank aft of

the bomb-bay. In an aircraft configured for military purposes, standard fuel- and bomb-loading procedures also had to be followed to ensure that undue stress was not imposed on the nose-wheel oleo.

Commerce Destroyer

To offset his shortage of aircraft, Kenney made it widely known that he intended to overwhelm the Japanese with as many bombs and bullets as the available bombers could carry – and as regards the B-25, this policy was soon to bear fruit. Pappy Gunn's team, working closely with Jack Fox, rigged up a system of angle-iron bars and struts fashioned into supports for four 0.5in machine guns. Bolted rigidly into position, this battery fired forward from the bombardier's 'glass' nose, the transparent panels usually being painted over. The additional guns came primarily from the decommissioned B-25 belly turrets, and various layouts were tested.

Various strafer combinations were tried out; Gunn used B-25C-NA 41-12437 – aptly named 'Pappy's Folly' – for the initial installation. An ex-Dutch order aircraft coded N5-136, it was joined by another Dutch contract aircraft, the famed 'Mortimer' 41-12443 which had flown the Royce mission. Other early B-25 strafers almost certainly included 41-12515 'El Aquila' and 'Margaret', which is otherwise unidentified. The latter aircraft had all four nose guns located close together in the plated-over bomb-aiming panel, which made sealing off the installation from excessive airflow easier than with more widely spaced guns.

The heavy forward firepower was beefed up even further by fitting package guns. The fuselage sides of the B-25C are virtually flat below the cockpit, providing an ideal place to bolt on a pair of 'fifties', giving the pilot a total battery of eight guns under his thumb.

The early gun package consisted of a single fairing to reduce drag, enclosing two Brownings, one above the other. Each dual pack had four slots, the ammunition belt links being ejected via the smaller pair, and the spent shell cases passing through the larger two. Early B-25 gun packs were made in Australia at Townsville, but as the required number increased, Consolidated undertook the fabrication work in the US.

Rigging the first B-25 strafer took twelve days in the workshops at Eagle Farm near Brisbane. Onlookers seemed sceptical, and

(Above) B-25C (41-12437) was the first of the SWPA strafer conversions enthusiastically supported by Gen George Kenney. Paul 'Pappy' Gunn was one of the driving forces behind the work to turn the Mitchell into an awesome ground-attack weapon, and the aircraft was named in his honour. NAA via N. Avery

With some variations, this was what the crews ended up with: a B-25C with four nose 'fifties', plus four more in packages on the fuselage sides. By converting the bomb-bay to take racks of parachute-retarded fragmentation bombs, US crews had their 'commerce destroyers'. via NAA

said the contraption wouldn't fly with all those guns. Fox, however, was prepared to await the outcome of practical tests – and when he went along as co-pilot on a dummy strike on the beached hulk of a Japanese freighter abandoned on a reef off Port Moresby, the results were spectacular: 'We could see splinters flying all over it when we cut loose with those eight .50s throwing ½in slugs', he reported.

Kenney was delighted, and asked for twelve more B-25s to be turned into strafers as quickly as possible – there was plenty of Japanese commerce to be destroyed. To do so effectively and on any scale, the necessity of having to stage any kind of long-range mission through Port Moresby was far from ideal; but these were early days. As the Fifth Air Force gradually brought more organization to its area of operations, its bomber crews showed great enthusiasm for low-level bombing and strafing, which was really the only way to destroy enemy targets with any degree of certainty. With a mix of B-25s, A-20s and B-26s, all of them highly suitable for attacking numerous enemy installations, Kenney had the weapons. They were all in short supply, but a start had been made.

Communications

As built, the B-25 was progressively equipped with a full range of radio sets to US standards – three command sets tuned to three different frequencies. These were for close air-to-air communications in bad weather and over the target, for receiving take-off and landing instructions, and an emergency channel to assist crippled aircraft in reaching a base. All members of a B-25 crew wore a throat mike and headset connected to the intercom system. Throat mikes, while convenient, often tended to garble transmissions and a switch was provided to call any crew member by name over the intercom; provided he was wearing his headset, he would hear the message clearly.

When replacement B-25s arrived in the Pacific, the groundcrews removed the marker beacon as there were no en route transmitters in the theatre to guide Allied aircraft. The B-25C had originally been fitted with only a radio compass, which in the US was tuned to a remote station. Combat crews flew with the needle pointed towards that station, the signal gradually increasing to indicate when they were flying towards it. A 180-degree turn meant they were heading directly away from it, and pilots had to judge from varying signal

strengths the direction in which they were heading – which was not always easy. An IFF (identification, friend or foe) set automatically transmitted a signal to a ground station indicating that the aircraft was 'friendly'.

The navigation problem was compounded in that many Fifth AF missions required the medium bombers to avoid radio transmissions of any kind: even the IFF equipment was switched off to prevent the Japanese obtaining any advance warning of an attack. Aircraft with no IFF transmission triggered an 'alert' message by a red light on the 'panel' of a ground receiver, and were assumed to be hostile.

NAA field representative Jack Fox was on hand in Australia to ensure that the B-25 strafer conversions did not impair flight safety. This B-25G was named for him. J.V. Crow

This also happened when B-25 crews forgot to turn on the set when they approached a friendly base, and occasionally the explosive charge built into every set to prevent it falling intact into enemy hands, detonated without warning.

B-25 radio operators were assisted in their long-range communications by reeling out a trailing-wire antenna under the aircraft. Transmitting by Morse code, in clear weather the operator could reach stations up to 1,000 miles (1,600km) distant, although transmission ranges were usually considerably shorter than that. Message codes were changed on a daily basis, the airborne operator also being able to transmit 'in the clear' in an emergency. On the forward Pacific airstrips, the communications ground station was usually located next to the communications office,

enabling messages from the airborne mission to be quickly passed on to, for example, rescue services.

The B-25 radio operator could also call a Catalina rescue flying boat (which set out in the general direction of the target when missions were on) and pass precise location details of ditched crews. The Cat could also be contacted via the command set, or on a VHF frequency. If an SOS were passed, other aircraft in the area were able to pick it up and re-transmit, if necessary. Later model B-25s were fitted with Loran ('long range navigation') radio, which was a great improvement on the basic radio compass.

Arrival of the Sun Setters

On 15 September 1942 the Fifth Air Force gained more muscle when Lt Col Theodore C. Castle's 38th Bomb Group, known as 'The Sun Setters', entered combat. Having endured a frustrating period of delays at various points in the US and Australia, the group finally flew its debut operation with twelve B-25Cs. Taking off from Australia's Horn Island, aircraft of the 71st and 405th Squadrons bombed the Buna area after staging through Port Moresby.

The continuing Japanese threat to New Guinea forced an Allied counter-offensive, part of which saw the 38th moving into Rogers aerodrome at Rorona. Otherwise known as Thirty Mile, this nightmare of a base was so inadequate that an advanced echelon of the group shipped out to Seventeen Mile, alias Durand, where operations were initiated. The 38th soon began skip-bombing ships at 'less than masthead height', and using parademos and parafrags on land targets; it also kept its hand in with medium altitude B-25 sorties. The crews thus gained wide combat experience with a flexibility born of necessity.

The ground battle to hold Buna was intense and bloody, with the B-25s in the thick of the air strikes to keep the Japanese at bay. On 14 December the 38th flew seven missions to ruin an enemy attempt to land at Mambare along the coast from Buna. Barges and troops were cut to pieces by the heavy fire of the B-25s. Now under the energetic leadership of Lt Col Brian 'Shanty' O'Neill, the 38th's crews could only guess at the results of some low attack runs, so dense was the jungle surrounding most targets; furthermore the weather inevitably played its tricks by shrouding the Owen Stanleys in dense cloud.

Despite the hazards, the pressure was maintained. The 38th hit airfields, dumps and enemy shipping until finally, on 2 January 1943, Buna was declared secure. This gave Allied aircraft access to airfields on the Moresby side of New Guinea's mountain range.

Bloody Bismarck: January–February 1943

With the official cessation of the Papuan campaign on 23 January, the Fifth Air Force began to reach out to enemy strongholds in the Huon Gulf area, and to Lae, Salamaua and Finschhafen. Good ground support of Allied troops ensured that the Japanese were contained – but on 28 February they made what turned out to be a last desperate attempt to reinforce Lae. Standing out of Rabaul came a Japanese convoy of eight transports carrying 6,900 troops and enough food, fuel and supplies to sustain 20,000 men. Eight destroyers provided the escort. There was no question that it had to be utterly destroyed, and on their first major operation of the war,

the Sun Setters excelled. Escorted by RAAF Beaufighters and AAF P-38s, and supported by B-17s bombing the ships from high altitude, on 3 March the converted mediums had their chance.

Making rendezvous over Cape Ward Hunt, the fourteen B-25s from the 71st and 405th Squadrons began their attacks at 09:55. Opting to hit the convoy from the port quarter, the 71st dropped thirty-five 500lb (230kg) bombs from 5,300ft (1,600m), while the 405th dived through cloud to hit the transports. Boring in at 275 to 300mph (440 to 480km/h), the pilots selected their targets, strafing as they came. Pulling away, the Green Dragons left three Japanese ships crippled and a fourth in trouble from a near miss – which was often as lethal as a direct hit. Two enemy vessels rammed each other as the B-17s bombed again, while the P-38s fended off intercepting Zekes.

In the afternoon the Sun Setters returned for a second stab at the convoy. This time the Wolf Pack crippled a destroyer, and the Dragons followed up with hits on two more. This mission was grim, in particular because in order to deny the enemy any chance to reach land, regroup and threaten Allied troops, survivors were strafed in the water. Yet this process became routine, as depleting the Japanese Army and preventing it from reinforcing was the object of the entire exercise. It was repeated on 4 March, by which time fewer than 3,000 Japanese troops were

left. Kenney and MacArthur had nothing but praise for the group's work.

In total, 355 Australian and American aircraft participated in the Bismarck Sea battle, with surface support by PT boats. The 38th's B-25s were credited with sinking four of the IJN destroyers – *Shirayuki*, *Arashio*, *Asashio* and *Tokitsukaze* – on 3 March.

Late spring missions for the modified B-25s and A-20s emphasized the merit of the 'low level' policy favoured by Kenney: the enemy, while showing little sign of withdrawing from its furthest Pacific outposts, was not going anywhere. By staying put, the Japanese had little choice but to accept the casualties inflicted by US forces, particularly through air attack. And the Fifth Air Force could all but guarantee to deny the Imperial Army the reinforcements it increasingly needed, barring any unexpected upturn in enemy fortunes.

Summer/Autumn Campaign 1943

June

The 38th continued its run of success, and on 22 June the 822nd and 823rd Bomb Squadrons joined the group at Moresby. And on 21 June the 345th Group, which was to win widespread fame as the 'Air Apaches', had flown its first B-25 mission,

Scourge of the enemy in the SWPA, members of the 345th Group, the famed Air Apaches, indulged in striking nose-art designs to identify each of the four squadrons. This B-25C wears the blue bat marking of the 499th BS. USAF

a 'biscuit bombing' supply run (repeated daily) for Australian troops slogging their way across New Guinea. Despite the tame name, these sorties could be anything but milk runs. Dropping canisters of food and supplies into a tiny jungle clearing from 250ft (76m) through cloud that barely broke to show the ground, was far from easy. The 500th lost its first B-25 on one such sortie when the pilot charged into dense cloud and struck a ridge, with inevitable results. As other pilots flying over New Guinea had come to realize, 'every cloud has a rock in the middle of it'. It was sound advice, to be ignored by crews unfamiliar with New Guinea at their peril.

The 345th flew its first bombing mission on 30 June. The target was an enemy airstrip at Logue near Salamaua, the mission itself the curtain raiser to a month of similar attacks on airstrips, supply dumps and troops. Using 500 or 1,000lb bombs, the mediums successfully worked over enemy targets in support of an Allied drive aimed at finally clearing the Japanese from New Guinea.

Flak protecting the targets was at times heavy, forcing the attacking crews to spread formations, which diluted the concentration of bombs. It was a ruse the Americans soon overcame with revised tactics. Groundfire remained the major hazard; spread thinly, certainly in terms of mounting defensive fighter patrols over much of New Guinea, the Japanese could not directly counter many of the medium bomber attacks, despite the JNAF occupying five airfields around Rabaul: Lakunai, Tobera, Vunakanau, Keravat and Rapopo, while the JAAF had substantial forces at Wewak.

Rabaul's Simpson Harbour was the main enemy seaborne supply base in the area, but with the AAF increasingly taking the initiative, traffic was monitored and repeatedly attacked. Watching out for any significant moves made by the Japanese became a vital Fifth Air Force preoccupation, attrition driving the enemy to sneak in supplies for the forces in New Guinea. Using small freighters and barges which they hoped would not attract so much attention, the Japanese were largely thwarted in this, as all vessels became frequent targets for the Army medium bombers-turned-strafers, ably supported by fighters.

July

Using at that time virtually standard B-25C/Ds, twenty-seven of the 345th's crews

were briefed for a mission on 8 July. Racing down the runway to take off, the 499th aircraft, with the squadron CO, Capt Edison K. Walters, as co-pilot, failed to gain enough airspeed and promptly settled back to go off the end of the runway and wreck itself in a swamp. Three men were hospitalized, including Walters, and Capt Julian B. Baird took over the squadron.

August

Four of the enemy airfields in the Wewak area were hit hard by the 38th Group on 17 August, with no opposition. It was a different story on the 18th, however, when the 405th BS went to Dagu. As the American bombers ran into the target, alerted Japanese fighters attacked and hit the lead B-25,

bases at Wewak. This Fifth Air Force attack was aimed at rendering an enemy air build-up impotent before it could be used against Allied forces, and it succeeded well – by the end of the month the counterblow had destroyed about 200 enemy aircraft.

September

These strikes culminated in an Allied invasion of Lae in September, a concurrent parachute drop into the Markham Valley being designed to seize Nadzab as a forward base. To persuade the enemy to give it up, forty-eight B-25s of the 38th BG opened the proceedings on 5 September with widespread strafing and parafrag attacks. Lae was secured on the 16th, and by October the entire Huon Peninsula was

Looking for trouble on 5 September 1943, B-25C 'Runt's Roost', a 90th Squadron strafer, overflies Cape Gloucester, one of the hotspots in the 3rd Bomb Group's operational area. F.F. Smith

flown by the CO, Maj Ralph Cheli. Holding the blazing aircraft long enough to complete his attack run, Cheli then ditched: he perished along with his crew (*see* box, page 76).

For the 345th, much of August was spent in Australia while the Townsville depot rigged the B-25s as strafers. As well as the standard 'commerce destroyer' modifications, the Mitchells were fitted with a new bomb rack able to contain up to 207 cylindrical 23lb (10kg) parafrag bombs in triple clusters. Attached to parachutes, the bombs burst into some 1,600 fragments upon contact with the ground, making them devastating against aircraft and vehicles.

The 345th returned to Moresby to learn that the 3rd and 38th Groups had followed the heavy bombers in to blast enemy air

in Allied hands. By then the 38th's four squadrons had for the first time been brought together at Moresby.

October

The 38th was to be one of the first AAF groups to deploy the B-25G – although this was not exactly out of choice. Equipping the 822nd and 823rd Squadrons, the cannon-armed Mitchells were converted to standard strafers at Townsville, work that caused some operational delay. It was nearly the end of the year before both squadrons went back into action.

On 12 October the Fifth mounted a huge attack on the Japanese air bases at Rabaul and the shipping in Simpson

On 2 November 1943, Fifth Air Force B-25s carried out one of many raids on Rabaul, the Japanese stronghold on New Britain. Bombs plastered port areas and shipping in Simpson Harbour in a typically low-level attack that claimed hits on eleven ships. USAF

Harbour. Kenney mustered no fewer than 114 B-25s (out of a total force of 349 bombers and fighters) to pulverize the enemy bastion on New Britain. The 345th and five squadrons from the 3rd and 38th Groups constituted the B-25 element, all aircraft being briefed to make strafing attacks on their primary targets, the Rabaul airfields. Taking the Japanese by surprise, the Mitchells shot up bombers in the landing pattern, strafed them in revetments, and showered the dispersals with parafrags. A few Zekes did manage to take off and one shot down a 71st BS machine, the single B-25 casualty of the day. While the mediums rained fire on the aerodromes, B-24s bombed shipping in Simpson Harbour with some success.

Although Rabaul was down, it was far from out, and it would be the target for many more US bombs and bullets before the end – but this attack and others like it imposed an aerial blockade that was continually reinforced. The decision not to mount what might have been a costly and time-consuming amphibious assault on that part of New Britain proved sound, the air campaign successfully denying the Japanese any attempt to use the base as a springboard for offensive operations.

Mitchells in the Islands

While the Fifth Air Force went toe to toe with the enemy in New Guinea, two other US air forces, the Seventh and Thirteenth, undertook initial operations in their respective sectors of the Pacific. Both were considerably smaller than the numbered air forces that fought on the other side of the world – one manifestation of the necessity of giving Europe priority in combat groups. Also, in an area as vast as the Pacific, the emphasis was on long-range heavy bombers rather than tactical mediums, at least until suitable bases could be utilized from which to deploy shorter-range aircraft on offensive sorties where they could be most effective. Most of the targets were of a tactical nature, whatever the means of attacking them.

The forerunner of the Seventh Air Force, given the responsibility of guarding Hawaii, had been savaged at Pearl Harbor, and the Thirteenth had not existed in December 1941 – later it would see action in the Solomons, mostly after the bitter battles to secure the main island of Guadalcanal were over. But to begin with it took time to reorganize the available combat groups from the old Air Corps 'regional command' structure into the new air forces: each air command would be responsible for conducting combat operations in a particular geographical area, and in order to carry out its mission effectively, each had ideally to be equipped with fighter, medium and heavy bomber groups plus the necessary transport and liaison units. This 'standard' complement of groups was understandably modified according to local requirements and the availability of new squadrons – which of course always began with trained crews, and maintenance and ground echelon personnel without whom few combat units could have functioned efficiently.

By 1943 the Seventh had been allocated the Central Pacific as its main combat area and, as one of the smallest air forces, it had a single medium bomber unit assigned. In December 1943, the 41st made its combat debut with the B-25G. New groups joined the Seventh in preparation for the important Operation *Galvanic*, aimed at wresting Tarawa and Makin in the Gilbert Islands from the Japanese; the recapture of these islands was of considerable strategic importance in that they could be developed as air bases. In November, the Army and Marines had stormed Tarawa: it was the first major operation on the 'road back' to Japan, and was a bloody, protracted battle. Much was learned at considerable cost – not least that the recapture of these islands would require overwhelming air and seapower deployment in the early stages, before the troops went ashore. Combat operations with broadly this same purpose were to be repeated often, and would occupy hundreds of bomber crews in many thousands of flying hours over the largest ocean on earth.

The 41st Bomb Group left its home at Hammer Field in California on 16 October 1943, and headed for Hickam Field, Hawaii; its war in the central Pacific began quietly enough. To place its aircraft within range of the Gilberts, the Seventh occupied part of the Ellice Islands and also used airfields on Funafuti and Baker Islands. It was the end of the year before Tarawa airfield was ready for occupation, by two squadrons of the 41st; the group's other two squadrons went to Abemama, also part of the Gilbert Islands chain. The unit, which was commanded by Col Murray A. Bywater, had the 47th, 48th, 396th and 820th Squadrons assigned.

The 41st went operational on 28 December 1943: the next objective in the area was the invasion of the Marshalls, and as part of

Seventh Air Force B-25s undertook the reduction of the Gilbert Islands after establishing bases on Makin where a service for B-25G 'Little Joe' (42-64896) flown by Lt Allen Davis and crew, provides interest for the islanders. IWM

the 'softening up' process B-25s of the 820th Squadron attacked targets in Milli Atoll. From 250ft (76m) altitude the nine B-25s, escorted by P-39s, spread demolition bombs and parafrags over enemy airfields. All returned safely. Dozens of similar missions were flown against the string of atolls that constituted the Marshall and Gilbert Islands – Jaluit, Taroa, Maloelap, and others. Mostly they were low-level sweeps to avoid Japanese flak, and flown unescorted owing to the distance the targets lay from Tarawa, the 41st's main base. They were not without losses – or reprisals by the enemy, who executed several members of the group whose aircraft had been brought down. Such behaviour on the part of their antagonists was a grim aspect of the war in the Pacific that all American aircrews had to come to terms with.

Crusaders in the Solomons

The B-25 medium bomber group assigned to the Thirteenth Air Force was the 42nd. Comprising the 69th, 70th, 75th, 100th and 390th Squadrons, the group, which adopted the name Crusaders, was unusual – though not entirely unique – in having five squadrons under its command for part of its existence. The 69th and 70th Squadrons had begun combat operations with B-26 Marauders, these being generally, but not entirely, replaced by B-25s from the spring of 1943. Based on Guadalcanal, and flying combat operations from 14 June, Col Harry E. Wilson's 42nd Group operated with four squadrons for the rest of that year. The 69th BS flew the debut mission, an attack on the enemy airfield at Vila, with the crews enjoying the luxury of fighter escort in the shape of Marine Corps F4U Corsairs.

In late 1942 the US had won the bloody battle for the possession of 'Cactus' (codename for Guadalcanal), and since then the island airfields had been developed as part of a major base complex in the south-west Pacific. Although the Japanese had been ejected from the immediate area of Guadalcanal, they remained very much in evidence on neighbouring islands, and considerable air action took place before the war moved on during 1944. The 42nd had the 106th Recon Squadron (Bombardment) attached from 1 January 1944; having operated a variety of aircraft over many years in an observation (later reconnaissance) role, the unit became a B-25 outfit and was re-designated the 100th BS on 9 May 1944. Four pilots of the 106th flew with the 390th to mark their personal combat debut on 13 January, with a mission to the Bonin Islands. Eventually the 100th BS flew 405 missions out of a group total of 1,481 for the five squadrons.

At that time the 69th, 70th and 100th Squadrons flew from Sterling Island in the Russell Islands, and were occupied with attacks on Rabaul; the 75th and 390th Squadrons were based at Banika, also in the Russells.

Decimating the Japanese air forces was vital to ensure safer Allied ground and amphibious operations. In this the B-25 groups more than did their bit, as a strike photo of Jofman airfield shows. Situated at Sorong on the north-western tip of New Guinea, it became an inferno on 16 June 1944 when the enemy was being cleared from the area. IWM

At every opportunity the Fifth Air Force medium bomber/strafers made life difficult for the Japanese. In this attack, also at Sorong, the US crews surprised enemy building work on barracks, gun emplacements and stores. USAF

Medal of Honor (II)

Major Ralph Cheli of the 38th Bomb Group, Fifth Air Force, won a (posthumous) Medal of Honor on 8 August 1943. His aircraft was a B-25D-5, and was part of a large force of medium and heavy bombers charged with reducing Japanese effectiveness in New Guinea by destroying enemy aircraft on the ground. On 8 August Cheli's flight was approaching the aerodrome at Dagua near Wewak when it came under attack by Ki-43s and A6M Zekes. A part of the citation accompanying the award describes what happened to his aircraft:

> The enemy aircraft centred their fire on his plane, caus-ing it to burst into flames while still two miles from the objective. His speed would have enabled him to gain the necessary altitude to parachute to safety, but this action would have resulted in his formation becoming disorganized and exposed to the enemy. Although a crash was inevitable, Cheli courageously elected to continue leading the attack in his blazing plane. From a minimum altitude, the squadron made a devastating bombing and strafing attack on the target. The mission completed, the major instructed his wingman to lead the formation, and crashed into the sea.

Despite the flames streaming from his right engine, Cheli went on to strafe a row of Japanese fighters before steering his B-25 out over the coast and ditch-ing. In one of the cruel ironies of war, Ralph Cheli in fact survived the crash, but was captured by the Japanese and taken to a PoW camp on Rabaul. He died on 6 March 1944 — not at the hands of his cap-tors, but because Allied aircraft bombed and sank the transport bearing him to Japan.

Medal of Honor (III)

Major Raymond H. Wilkins, commanding officer of the 8th Bomb Squadron, 3rd Bomb Group, became the third recipient of a Medal of Honor awarded for a B-25 com-bat mission, on 2 November 1943. Flying B-25D-10 (41-30311), Wilkins' target that day — along with other Mitchells of his group — was the notorious Simpson Harbour at Rabaul; heavily defended, the harbour was a frequent anchorage for Imperial Navy ships. On this occasion, to get at their intended merchant shipping targets, the American bombers had to run the gauntlet of heavy cruiser fire. As the B-25s ran in, the warships opened up with everything they had, shell splashes from large calibre guns creating geysers of water that could easily bring down a medium bomber. Hits were taken by the B-25 flown by the 3rd Group commander Maj John P. Henebry, but he managed to ditch. Wilkins, however, had positioned his aircraft on the left flank of his formation to draw fire from the cruisers, and he was not so lucky: his Mitchell drew plenty of fire and was badly hit, and went straight into the harbour.

Ray Wilkins' B-25 was one of eight lost in the Simp-son Harbour attack – this was a high figure for the Fifth Air Force. Nevertheless, the attack was successful: six enemy vessels were destroyed, and three freighters, a minesweeper and an oil tanker were damaged.

CHAPTER EIGHT

Allied Mitchells

As part of the wartime build-up of the AAF, the B-25 entered service with training units destined to remain in existence in Conus – continental United States – for the duration of hostilities, or until sufficient replacement crews had been trained for the combat units overseas. The earliest model B-25s undertook training duty, the entire series eventually seeing service in this second-line role. Medium-bomber training was generally completed by 1944, resulting in the inactivation of a number of groups.

The B-25 otherwise joined the AAF in a host of variable roles, one of the most important of which was that of antisubmarine warfare. As part of the six Conus-based air forces, the Antisubmarine Command was faced with the very real threat of U-boat attack off the eastern seaboard from late 1941. Panama, too, faced a potential threat from the sea, and the Sixth Air Force was consequently reinforced, primarily to guard the Panama Canal. The following year B-25 C/D and G model Mitchells could be seen in the distinctive white and olive drab camouflage scheme which by that time had been adopted for overwater patrol aircraft.

As events transpired, the B-25's record as a U-boat killer continued to amount to zero, the 1941 'false alarm' mentioned in an earlier chapter being followed by a single attack on U-848 on 5 November 1943 in the South Atlantic off Ascension Island. This was the only confirmed instance of a B-25 attack on a German submarine coming anywhere near to success – though it still left the aircraft's record of non-success intact: the two participating crews from the 1st Composite Group dropped 500lb (230kg) bombs from 4,000ft (1,220km), but they resulted in clear misses. In fact this particular U-boat exploded and sank after repeated attack by Navy PB4Ys.

The foregoing is certainly not meant to imply that the thousands of AS sorties flown by B-25s attached to the command were not effective in keeping the U-boats in check: by their very presence, AS patrols were a deterrent to overt attack by underwater

craft. And it was a different story in the Pacific, where B-25s participated in the sinking of several IJN submarines. Furthermore, the AAF School of Applied Tactics at Orlando counted Mitchells among its varied aircraft inventory used to test equipment and techniques to improve the offensive capability of Army aircraft against the underwater menace.

Orlando was also home to the 5th Antisubmarine Squadron, which in 1943 operated some of the few B-25Cs in Army inventory to be fitted with centimetric radar. Housing the scanner of the sea-search set in a ventral radome in place of the lower gun turret, several of these converted examples came from the production batch of the one hundred B-25C-25s, sixty-three of which were completed as G models with the 75mm cannon. This weapon was potentially effective against surfaced submarines, although as far as it is known, there was no opportunity for a B-25 crew to prove the fact, at least off the US east coast.

While many hundreds of B-25s were delivered to combat and training commands within the USA, NAA continued to build the aircraft for America's wartime allies. Countries that eventually received the highest allocations during the war were respectively Britain (881), Russia (732), the Netherlands (162) and China, which had an initial Lend-Lease allocation of 161.

Other examples were used during the war by Brazil, Canada and Australia, most being supplied under Lend-Lease, which passed into US law on 11 March 1941. Russia received US military equipment under a scheme of interest-free credits totalling one billion dollars and released during four Soviet Protocols, the first of which lasted from 1 October 1941 to 30 June 1942. The three others, each of about a year's duration, covered the remaining war years, with the fourth one ending on 12 May 1945.

RAF Reconnaissance Mitchells

Although the main operational area for British Mitchells was to be Europe, the first sorties by the type in the hands of RAF crews took place on the other side of the world, more than six months before the first sorties by 2 Group. Having suffered humiliating defeats in Malaya and Burma during 1941–42, British forces fell back to the relative safety of India where a military command structure was gradually rebuilt. RAF assets were modest, but to gather vital intelligence data for future operations against the Japanese, No. 5 Photographic Reconnaissance Unit was formed at Dum Dum near Calcutta on 11 April 1942. Commanded by Flt Lt A.C. Pearson, this was the first RAF unit to fly the B-25C operationally, albeit on

Pre-flight check for B-25C (N5-145) serving with No. 3 PRU in India during June 1942.
F.D. Procter via G. Thomas

a rather ad hoc basis, with aircraft transferred from Dutch orders.

While twenty aircraft from the original Dutch order for 162 B-25Cs had been ferried to Brisbane to be partially taken over by the US 3rd Bomb Group, eight had concurrently arrived in India. There was then a desperate need by the RAF to mount long-range PR sorties over Japanese targets, and because there were no other suitable aircraft available at the time, negotiations were opened to use these Mitchells for the purpose. There was some resistance, both from the USAAF which also wanted them, and from the Dutch, who actually owned them and wished to fly combat sorties. But when the Dutch situation eased a little with the fall of Java, the transfer was agreed.

Five of the Mitchells were despatched to Bangalore where they were stripped of all armament, including the dorsal turret; the latter was replaced by an astrodome. A four-man crew consisting of two pilots, a navigator and a camera operator could thus operate the aircraft. The least enviable job fell to those who manned the fuselage camera station, which at first posed problems, one of the most significant being that nobody with experience was available. This was solved by a call for volunteers – who found that although the temperature on the airfields was typical of the tropics, at 25,000ft (7,600m) European-type weather prevailed, and it was bitterly cold. Thus an activity that involved being perched over an open camera hatch was not to be recommended without heavy clothing.

Whatever their shortcomings as PR aircraft, the Mitchells could be relied upon to cover potential targets 1,000 miles (1,600km) from Dum Dum, and they were consequently well utilized during the rest of 1942. One detail that occurred at this time was that on 16 May, No. 5 PRU was renumbered as No. 3 PRU.

Reorganization

RAF PR sorties with the ex-Dutch Mitchells continued when No. 681 Sqn (the renumbered No. 3 PRU) was formed at Dum Dum on 25 January 1943. The unit remained in the Calcutta area for the duration of its period with Mitchells, which included N5-144/B, N5-145/C, and N5-148/A (later coded M). To these were added several Mk IIs from British Lend-Lease deliveries, including MA956/E and

A poor-quality but interesting photo of B-25C (N5-148) which was shot down over Rangoon in 13 February 1943. via G. Thomas

(Below) LAC Eddie Smith holding an F.24 camera in front of the B-25C he died in when the Mitchell went into the sea on 5 November 1944. The B-25 was an ex-Tenth Air Force aircraft that boosted the RAF's modest PR force in South-East Asia at the time. via G. Thomas

MA957/K (later coded Z). Of these, N5-148 (41-12508) – coded 'A' – did not last long, for on 13 February 1943 it was shot down near Rangoon.

Wing Commander S.G. Wise commanded the squadron during 1943, and his aircraft flew many sorties to cover targets, those in Burma, Rangoon, Mandalay and the Adaman Islands being among the most frequently visited. Depending on the weather, between fifty and ninety sorties a month were flown, many of them at the request of the Army at Mandalay. No. 681 had begun to use single-seat fighters and Mosquitos before the end of 1943, and the Mitchells were passed to what was, in effect, a new unit; this was also formed at Dum Dum, on 29 September, and designated No. 684 Sqn. This move – in effect the splitting of No. 681 Sqn's 'C' Flight to form a new squadron – represented a degree of rationalization in PR coverage, in that No. 684 (initially commanded by Sqn Ldr D.S. Jones) undertook all the longer-range flights with, initially, four Mitchells and five Mosquitoes, though the British aircraft had superior range.

No. 684's inventory included 'inherited' Mitchell IIs MA956 and MA957/Z, as well as the Dutch N5-144 and N5-145. In fact the unit soon had more Mosquitos than Mitchells, but the former type's suspected structural problems under Far Eastern conditions ensured that a few Mitchells soldiered on. Neither of the Lend-Lease Mk IIs were destined to be around until the cessation of hostilities, however. On 5 May 1944, MA957 went into the Bay of Bengal during an ASR sortie, and fire engulfed MA956 while it was at Alipore on 16 December 1944, when petrol-soaked ground around its dispersal ignited. Of the two Dutch-contract Mitchells known to have been taken on charge by No. 684, N5-144 (believed to have been 41-12495 or 41-12509) was converted for courier duties with the squadron on 9 March 1944; and N5-145 (41-12507) survived the war and was finally passed to No. 162 Repair and Salvage Unit at Alipore on 19 September 1945.

In December 1944, Wg Cdr Wise was placed in command of the joint USAAF-

RAF organization to handle all South-East Asian PR sorties, this being known as the Photographic Reconnaissance Force (PRF): it included the two British units, and the 9th Photo Recon Squadron, which also had some B-25s on strength. PRF's blanket coverage of Burma and Malaya involved an increasing number of sorties by Lightnings, Mosquitoes and Spitfires, types with which a handful of war-weary Mitchells – at least those belonging to the RAF contingent – could hardly compete. That said, when stripped of all its guns, other surplus (and weighty) equipment, and with both engines in good condition, a B-25 could generally show enemy fighters a clear pair of heels. And its greatest asset in PR work was undoubtedly enough fuselage space to accommodate the largest cameras.

Change of plan

Dutch crews in Australia had planned to operate Mitchells in conjunction with their own coastal craft in naval operations around Java. In fact this came to nothing, as the rapidly changing war in the Far East brought almost daily revision of all such plans. Finally the Japanese secured all the important locations in Java, which surrendered on 9 March 1942.

Denied this early chance to fight the enemy, the Dutch airmen who might well have been among the first to fly the B-25 in combat, were obliged to sit on the sidelines for about eight months. Having little choice but to postpone their entry into combat, the Dutch crews were organized as No. 18 (NEI) Squadron, and trained under the programme initiated in Australia by Jack Fox early in 1942. It was decided that the squadron would become operational as soon as enough B-25s arrived, the intention being for No. 18 to remain an all-Dutch unit, but to be incorporated into the Royal Australian Air Force. This was agreed to, in spite of the fact that Dutch methods of operation differed to those of other air forces in a number of respects. The RAAF badly needed the extra manpower: being expanded in line with most other air forces, it had a substantial commitment overseas, as well as a prime responsibility to defend the country against incursions by the Japanese.

The ferry route to Australia soon brought No. 18 Sqn new B-25Cs, the first five of which arrived at Archer Field, Brisbane, on 12 April 1942. The squadron had officially formed on 4 April, with Lt Col B. J. Fiedeldij in command. Five B-25Cs were then taken on strength, with another five on hand by early July. These were the first of the agreed replacements for the Dutch aircraft taken over by the 3rd BG.

In flying terms, being under RAAF control meant that the Dutch unit was organized along basic Australian lines, with an establishment of twelve aircraft divided into three flights of four, and an additional six machines in reserve on the strength of a maintenance flight. All crews, including three in reserve to make good combat losses, were allocated their own aircraft.

The attachment of No. 18 to the RAAF was a short-lived arrangement, as by early July it had been decided that it would revert to Dutch control, although retaining a number of Australian personnel. But the Dutch unit found that retaining its B-25s was not nearly as easy as might have been expected. To keep the accounts straight, the NEI serial numbers of the early (paid-for) aircraft passed to the

Crews of No. 18 (Netherlands East Indies) Squadron were the first Dutchmen to fly Mitchells after a substantial wait. Based near Canberra, these two aircraft, with a B-25C leading, make an approach after a training flight.
F.F. Smith

Americans were duplicated on the B-25Cs that had arrived in mid-year. As far as the Dutch were concerned, they had paid for 162 B-25s and fully expected to receive them all – but the war situation led to delays, and an attempt to exchange the five precious Mitchells with A-20As and, reportedly, a number of 'export' DB-7Bs. This 'unofficial' offer was refused. With B-25s in short supply, further deliveries to the Dutch were suspended and No. 18's personnel had no choice but to fly the A-20s which had arrived on 27 May. This they did only briefly – and reluctantly, for the aircraft were in poor condition with well worn engines. In any event, the Dutchmen considered the B-25 to be greatly superior to the Douglas product, which was why they had ordered it in the first place. The A-20s were flown away by American and Australian crews between 18 and 23 June.

American pressure to prise away No. 18's five B-25s took a more devious turn when they refused to supply any spares; however, this action was to backfire. The arrival of more B-25s redressed a difficult situation, and by 17 September No. 18 Sqn finally had its eighteen aircraft. Then it was happy to release a quintet of worn-out Mitchells to the 3rd Bomb Group – which still accepted them. It seemed inevitable that some of the Dutch aircraft would adopt Australian markings, and this situation indeed materialized when No. 2 Squadron RAAF became a Mitchell unit in April 1944. For many Dutch airmen, the day they entered combat could not come soon enough

In the meantime, No. 18's crews flew training sorties, interspersed with antisubmarine patrols. These often fruitless flights yielded rare success on 5 June, when Lts Winckel and Van Loggen, flying a B-25C (41-12464; N5-151), attacked a Japanese submarine off Moruya, NSW. The crew were credited with sinking the boat, although this appears not to have been the case. At the time, however, such a boost in unit morale was more than welcome, and it was followed by the equally pleasing arrival of another eighteen Mitchells during August and September. These aircraft, which at long last formed the 'permanent' establishment of No. 18 Squadron, were fitted with Estoppey D-8 bombsights, which were apparently all that was available. There was some dismay over this, as not only was the sight unreliable, but many bomb aimers were unfamiliar with its function. Coupled with a lack of long-range fuel tanks, this situation was a big disappointment to the Dutch crews who had hoped that they were about to be declared fully operational. Things were partially redressed, however, by the arrival of an American instructor on the D-8 sight, and the news in October that the unit would move to MacDonald airstrip in the Northern Territory, in order to finally get to grips with the enemy.

In the meantime there was some further delay while long-range tanks were fitted in the bomb-bays by No. 1 Aircraft Depot at Laverton, Victoria; but by late November an advance party had left for MacDonald. The Mitchells, modified at the rate of one per day, followed during the last days of 1942.

In total the Dutch took nineteen Mitchells on strength in 1942, enough to get No. 18 Sqn operational. This long-awaited event took place on completion of the move to MacDonald, on 18 January 1943. The squadron's brief was to help in the defence of Australia's northern coastline and the Torres Strait area. Under RAAF North Western Area command, No. 18 (NEI) Sqn shared this duty with six Australian, one US and one British squadron. The Dutch Mitchells needed their long-range tanks because they were based, like the other units, to the south and south-east of Darwin, the strip the furthest away, known as MacDonald strip, lying about 105 miles (170km) from the town.

Under the command of Lt Col B.J. Fiedeldij, No. 18 Sqn prepared for its part in defending Western Australia, with the overall aim of securing the flank of MacArthur's drive into the south-west Pacific. Japanese bases and shipping were priority targets for No. 18 Sqn crews, operations beginning on 18 January with a shipping reconnaissance of Tanibar Island in the Arafura Sea, north of Darwin. No worthwhile targets were found, but the following day a bombing raid was made on Portuguese Timor, when Japanese AA fire caused some damage to the participating Mitchells. On the 20th, sorties to the enemy air base at Fuiloro on Timor resulted in claims against two Mitsubishi Zekes and a Nakajima E8N *Dave* seaplane by the Mitchell gunners.

Dutch Mitchell operations developed similarly to those pioneered by the US Fifth Air Force: low-level bombing and strafing, for which some aircraft received extra nose guns in the bombardier's station. Inevitably combat resulted in damage to aircraft and in accidents, some with fatal casualties. The first operational loss of a No. 18 Mitchell was on 18 February 1943 when B-25D (41-29717; N5-144) was shot down by A6Ms which attacked a force of six Dutch aircraft during a bombing raid on Dili, Timor. In the running combat, the pilot and bombardier were killed by enemy fighter fire, whereupon the co-pilot managed to ditch the aircraft which stayed afloat just long enough for the remaining members of the crew to be rescued.

No. 18 Squadron remained at MacDonald until 9 May 1943, when a move was made to Batchelor Field, south of Darwin. This was to remain the unit's home for almost the duration of the war in the Pacific, during which time it took on charge a total of 139 Mitchells, seventy-nine B-25C/Ds, and sixty Js. Some of the B-25Js were fitted with the eight-gun strafer nose for the low-altitude attack role.

School at Jackson

So as not to overload heavily utilized Australian bases with additional training regimes, a scheme was agreed whereby Dutch crews would be trained in the US at Jackson Army Air Base in Mississippi. Accordingly, the Royal Netherlands Military Flying School was established in the spring of 1942. Under the auspices of the Flying Training Command, classes began without delay, trainee crews using loaned aircraft pending delivery of twenty B-25Cs and Ds and ten B-25Gs assigned to the school and paid for by the Dutch. The first of these B-25s arrived on 19 November 1942, the initial class having graduated that September. The school's main commitment was to provide replacement crews for No. 18 Sqn in Australia, and it continued to operate until February 1944; from then on there was little further need to train more Dutch crews, and so it closed. The majority of the Mitchells used for training purposes were returned to US control, although at least one B-25D-15 (41-30500) had crashed during the period.

Since 11 June that year, No. 18 had been led by Lt Col J.J. Zomer.

By March 1944 the squadron began to receive new B-25Js with improved defensive armament – just at a time when Japanese fighter opposition was growing ever scarcer. No. 18's anti-shipping exploits in support of MacArthur's drive to recapture New Guinea and part of Papua brought about an unofficial unit badge: known as the 'Dutch cleanser', it depicted a girl in traditional Dutch costume wielding a broom. It was more than appropriate, as anti-shipping sweeps between 17 November 1943 and 4 January 1944 had resulted in the Japanese losing 25,545 tons of shipping, either sunk or left burning.

On 1 May 1944, Lt Col E.J.G. teRoller, who had represented the Netherlands Purchasing Commission and negotiated the purchase of Mitchells back in June 1941, took over command of No. 18 Sqn. In fact his tenure was brief, for he was killed in action on a mission in June; so from 1 July, Lt Col D.L. Asjes led the squadron. During July No. 18's Mitchells flew 107 sorties, the highest number to date.

In the spring of 1944 the delivery of B-25s to Australia outgrew the requirements of No. 18 Sqn, and it was decided to make it part of 79 Wing RAAF and re-equip an Australian squadron with the surplus Mitchells. This was No. 2 Squadron, which took delivery of its first twenty aircraft in April: these were B-25Ds (A47-1 to -20), and they were followed by five more (A47-21 to -25) in June; another five (A47-33 to -37) were transferred in August. Otherwise No. 2 Sqn operated eleven B-25Js, although twenty were allocated, but from US rather than Dutch stocks (A47-26 to -32 and A47-38 to -50). The last two examples arrived in August 1945.

Based at Hughes in the Northern Territory, No. 2 was led by Wg Cdr L.A. Igram, and began offensive operations on 27 June after several sea-search missions. Understandably delayed by the need to train crews on an aircraft type entirely new to them, No. 2 operated within 79 Wing independently as well as in company with No. 18. Initially sorties were flown against Japanese targets in the Timor area, particularly the airfields at Penfui and Langgoer.

Although somewhat restricted to the targets that lay within range of their aircraft, the Dutch and Australian flyers continued to harass Japanese shipping, and bases in the Kei and Aroe islands as well as on Timor and Ambon. With the war moving closer to the home islands, No. 18 became less exposed to fighter attack – but Japanese AA guns were still dangerous.

Then on 7 October 1944, Lt Col M. van Haselen took over as CO of No. 18 Sqn. He was to lead it until almost the end of the war, when the reins passed to Lt Col R. E. Jessurun. It was during April 1945 that the Dutch Mitchell unit scored a notable success: on the 6th an enemy convoy was discovered in the Flores Sea, apparently engaged in evacuating troops from Timor and escorted by the cruiser *Isuzu*. The convoy was attacked by Mitchells of 79 Wing plus RAAF Liberators. Penetrating a Japanese fighter screen to get at the ships proved fatal to two Liberators, but the medium bombers pressed home their attack on the cruiser and inflicted serious damage, so much so that she was sunk by US submarines the following day, 7 April.

(Right) As No. 18 (NEI) Sqn came under RAAF control, Australian groundcrews serviced the Mitchells. These armourers are feeding in ammunition for the rear guns of a B-25J. IWM

The single Australian Mitchell unit was No. 2 Sqn, based at Batchelor in the Northern Territory in 1944 when this B-25D was photographed. F.F. Smith

(Below) In common with other air forces, the RAAF operated Mitchells without camouflage after late 1943. B-25J (A47-46) seen at Amberley, Queensland, in 1945 had standard Australian markings. F.F. Smith

Piloted by Flt Lt A. Egan, this B-25J-25 (44-30896/A47-44) was photographed over Brisbane on 19 July 1945. It was disposed of on 10 March 1950. RAAF via N. Avery

On 15 July 1945 No. 18 Sqn moved to Balikpapan in Borneo, mainly to fly humanitarian aid to PoW camps in Java, Borneo and the Celebes. Dropping food and medical supplies was not without risk, and one Mitchell (N5-255) was lost. This duty occupied No. 18 until the end of the war, by which time its Mitchells were also operating a repatriation service for prisoners throughout its operational area. As recounted later, combat missions by Dutch-operated Mitchells in the East Indies merely paused with the surrender of Japan.

A similar tailing-off period was experienced by the crews of No. 2 Sqn, which was to have supported the campaign to recapture Borneo, but was forestalled by the Japanese surrender. After three months of inactivity during wartime, No.

2 joined No. 18 in flying numerous peacetime humanitarian sorties. For the record, thirteen Australian Mitchells were lost to all causes during the war, and two more crashed after hostilities had ceased.

Gifts through Alaska

Although the B-25B did not see lengthy first-line service with the USAAF other than for early antisubmarine patrols off the US coast and the Tokyo raid, an example of this Mitchell sub-type became the first to pass into Soviet hands. It has to be assumed that 'Ski' York's B-25B was evaluated by the VVS (Vienno-vozdushnyne sily – Soviet Air Force); their personnel had also earlier examined the aircraft flown by the 17th BG in the spring of 1942.

Flying into Bolling Field, Washington, Capt Ted Lawson, later one of the Tokyo raiders, was obliged to loan his B-25B to a visiting Russian general. Secretary of War Harry Stimson told the B-25 crew that the government had offered the Russians a choice of ten multi-engined combat aircraft, and as the Mitchell was on that list, this would be a fine time to give the general a check ride. In fact it was Lawson who got the ride: the Russian was an outstanding pilot who thought nothing of stunting directly over Washington and holding the medium in a 90-degree bank. The American crews had never seen anything like it, and had to admit that their comrade-in-arms was, as Lawson put it, 'A wild man, but one hell of a flyer!'.[1]

Lawson had earlier been impressed by Russian enthusiasm for the B-25, a fact that was later borne out by what is known of VVS combat missions in the type. Every effort was made to place American bombers at the disposal of Red Air Force crews, but neither they, nor the US ferry crews, probably realized how much diplomatic effort the actual transfer would involve. Even with his country continuing to be put under extreme pressure by the German invasion, Josef Stalin showed a marked lack of enthusiasm – much less practical co-operation – in taking delivery of Lend-Lease supplies, and no workable plan was put forward for Allied aircraft to be flown directly into Soviet airfields by Western pilots.

During 1940 the Americans, worried by the events in Europe, looked to the defences of Alaska. An agreement was made with

Canada to expand former gold-mining strips in the Yukon Territory into air bases capable of handling substantial numbers of aircraft. To reduce any diplomatic tension as a result of Stalin's mistrust of anything foreign (even the lifeblood of Allied war material), Project *ALSIB* (Alaska-Siberia ferry route) was established. Under this programme US aircraft would be ferried to Ladd Field in Alaska, the nearest point to Soviet Russia on the US mainland. At Ladd they were officially handed over to Russian ground personnel and aircrews, who flew them back to the Soviet Union via Siberia.

On 24 September 1942, five transports and one B-25 arrived carrying Russian ferry crews experienced enough to need only cockpit checks and a few practice

landings to enable them to fly the American aircraft home. Enough men were carried on this initial trip to crew four B-25s, fourteen A-20s, twenty-eight P-40s and seven C-47s. During the succeeding years of war, several hundred Mitchells were handed over to the Russians via the Alaska ferry route, the total figure having been variously quoted as between 732 (Ladd Field's own figures) and 733 by respected authors/ researchers (one of whom in fact downgraded the figure to 726). Other sources add another 100 aircraft, to place the B-25 total as high as 862.[2] In terms of medium and attack bombers, *ALSIB* deliveries of Mitchells were second only to the 1,368 (2,908)[3] A-20s passed to the Russians.

(Top) Marked to signify an initial Russian military mission to Alaska in the late summer of 1942, this B-25B accompanied the C-47 at right. The purpose of the visit was to help establish the Alaska–Siberia ferry route for US military aircraft, including hundreds of B-25s, to be delivered to Russia. USAF

(Above) As they did for all their customers, NAA painted the Russian B-25s at the factory. Many of them stayed in this basic light green/tan brown colour scheme with gloss black undersides when they entered VVS service. via NAA

The delivery rate of aircraft through Ladd Field increased steadily throughout 1943, although this brought an inevitably rising accident rate in such inhospitable conditions. To begin with, an efficient search-and-rescue organization lagged behind the setting up of the ferry route, but this was established in January 1944. It was certainly needed. Appalling weather often got the better of pilots – although a lack of flight discipline was the apparent cause of some accidents. There were occasions when aircraft simply disappeared without trace in the white wilderness of Alaska. This fate befell a B-25 belonging to the Cold Weather Testing Detachment (CWTDet), which went missing in February 1944 en route to Ladd Field from Kodiak. It was never found. A B-25 flown by Maj Peter Zotov of the VVS is known to have gone down in bad weather east of Nome, killing three crewmen. As can be seen from mention of the CWTDet, not all the US military aircraft in Alaska were destined for the Russians, as the eleventh Air Force also received a number of replacements via this route.

On 15 September 1944 another B-25 was reported overdue between Edmonton to Fort Nelson, and a search was initiated. The Mitchell had gone down about 70 miles (110km) east of Grande Prairie, and had ended up between two small muskeg lakes. It was only just spotted from the air when an observer caught sight of a small tongue of flame. An overland search party out of Edmonton took two days, using vehicles, horses and wagons, to reach the wreckage and extract the bodies of the crew.

On 14 August 1944 further rationalization of the AAF ferrying service took place with the activation of the 7th Ferrying Squadron (later Group). This unit embraced the personnel of the three squadrons which had previously supplied flight crews, and for convenience, it adopted the Air Transport Command method of classifying pilots by the type of aircraft they were qualified to fly. Graded by their qualifications, individuals would be grouped in Classes I to V, aircraft such as the B-25 coming under Class IV, 'heavy twins'.

Not surprisingly, the generally smooth *ALSIB* operation was occasionally hampered by technical troubles on the aircraft being ferried. This happened to the B-25 in October 1944, when carburettor malfunctions led to the Russians refusing to accept nearly half the J models coming through Ladd Field. Deliveries resumed after all carburettors had been changed at Fairbanks.

Russian pilots generally impressed their American counterparts with their flying skills – though the US crews did have some reservations as to the wisdom of hauling aircraft with cold engines off the runway and immediately throwing them into wild aerobatic manoeuvres: it was not exactly a recipe for accident-free operations. But the pilots who came to collect US aircraft in Alaska were combat-experienced men who had seen at first hand the harsh conditions on the Eastern front, and their fatalistic, reckless approach to ferry flying was generally regarded as a mere interlude, and nothing to get excited about in a war that was far from over. There was, however, a perceptible change in this 'gung ho' attitude as Russia's war successes became unstoppable; American personnel noted an increasing reluctance by ferry pilots to fly in less-than-perfect visibility, whereas previously they would literally take off in any weather conditions.

Russian B-25 Operations

Full service records by VVS units fully or partially equipped with the B-25 are as yet sketchy, although at least one Guards Aviation Corps (4 Gv AK)[3] of the ADD (*Aviatsiya dal nego deistviya* or 'long-range air force') equipped with the B-25J gave a good account of itself in combat, enough for the unit to display the Order of the Red Banner on the forward fuselage of its Mitchells. Apparently well thought of by its crews, the B-25 was integrated into the ADD to become part of the typically mixed aircraft complement of these formations.

Operations were equally varied, and included strategic bombing and tactical close support as well as transport and supply flights. Contemporary Luftwaffe accounts include mention of night interception sorties against ADD Mitchells on the Eastern front when such aircraft were engaged upon supply flights to partisans. Indeed there was some indication of impending night operations by the B-25s handed over to the Russians even in the NAA factories that built them, as many B-25s destined for Soviet service were camouflaged and given black undersurfaces: the Russians rarely repainted Lend-Lease aircraft, and it is known that they flew these in combat without much alteration to this basic airframe finish. And on 6 September a change was made to the Russian national insignia: from then on the red star was applied with a white outline,

replacing the former marking of a star on a white disk. Later, the Russian penchant for applying badges and slogans to their combat aircraft extended to B-25s in VVS service.

During the late autumn of 1944 a major part of the ADD was transferred to airfields around Leningrad – Gzhatsk, Andrepol, Volkhov Toropets and others – for strategic bombing attacks on Helsinki. Accompanying the force, which was predominantly equipped with Russian aircraft, were the B-25s of 4 Gv AK (consisting of two air divisions: 4 Gv AD and 5 Gv AD) commanded by Col S.P. Kovalev. For a war front that did not see many large-scale strategic bombing operations by the VVS, this short campaign involved a substantial number of aircraft, around 600. Its purpose was to force the Finns to sever their alliance with Germany and to negotiate an armistice with Russia.

The offensive began on the night of 6/7 February 1944: on this occasion some 200 aircraft were involved, and raids were repeated on the nights of 16/17 and 26/27 of that month when, according to Finnish estimates, 420 and 600 Soviet aircraft respectively were deployed. Exactly to what extent the B-25 units were involved is unknown, but the proximity of the Leningrad bases to the Finnish capital meant that some aircraft flew up to three sorties per night.

For all this effort the Soviets achieved little, because with advance warning of the raids, the Finns put up spirited AA fire, and as a result, many of the bomber crews were obliged to jettison their loads over the sea before they reached the city. Only 711 bombs out of 10,681 dropped in a total of 2,120 sorties exploded in Helsinki, killing just 120 people.

It was a rather different story on the night of 10/11 March when the ADD bombers were briefed to attack the German-occupied Estonian capital of Tallinn. This time the Russians were greeted with only weak defences, and with 300 aircraft they proceeded to destroy over half the buildings in the city, causing over 1,000 casualties. But what appeared to be a successful operation in terms of bombing results in fact quickly turned sour for the ADD, as unbeknown to the returning Soviet pilots, Finnish bombers tailed them as they withdrew: thus unsuspectingly they led their adversaries straight into their airfields at Levashovo, Kasimova, Gorskaya and Yukki, which the Finns systematically bombed, destroying runways, aircraft, fuel stocks and ammunition, without any cost to themselves.

CHAPTER NINE

Desert Debut

Equipped with B-25Cs and Ds, the first American medium bomber group arrived in the Western Desert in mid-August 1942 as part of the Ninth Air Force, United States Army Middle East Air Force (USAMEAF). After the 98th with B-24s and the 57th with P-40s, the 12th BG was the third AAF group to arrive in Egypt, the fighters flying from aircraft carriers, and the fifty-five B-25s, under the command of Col Charles G. Goodrich, travelling via the southern ferry route. Egypt was identified by the USAAF as part of the Mediterranean Theatre of Operations (MTO), and the 12th had come specifically to aid the British in the fight against Erwin Rommel's Afrika Korps. Sterling work had already been undertaken in this area by RAF and SAAF medium bomber squadrons, which were then equipped either with Blenheims or the US 'export' mediums, the Baltimore and Maryland. Douglas Bostons of No. 24 Sqn SAAF had been in the area since October 1941.

The 12th and the other groups in USAMEAF became in effect the advance guard for a substantial American build-up which occurred in the desert after the Operation *Torch* landings in French North Africa in November 1942. In the wake of *Torch* came the 319th Bomb Group with B-26s, followed by the 17th Bomb Group, the unit that had provided the majority of crews for the Tokyo raid. But it was not flying Mitchells: continuing to fly AS patrols after the carrier strike, the group had been

(Top) In their overall 'desert pink' colour scheme, the B-25s of the 12th Bomb Group were an increasingly numerous sight over North Africa from the summer of 1942. Early on the US crews operated with RAF and SAAF squadrons to gain experience. B-25C No. 33 (41-12863) in company with Baltimores, was assigned to the 82nd BS. IWM

This desert service for a 434th BS B-25C included removal of the transparent turret dome. Gun malfunction was not uncommon on the early model Mitchells. IWM

switched to Marauders due to a shortage of B-25s. The 17th would be joined in April 1943 by the third B-26 group in the MTO, the 320th. In addition, the 47th Bomb Group, with A-20s, had arrived in November 1942, to be followed by the 68th Observation Group with a mix of types including A-20s.

Fighter escort for the bombers was vested in the new tactical Twelfth Air Force (formed to support *Torch* operations), with three squadrons of P-38s, two of USAAF Spitfires, one of P-40s and two of P-39s. The bulk of the fighter units was already in the theatre before the medium bombers arrived. Although a substantial enough force on paper, the deprivations of the desert would present numerous practical challenges for the USAAF, some of which took time to overcome. The 12th Bomb Group was allocated airfields along the line of the Suez Canal and was obliged to split up, the 81st and 82nd Squadrons taking up residence at Deversoir, and the 83rd and 444th Squadrons occupying Ismalia.

To gain all-important experience of the Allied medium bomber tactics that had already proven sound in the theatre, six B-25s were attached to each bomber squadron of 3 Wing, SAAF (Nos. 12 and 24 Squadrons). Even though they often had fighter escort, the SAAF squadrons adopted very tight formation flying for mutual self-protection. In this respect the more heavily armed B-25C could take better care of itself than the early model Bostons – but the principle was sound enough. The 12th began practice flying with eighteen-ship formations similar to those of its allies.

Although the group had flown its own aircraft to Egypt, a support unit, the 26th Air Depot Group, was established at Deversoir to supply and maintain aircraft allocated to USAMEAF units.

Debut of the 'Earthquakers'

The 12th BG flew several missions in company with the RAF, the first being on 16 August, but it made its combat debut in its own right on 31 August 1942 when it joined in the Battle of Alam Halfa, which had begun twenty-four hours before. Erwin Rommel's timely move was not all it seemed. In a last bid to take Egypt he had little choice but to attempt to break through the El Alamein line in the south and drive north to take the Alam Halfa Ridge. He failed; without effective enough

support from the Luftwaffe and starved of supplies, particularly fuel for his tanks, the 'Desert Fox' encountered loose sand south of the ridge which dangerously slowed the Panzers and inadvertently created a huge tank and vehicle 'chokepoint'. It was an ideal target for air attack.

Harassed by Allied aircraft for two days, the German tanks were forced to pull back. The 12th's B-25s contributed to this latest 'bomb carpet' – as Rommel himself called the cascade of high explosive – to the extent that AVM Coningham, commanding the RAF in the Middle East, sent a congratulatory telegram to Col Goodrich:

Many thanks for your assistance in a record day's bombing. We are full of admiration for the grand work of your crews, and I know our squadrons are delighted. Well done and good luck.

On 1 September, three 12th BG aircraft, led by Goodrich, joined fifteen Bostons from No. 24 Sqn SAAF to hit the German tanks. Finding an estimated 1,000 enemy vehicles badly dispersed three miles northwest of Qaret el Himeimut, the mixed formation bombed at 09.05hr, with reportedly effective results. On the down side, flak found the bombers, and one accurate burst almost simultaneously tore the wing off the Mitchell piloted by Lt J. A. Pocock and severed the tail of a Boston. A single crew member managed to jump from each of the ill-fated aircraft.

The crews of the 12th soon found themselves flying night missions to such locations as Matrah and the Axis aerodromes at Daba and Fuka; however, they had not been trained for this, and worried that the poor flame-damping properties of the Wright R-2600 engines of the B-25 would become a 'flak magnet' for German groundfire. And some aircraft were indeed lost – two had even gone down during night-flying training on 6 August – before bombing altitudes were varied from 8,000 to 10,000ft (2,450 to 3,050m), statistics having shown that enemy fire could be marginally less effective below 10,000ft. But the 'blue-tinted comet', as one observer dubbed the large, full-ring exhaust collectors of the B-25C, were found to be visible from the ground, even with the aircraft flying at 10,000ft. This unfortunate drawback was indirectly to rob the Earthquakers of their first CO within weeks of the group's combat debut.

Despite the bad flame-damping of its engines, the B-25C began to excel at night bombing; in this, the 12th adopted a sys-

tem of strict target times under which each pilot was briefed to release his bombs within a timeframe of a few seconds. The plan was for individual B-25s to carry out as many as four runs on the target, the number being pre-arranged. After its initial bombing pass each aircraft would depart the target area on a set heading, fly for a given time and then double back to bomb again, adopting the strict procedure it had followed the first time. By staggering the group attack in this way, a second aircraft would be on its bomb run as the first turned away, then a third would follow the same procedure, and so on for each individual crew. Split-second timing and adherence to the different headings was required by the pilots of all forty-eight aircraft.

Such tactics could only minimize, rather than entirely prevent, losses as a result of the enemy defences, and on the night of 12/13th September the 12th lost Col Goodrich, his aircraft brought down by flak during a mission to bomb three Luftwaffe landing grounds near Sidi Haneish. Goodrich himself survived, however, to become a PoW for the duration of the war. Just three days later, on 16 September, Col Ed Backus replaced Goodrich as CO; he was destined to lead the 12th Group throughout its North African period of operations and into early combat in the campaign to secure Sicily.

October Campaign

Part of the substantial build-up of Allied air forces for the battle of El Alamein in October 1942 was to position combat units as closely as possible to their intended targets on and behind Rommel's lines. The 12th was therefore located at LG 88 from mid-month, the B-25s adding their strength to the preliminary campaign to destroy Axis aircraft on the ground when their own forward landing grounds around Daba and Qattara became waterlogged following seasonal heavy rainfall.

Although these sorties resulted in the destruction of no more than a dozen enemy aircraft, every little helped. Before Alamein the Allies had 940 aircraft – USAMEAF's contribution including thirty-five serviceable B-25s out of forty-six on strength – while the Axis had 603. Notwithstanding unserviceability (on both sides), the ratio was clearly favourable to the RAF, USAAF and Commonwealth squadrons, which could make good their losses more readily than their opposite numbers.

**In standard desert markings of 1942–43, including the RAF fin flash 'theatre marking',
a 434th Squadron B-25C crosses the proverbial 'sea of sand'.** H. Levy

If the desert brought deprivations, it also had many advantages when fighting a fluid, ground-support war. For one thing it was huge and sparsely populated, and B-25 crewmen who hailed from the American states with those legendary 'wide open spaces' felt quite at home in this respect. They soon devised a variation on the USAAF doctrine of precision bombing, which was useless in the desert as the Germans avoided grouping their vehicles closely together. As it was clearly unrealistic to attempt to attack every vehicle individually, at least with mediums, the AAF devised the 'bomb carpets' so despised by Rommel.

More correctly known to the AAF as 'pattern bombing', it was achieved by identifying on a map the areas of known enemy activity, and marking them into rectangles half a mile long by a quarter of a mile wide. Group aircraft would then drop all their bombs into the rectangles, thus swamping everything caught inside them. German reaction was to liken the rain of explosive to an earthquake, a statement later seized upon by a war correspondent recording the 12th's combat exploits. The name stuck, and the 'Earthquakers' were born.

If the lead bombardier's aim was good, the 12th would invariably cause widespread damage and destruction inside the boxes. Attacks were generally made from 6,500 to 8,500ft (2,000 to 2,600m) altitude, the B-25s spacing out to fly a prearranged formation prior to the bomb run.

The object was to cover the entire box – which did sometimes vary in area – and to meet a requirement for all bombs to hit no more than 50ft (15m) apart. If the enemy vehicles were travelling in columns, the American mediums dropped on a parallelogram pattern at half-second intervals, which on average enabled two more bombs per aircraft to be dropped.

To make the 12th Group's move to LG 88 as smooth and rapid as possible, only essential aircrews and ground personnel were transferred. It was their misfortune to arrive just in time to experience the worst sandstorm in living memory, the swirling sand cutting visibility to five feet or less.

As a prelude to the battle of El Alamein proper there was a curtain-raising air offensive to soften up the enemy: this began on 19/20 October, three days before the ground assault began. The purpose was to deny Rommel his air support, reduce his supplies even further, and to protect the movement of Allied troops into their forward positions. Most of these objectives were achieved in hundreds of sorties before the ground battle opened. When it did so on the 23rd, the largest concentration of artillery yet amassed thundered out over the desert to shatter the Afrika Korps.

Hard on the heels of the gunfire came the Allied air forces, the 12th Group's B-25s being in the thick of the action. LG 88 began a week-long bomb shuttle, sending off an eighteen-ship formation of B-25s at thirty-minute intervals throughout the hours of

daylight. The aircraft took twenty minutes to cover the 50 miles (80km) between their base and the front line, which stretched southwards from the Mediterranean for about 30 miles (50km) to the Qattara Depression. On 24 October the Earthquakers set a record by flying seven missions during a single day. In total the group dropped well over 100,000lb (45,360kg) of bombs (96,000lb/43,500kg on 24 October alone) during this hectic period, the intention being to wreck so many of Rommel's tanks, trucks and guns that his offensive capability would be broken.

However optimistic the results of the El Alamein artillery barrage may have been, Rommel was still far from 'out', as his counter-attack on 27 October showed. But pounded ceaselessly from the air, he failed to gain ground, and ultimately Allied bombs broke the back of the 90th Light Divn, which was almost the Afrika Korp's last hope. No further counter-attack could be made in strength, and by 4 November the battle was over. Rommel began a 2,000-mile (3,200km) retreat to Tunis.

Though eager to pursue the enemy, the Earthquaker B-25s soon ran out of ground transport. In fact, so acute did this situation become that the Mitchells, which had moved from LG 88 to an airstrip formerly occupied by the Germans, were obliged to ferry their own bombs before they could drop them on the Axis vehicles choking the coastal road. They also hauled bombs for B-24s engaged on a similar mission.

Blasting Rommel's transport and communications occupied the 12th to the end of the year, the group ranging out to Crete to reduce the effectiveness of the Luftwaffe. It also flew some of the last sorties in the Libyan campaign, which ended in Axis defeat on 23 January 1943. The focus now turned on Tunisia.

The 310th Bomb Group

On 2 December 1942 a second Mitchell unit, the 310th BG, had made its combat debut in the desert. This was a relatively quiet period due mainly to prevailing bad weather over the front in Libya. Also flying B-25Cs and Ds, the 310th, under the command of Lt Col Anthony G. Hunter, comprised the 379th, 380th, 381st and 428th Squadrons. Initially flying missions from Maison Blanche, they were soon on the move. By 21 December the group was established at Telergma, but then on 1 January

1943 it occupied a third Algerian base at Berteaux.

These moves firmly established the 310th in the MTO, rather than the ETO, previous definite orders having 'confirmed' that it would become part of the Eighth Air Force. But having flown its B-25s to England via the northern ferry route and assembled at Hardwick in late 1942, the 310th was instead headed for North Africa early in November.

After an uneventful eight-ship first mission to the latent hotspot at Gabes on 2 December, mission two on the 5th brought Luftwaffe reaction, when in an attack on Sidi Ahmed aerodrome one B-25 was shot down. The missions achieved gradually accumulated, and by 19 January, Tunis, Sousse, Sfax and Medenine had all been attacked. In that time the group had also conducted ten low-level sea searches for Axis shipping, which boosted the mission total to twenty-five to date.

The 310th benefited from the experience of a Royal Navy officer on sea-search missions. He advised the American crews that the best method of attacking enemy vessels involved approaching the target at 50ft (15m) off the sea, then climbing and using the 'eyeball' method of sighting before attacking with standard 500lb (225kg) bombs. By adopting such tactics, the 310th's Mitchells helped put enough freighters on the bottom of the Mediterranean to ensure that the Afrika Korps never received an over-abundance of supplies.

Although the crews of the American mediums were alert to the possibility of attack every time they went out, it did not follow that they would encounter enemy fighters in force on every mission – but on 8 February, fifteen of the 310th's aircraft stirred up a veritable hornet's nest during an attack on Gabes aerodrome. Escorted by eighteen P-38s of the 82nd FG, and led in by fifteen 17th Group Marauders, the AAF formations encountered between twenty and thirty Bf 109Gs from the Stab and I./JG 77. A running battle ensued – and it did so because, in that time-honoured American phrase, 'someone goofed'. Having climbed to altitude immediately after take-off – which was in itself unusual – the 310th flew right over the target in straight and level formation, then turned north, before doing a 180-degree turn prior to the bomb run. All this gave the German flak gunners ample time to adjust their sights, and enabled the fighters to take off in almost leisurely fashion.

The 310th lost four B-25s in this combat; for the record, the German pilots somewhat over-estimated the number they destroyed: Ltn Armin Kohler and Fw Karl Hosmann of 2. Staffel claimed one each, and Ltn Edgar Berres of the Stab claimed one, making his thirtieth kill. In 1. Staffel, Oblt Helmut Goedert claimed two, and his colleague Fw Horst Schlick one – making six B-25s in all.[1]

The German fighter pilots were certainly distracted by the P-38s, which claimed eight enemy aircraft downed, while the Germans put their own losses at three, and additionally claimed two P-38s – but the B-25s again proved their ability to withstand combat damage, since repeated fighter passes were necessary to bring them down. All the 310th's aircraft retained the lower turret at that time, the group following the sound principle of the more guns,

the better. And they were certainly needed, as evidenced by one ship that came back with more than 500 holes!

This operation was followed by a number of others, and although they could hardly be described as 'milk runs', they did not incur the level of aerial opposition experienced by the 310th on 8 February. As its fighter losses increased, and transfers away from the southern war front depleted units for lengthy periods, Luftwaffe reaction to raids was inevitably uneven; the Mitchells were usually escorted to those targets which the enemy was expected to defend, and whilst losses were of course serious, the number of bombers lost in any given month was generally relatively small. The 310th remained in Tunisia for most of 1943 before it moved back to Algeria in November, thence to Corsica, and finally to Fano in Italy where it remained until the end of the war.

With a single yellow tail stripe identifying the 310th Bomb Group, these B-25s en route to a target belonged to the group's 428th BS. J.V. Crow

Low over the Mediterranean during a 1943 mission, this B-25C belonged to the 82nd BS, 12th BG. According to the original caption, it was about to ditch. H. Levy

(Above) One of the B-25Cs that had armament modifications at a North African depot, this aircraft, named 'Lucky', may have been part of the 310th Bomb Group. It has new waist positions with armour plate attached to each gun and a single gun in a heavily braced tail position. H. Levy

Roman numerals identified B-25s of the 321st Group during 1943. 'IV' on the nearest field-modified B-25C-20 indicated the 448th Bomb Squadron, part of which is peeling off to land. USAF

The 321st Bomb Group

In November 1942 a third B-25 unit, Col Robert D. Knapp's 321st Bomb Group, was assigned to the MTO. Comprising the 445th, 446th, 447th and 448th Squadrons, the group conducted a phased move from its 1942 base in French Morocco, to Algeria and its designated base at Ain M'lila. The unit also used two other Algerian bases, Berteaux and Dar el Koudia, the latter being occupied after some six months of combat flying in the theatre.

Operations for the new Mitchell group during the first three months of 1943 were mainly of an anti-shipping nature. These sea sweeps often brought the B-25s into contact with the notorious Siebel ferries, shallow draft vessels bristling with short-range AA guns; these could be lethal to attack aircraft when acting as 'shotgun guards' to small convoys. Robert Knapp solved that particular wrinkle by suggesting a double approach to the target convoy: a high-level attack by about twelve B-25s, which would bomb from around 8,000 to 10,000ft (2,430 to 3,000m) to give the

German gunners something to shoot at; and at the same time six more B-25s would be poised to attack at masthead height. By timing their strafing and skip-bombing runs to the second, strafing and releasing their bombs just before the cascade of high explosive from the higher elements, they could smother the target before the gunners could retrain their weapons.

Like other US medium bomber units, the 321st used standard 500lb bombs with delayed-action fusing for skip-bombing, to allow just enough time for the aircraft to get clear of flying debris. This type of attack was not without casualties, and sometimes heavy ones. Nobody fooled the German flak gunners for long. As soon as they realized that the greatest danger lay with the low-level bombers, they would put up walls of fire. The 321st counted it

a lucky day if this type of attack did not result in two out of six B-25s being shot down.

Knapp had also to judge his sorties with that ever-present hazard, the weather. He did his best to fly missions when the Germans would least expect him to, and even if the conditions were bad, if the crews could see their targets, they went out. For various reasons, missions did not take place on every consecutive day.

Despite his protests, Robert Knapp was in effect 'kicked upstairs' by his squadron commanders after leading a couple of low-level attacks. They offered to take it in turns to lead the strafing runs, horrified at the prospect of their CO – and, incidentally, the commander of the entire 57th Bomb Wing – being shot down. It made sense, and Knapp reluctantly complied.

Spring Offensives

On the ground, the retreating Germans were now trapped in north-eastern Tunisia, which meant even greater reliance on airborne supplies. Their regular shuttle service between Sicily and Tunisia was quite reliable, but the Allies sought to stem these supply flights with Operation *Flax*, and accordingly attacked on 10 April 1943. An armada of Ju 52s was intercepted by P-38s and crews of the 310th, who took their B-25s down to wave-top level in order for the gunners to shoot up the enemy aircraft: nine gunners were credited with Ju 52 kills. And a week later, on 18 April, the Luftwaffe transport aircraft again suffered heavily at the hands of fighters in the 'Palm Sunday Massacre'.

With the termination of the battle of Tunisia in May 1943 the Afrika Korps, then under the command of Jürgen von Arnim after Rommel's return to Germany in March, lost its last foothold in Africa. It surrendered on the 13th, and this meant the end of all organized Axis resistance in this area. Contributing to that satisfactory situation for the Allies, the 321st BG had by that time completed fifty-one missions, and a breakdown shows a typical spread of offensive operations for the US mediums: thirty missions were anti-shipping strikes in the Sicilian Straits, fifteen were against Axis air bases, four were aimed at silencing the communications centre at Mateur, and there were single missions against harbour installations and a rail junction.

By blockading the sea lanes the B-25s helped stop the flow of supplies to German troops in Africa, the 321st Group sinking at least ten sizable vessels and damaging thirteen so badly that they were unlikely to have delivered their cargoes intact. Pinning the Luftwaffe to the ground under myriad bomb explosions prevented Allied casualties both in the air and on the ground, particularly when they were timed to take place just before army offensives. A rain of bombs destroyed and disabled valuable aircraft, and on some occasions, killed pilots. Superior Allied intelligence frequently paid dividends in this particular aspect of the air war.

To complete the complement of the 57th Bomb Wing, the 340th Group had by April become the fourth and last unit with the B-25 as its original equipment to see combat in the MTO. Flying its first mission on 19 April, the 340th made its debut sorties against Korba South LG, destroying four Italian fighters in the process.

The 57th Wing thus encompassed the 310th, 321st and 340th plus the 319th with Marauders. In the interests of standardization the 319th later became a B-25 outfit – much to the chagrin of many of the crews! The 12th BG remained under the control of the Ninth Air Force until it was transferred to the Twelfth in October 1943; in the re-alignment of AAF groups after the Axis surrender in North Africa, the 12th was posted to Burma for a further round of operations with the Tenth Air Force.

On 6 May the 340th was handed an extremely important mission. American ground forces had been stopped on the Medjez-el-Bab to Tunis road by heavy German artillery fire. The source of the trouble was located about 17 miles (27km) east of Medjez, and the 340th – on its first full group mission – was briefed to remove it. An early take-off was made by fifty-plus B-25s, with Col Mills flying in the lead Mitchell which was piloted by Capt Donald J. Marcan; it was he who ensured that a good bomb pattern was achieved. Turning north towards Mateur to avoid concentrations of flak, the group's B-25s were fired on, and about fifteen seconds after making the turn, at 07.45, the aircraft in which the CO was riding took hits from flak.

Severe damage was done to the rear of the aircraft, the tail gunner being killed instantly. With smoke filling up the flight-deck, navigator Lt Joe Zerega prepared to bail out. He recalled that the colonel probably had no chance to reach his detachable parachute pack and attach it to the harness before the B-25 became engulfed in flames. Within seconds its fuel tanks exploded, and the next thing Zerega remembered was being in mid-air with pieces of the aircraft falling all around him. Only Marcan, Zerega and radioman Lt Gordon Warren survived the loss of their ship, furthermore it was the only one that did not return from the mission.

Everyone who had known Courtney Mills was saddened by his loss, not least his comrade and friend, Adolf Tokaz who assumed command of the 340th for the second time on 7 May. A posthumous Silver Star seemed small compensation for the life of a respected commander.

Summer Offensives

During the summer months of 1943 the four B-25 bombardment groups of the Ninth and Twelfth Air Forces continued to harass the Axis to the point where their military ambitions in North Africa were all but finished. Most significant was Operation *Husky*, initiated on 10 July and involving the Allied invasion of Sicily – indeed, so overwhelming was the combined might of the US, British and Commonwealth air forces that only two Axis airfields remained usable after the pre-invasion bombardment. The B-25 groups were in the thick of the fighting, flying missions against such important targets as the Naples marshalling yards. The operation launched against these yards was huge, involving seventy-two Mitchells escorted by sixty-seven P-38s following up the heavies and B-26s to add their contribution to the 868 tons of bombs already dropped to cripple the yards. Rome's marshalling yards were attacked two days later, the crews being carefully briefed to avoid collateral damage to the historic buildings in the 'Eternal City'.

On 5 August the first MTO attack by B-25Gs of the 'gun squadron' of the 321st took place, a flight of four attacking the rail switching station at Guspini. Sweeping in from 300ft (90m), they blasted the vital switchgear with thirty-six 75mm shells.

Operation *Dragoon* involved the invasion of southern France, and took place on 15 August; Axis forces in Sicily surrendered on the 17th – and these Allied successes all but guaranteed a swift end to the fighting in the Mediterranean region. A week or so later the Ninth Air Force began to lose its combat groups in preparation for a headquarters move to England to create an entirely new tactical force for the invasion of Europe.

The capitulation of Italy on 8 September was not the victorious event it first seemed to be, as Germany fortified key points of the country and fought on. Initial Allied landings in Italy took place on the 3rd, followed by the main invasion at Salerno on the 9th. In the meantime more B-25Gs had arrived in the theatre, and it was at this juncture that the 310th's 379th Squadron, led by Maj Manford Wetzel, found itself assigned to Coastal Air Force, flying out of Gambut Three. It was consequently based 500 miles west of Cairo, while the rest of the group was at Philipeville, Algeria, for some R & R and training to use the B-25G and H. 'Wetzels' Weasels' was the second unit in the eastern Mediterranean to be fully equipped with cannon-armed Mitchells, and worked alongside a wing of RAF Beaufighters (fighters and Torbeaus) to conduct (or so the crews assumed) anti-shipping strikes in the Aegean – at least, that was the theory.

In practice the B-25Gs found little to attack, and they were too slow (cruising at 200mph/320km/h) to effectively integrate their sorties with Beaufighters. By all accounts the American crews quickly realized the Aegean was a backwater of the war, despite a garrison of some 45,000 German troops on Crete and several of the smaller Greek islands. They actually posed little threat to anyone, least of all Allied shipping which was rarely seen in the area without a heavy escort. German supplies came in by small caiques, many using sail power with auxiliary engines, which were shadowed, shot at, routinely missed – and only very occasionally sunk by 75mm cannon shells.

The AAF/RAF combined operations gradually petered out, largely due to the disparity of performance between a medium bomber and a twin-engined fighter. The Mitchell crews were of the opinion that Allied planners had not thought the idea through: many men would dearly have liked to meet those who thought the Aegean to be an ideal theatre for flights of four B-25Gs at a time to regularly fly around at 50ft (15m) altitude, acting as Luftwaffe fighter bait when the occasion

Maj Gen Doolittle flew a 12th Bomb Group B-25D when he visited the group at Gerbini, Sicily on 20 October 1943. H. Levy

demanded. It *was* demanded on a few occasions, the B-25s effectively keeping the Bf 109s and Ju 88s occupied while the Beaus went in and sank ships. The Mitchells gave a good account of themselves in such situations, their heavy conventional firepower convincing the *Jagdflieger* not to press their luck too far. Yet it took the same planners about six months to reach the conclusion that such missions were not really very productive, much to the relief of the 379th's crews.

Having helped 'write the book' (such as it was) on low-level anti-shipping attack with the B-25G in the MTO, the 379th quietly forgot about it. Joined by its sister squadrons, it moved to Corsica to take up residence at Ghisonaccia, which was destined to be its home for the next fifteen months. The 310th Group then became a temporary part of the 63rd Fighter Wing for operations early in 1944.

Cannon-armed Mitchells arrived in the MTO in abundance, almost as though someone with authority had found a place to send them and had made the most of it. The 379th continued to be unimpressed…

At the end of 1943 an AAF statistician worked out that the 321st Group's B-25s had encountered a total of 421 enemy fighters during all combat missions up to that time, and of these, fifty-one were destroyed, twelve were probably destroyed, and twenty-eight were damaged. Although such figures compiled in wartime do have an immediacy, the enemy loss figures generally bear some re-examining – set against actual Luftwaffe losses, such claims are usually open to some downgrading. What does remain of interest is the number of encounters reported by crews: taken directly from

Weather-beaten Mitchells of the 321st taxiing out for another mission at Amendola, Italy, in December 1943. Following a B-25C-20 that shows evidence of having been transferred from the 310th Group, is 'Oh-7', a B-25 made famous by its nose art, shown in colour in various publications. USAF

En route to blast the monastery at Monte Cassino on 15 March 1944, the 340th Bomb Group's 488th Squadron flew B-25Cs with various colour schemes, but generally with uprated armament. USAF

Stormy Weather

Many of the B-25s issued to the MTO groups returned fine combat records. Dozens flew fifty or more missions, while numerous others reached the century – and at the same time possessed 'that certain something' that seemed to set them apart from other aircraft. One was the 310th's B-25C-1 (41-13053) named 'Stormy Weather'. A group original aircraft, it was brought to England in 1942 as part of the first contingent and flown to Berteaux, Algeria. By 1 March 1943 it had flown twenty missions. On 10 March it had a torpedo rack installed, the first in the group to be modified. On a sea search on 3 April its gunners were credited with two Bf 109s. In other encounters with German fighters the bomber emerged unscathed, and by 15 June some of the original crew had completed forty missions, and the aircraft forty-six.

While bombing Sicily on 7 July, its fifty-third mission, '053 encountered flak but again survived. The remaining original crew members completed their fifty missions on 12 July, and the aircraft got a new crew which flew it on their first mission on 8 August. Over Salerno marshalling yards on 17 August flak again got '053's range and put ten holes in her.

'Stormy Weather' was flown to Bizerte on 15 September to have the lower turret removed and new waist windows and tail position installed, the first Mitchell in the 310th to have these modifications. On return to base on the 23rd, a test-firing showed up malfunction of the tail gun due to ammunition jamming. The cause was traced to the over-long ammo track, which was far from unique to this one aircraft.

'Stormy Weather's' last few months have been chronicled as follows:

3 October: Target: crossroads north-east of Naples. Heavy flak plus fighters, tail-gun problems fixed – gunner credited with a fighter. Another credited to top turret gunner.
6 January: '053, now only remaining B-25C in group; taken off combat after 86 missions.
17 January: Back on combat status with guns reinstalled.
3 February: Taken off combat, de-armed prior to use as transport.
3 March: Back on combat status; guns remounted. Groundcrew comment: 'Wish to hell they'd make up their minds.'
5 April: Ferry sortie to Capri – fired on over Naples.
6 April: Returned with hole in left wing.
8 April: New wing-rib installed.
20 April: Stormy Weather flies 100th mission.
4 May: Target: bridge over Orvieto; flak hit in right wing-tip.
12 May: Two missions to road junction east of Cassino, flak hit in nose.
16 May: Grounded due to cracks in exhaust stacks; aircraft now oldest in 57th BW.
21 May: Off combat but guns remain, just in case.
24 July: Heavy crash-landing at Naples when pilot retracted gear too early; aircraft settled and skidded down runway. Hauled to boneyard after 125 missions.

combat reports, such figures should be reasonably accurate. With only five B-25s of this particular group having been lost to fighter attack, the above figures were projected to conclude that on average, ten fighters were downed for every Mitchell lost in air combat, an interesting but surely optimistic statistic – until the relatively small number of bombers lost to this cause alone is taken into account.

The number of enemy aircraft destroyed in encounters with bombers was always notoriously hard to determine with any accuracy, due to the multiple claims arising from the number of gunners who actually fired when their formation came under attack. All air forces realized that such claims, confusing as they sometimes were, were made in good faith; it was equally clear that German fighters often went down after being hit by machine-gun fire from multiple bombers, a small but steady part of an attrition rate that eventually proved disastrous to the Luftwaffe.

CHAPTER TEN

New Blood for 2 Group

In all honesty it must be said that the B-25 was probably not the first choice of the crews of some RAF light bomber squadrons when they had their first sight of the North American medium in 1942. They were more familiar with the Douglas Boston, which had been the first of the 'new generation' of American types to enter service in a tactical role with the daylight bomber force of 2 Group, Bomber Command; by comparison, the RAF men considered the Mitchell to be a little too large and ungainly. It was indeed larger than the more nimble-looking Boston – but looks can be deceptive, and not only could the B-25C carry double the bomb load (4,000lb/1,800kg as opposed to 2,000lb/900kg) over a greater range, but the Mitchell's configuration meant that crew members were not isolated from each other as they were in the Boston. The fact that another member of a Mitchell crew could fly the aircraft if the pilot were wounded or killed was a safety bonus that came to be highly appreciated.

When in 1942 it was decided to re-equip the squadrons of 2 Group with modern aircraft, the only effective types available in the required quantities were American. Supplied under Lend-Lease, the Mitchell and Ventura were to serve the RAF only in Europe, while Bostons saw service in Europe and the Middle East – where the Marauder served exclusively.

Training in the Bahamas

Apart from the ex-Dutch B-25Cs that had been operated by No. 5 PRU in the Far East, the first Mitchells to adopt RAF markings in any number were an incoming batch of twenty-three B-25Bs, designated Mitchell Mk Is with serials FK161 to FK183. Starting in May 1942, these machines were nearly all delivered direct to a new training establishment, No. 111 OTU, based at Nassau in the Bahamas. Formed on 20 August, about three months after Mitchell deliveries began, this OTU was intended primarily to

train crews on American aircraft types. Two airfields were utilized that were adjacent to Nassau, Windsor and Oaks Field, and a flying programme with Mitchells and Liberators was under way by December.

At the same time as they were training Mitchell crews in their own right, the OTU introduced another system whereby the medium bomber was also used to train crews on the 'heavies'. These were newly formed Liberator crews flying in Mitchells captained by their future second pilot, before they made the transition to Liberators.

The hazards of training were made only too clear on a number of occasions, 111 OTU's Mitchell 'crash log' including the following Mk IIs: FW148 which flew into trees near Nassau on 28 October 1944; FW150 which collided with HD330 on 24 November, both aircraft going into the sea; and FW149, damaged in a belly-landing on 3 May 1945 after a practice bomb exploded in the bomb-bay.

The Bahamas were an ideal training base for three main reasons: they were conveniently near enough to the US for direct

aircraft deliveries; they were comfortably distant from any war zone; and their skies were far less crowded than those over the UK. As far as the Mitchell was concerned, the OTU continued to function until 23 August 1945. But on that date flying ceased, and although the Liberators were flown to Kinloss, the medium bombers are understood to have been abandoned to their fate, all of them being struck off charge (SOC) that same day. Eighty Mitchells of all three RAF marks were despatched to the Bahamas during hostilities.

Testing in England

Of the first twenty-three Mitchell Mk Is allocated to the RAF, only three – FK161, FK162 and FK165 – arrived in England for testing during May 1942. Mitchell Mk Is were not intended for operational service with the RAF in Europe, that distinction being reserved for the Mk II, the B-25C/D.

A&AEE Boscombe Down's initial flight tests of the Mitchell Mk I covered take-off

The B-25B was not required for combat operations with the RAF, and only three were despatched to the UK to be used for testing by various service establishments. The first to arrive in the spring of 1942 was FK161, alias 40-2341, here exhibiting the common style of serial presentation on Mitchells, with a hyphen between the letters and numbers. IWM

As the second Mitchell to arrive in the UK, FK162 was among the examples used for a comprehensive evaluation programme before the type entered RAF service. IWM

performance and handling over a range of CG loadings. The aircraft was found to be satisfactory at all weights, and landings were reported as very easy, despite the tricycle undercarriage, which was then still something of an innovation. Stalls with landing gear and flaps down were found to occur at the relatively high speed of 100mph (160km/h) at the maximum loaded weight of just under 29,000lb (13,150kg). A minor adjustment was that the pilot's seat needed more effective restraints because it tended to slide backwards at inopportune moments – but apart from that, A&AEE pilots confirmed that the Mitchell should have few problems on RAF operations. FK162 did crash in November, when some reparable damage was caused, but this was attributed to the throttles closing too slowly, again a minor glitch.

These two Mitchell Is remained at A&AEE throughout their testing lifetime, both being finally struck off charge in May 1943. The No. 2 Group Communications Flight at West Raynham in Norfolk subsequently took FK165 on charge, later passing it to No. 98 Sqn (presumably for use as a unit hack); it was eventually SOC on 29 May 1943.

Boscombe Down's highly experienced test pilots cast an extremely critical eye over 'foreign' aircraft. By the time US Lend-Lease types began to arrive in the country, the staff had been exposed to more than two years of highly exacting evaluation of examples of aeronautical engineering, which in some cases left

much to be desired in terms of safety, performance and capability.

Because in technical support terms they operated alongside the front line squadrons, A&AEE staff were bound to be more thorough in their analysis than their opposite numbers at Wright Field, simply because they were acutely aware of what RAF crews needed in an effective military aircraft. This was particularly true of a medium bomber that was to operate against targets in occupied Europe in daylight. Given the quality of the opposition, it was widely considered that there were few more challenging tasks for aircrew, particularly in 1942.

Evaluation of new aircraft in the US in 1942 was rudimentary to say the least; a single test flight was deemed sufficient to pass each one as satisfactory for service in deference to a laudable, if slightly risky desire to despatch war material to overseas customers as quickly as possible.

Boscombe Down's flight-test pilots were well aware of the American system, and one is consequently left with the impression that while A&AEE's pilots tried extremely hard, they could not pass all US types as fully fit for immediate service with the RAF. Numerous small modifications usually accompanied the final test reports, their primary purpose being to ensure safety on operations, to ease the pilot's workload and improve the comfort and efficiency of the crews. While these remedies were often advisory, many were carried out before the aircraft actually entered service, depending on urgency.

Undoubtedly it was important not to delay the service entry of new combat aircraft any longer than was absolutely necessary, and fortunately the basic soundness of the B-25 and A-20 meant that both received A&AEE's approval relatively quickly. The Mitchell and Boston were to serve the RAF long and reliably, but the Ventura did not stand up well to the type of enemy opposition it faced in Europe, and it was soon withdrawn from service. Therefore apart from the Mosquito, which was in a class of its own, the Mitchell and Boston became the mainstay of 2 Group squadrons for most of the remaining years of the European war. Shortly before the end, the Boston was also withdrawn.

Between June and August 1942, B-25Cs and Ds arrived in the UK in three main batches (see Appendix IV), and by the end of August ninety aircraft had been taken on charge. Thereafter the North American medium arrived at a steady rate. Both early model B-25s were designated 'Mitchell Mk II' in RAF service, the only exception being an unknown number of Mitchells with waist windows and a rear gunner's cockpit in addition to the dorsal turret: these were identified with the suffix 'IIa'.

Two B-25Gs (FR208/209) also arrived in England: they were not given a separate mark number, although the designation 'Mk II Srs II' was allocated to identify them. The British service had no operational use for the 'big gun' Mitchell, but both were evaluated by A&AEE, after which they were sent in different directions: FR208 went to the Air Fighting Development Unit at Wittering, ending up at 2 Group Support Unit and becoming 4823M in February 1945. FR209 was taken on charge by the Empire Central Flying School at Hullavington, and remained with the renamed Empire Flying School before passing to the Met Research Flight based at Farnborough. The aircraft was subsequently allocated the maintenance serial 6891M on 13 September 1951, the culmination of a remarkably long career.

Into Combat

The need for 2 Group to initiate a thorough conversion training programme for its new aircraft, at a time when the whole command was undergoing drastic revision, meant that the first RAF Mitchell squadron, No. 180, did not fly its first operation until 8 December 1942. Formed at West Raynham on 13 September, the unit, led by Wg Cdr C.C. Hodder, had little time to work up to operational efficiency before moving to Foulsham, Norfolk on 19 October, from whence the first SAR sorties were flown. Foulsham was no place to be in winter: rain turned the airfield to a sea of mud, which hampered the servicing and arming of the aircraft. The squadron nevertheless rode out the weather, continuing conversion training in anticipation of the first bombing operation. Few crews counted ASR flights as the 'real thing', but men down in the sea were as pleased to be found by the low-flying Mitchells as any other friendly aircraft.

Behind the Scenes

Boscombe Down had meanwhile taken delivery of further Mitchell Mk IIs. As it turned out, events transpired to prevent FL191 yielding much valuable flight data, as it promptly cartwheeled (fortunately without causing any crew casualties) on the very night it arrived at the Wiltshire aerodrome. Premature retraction of the undercarriage was found to be the cause – normally the Mitchell's wheels came up in the respectably short time of just seven seconds. Boscombe Down already had Mk II FL671 which had begun performance trials as early as June, and this aircraft conducted numerous test flights without mishap throughout the war. It survived to pass to No. 13 OTU, and was not SOC until 5 June 1947.

RAF Mitchells were standard production aircraft, complete with the Bendix ventral turret, which the RAF retained. A&AEE had stressed the drawback of the complex sighting system and the slow extension and retraction, noting that in the down position the turret clipped 8mph (13km/h) off the Mitchell's speed. Later, when 2 Group developed a unique close formation for its Mitchell squadrons, the ventral turrets successfully formed an integral part of the defensive gunnery. Incidentally, Boscombe Down also noted that the Mitchell lost another 8mph with the bomb doors open.

Tests with various aspects of Mitchell turret armament were exhaustive, and the aircraft used included Mk IIs FL189 and FR370, from July and November 1942 respectively. By July 1943 two more Mk IIs, FL215 and FL185, were also being used by A&AEE. The latter was a standard service machine borrowed from No. 180 squadron for the purpose of addressing severe RAF criticism of the poor access for the gunner, and the slow rotation of the Bendix dorsal turret. Despite its excellent, virtually frameless all-round vision, this turret dome was apparently so difficult to turn at any speed that replacement by a Boulton Paul-type was strongly recommended.

The Mitchell Mk II's top turret continued to give trouble, and in a later gunnery report on the Mk III (B-25J) turret in its revised, forward location, A&AEE made the educated comment that any comparison between the two had to be biased towards the Mk III, as this was part of an integrated re-design of the Mitchell, whereas there had been no turret provision in the original design. The later-type turret was therefore more rigidly mounted, and this undoubtedly improved its overall operation.

Some temporary 'fixes' were carried out on the dorsal turret, but in the event, neither this, nor the lower solid cupola, were changed on RAF Mitchells. This was the kind of compromise Boscombe Down staff constantly faced: problems that were only highlighted by operations over a period of time ran headlong into the prospect of first-line aircraft being grounded pending time-consuming modification. More often than not there was no choice but to continue using below-standard equipment, and to make due allowances. Minor problems with the Mitchell did not appear to affect RAF operational use adversely, but some delays were inevitable when aircraft had to be kept hangared longer than expected pending modifications.

Second on Ops

As well as equipping No. 180 Sqn, Mitchell Mk IIs had also been taken on charge by No. 98 Squadron at West Raynham, deliveries beginning on 27 September 1942. The unit had also moved to Foulsham, on 15 October. Then led by Wing Commander L. A. Lewer, No. 98 Sqn personnel collectively cursed the muddy conditions at their new airfield. While working-up continued, the squadron recorded the loss of Mk II (FW206), which spun in on 17 October. No. 98 had actually been declared operational in December 1942 and its aircraft, like those of No. 180, undertook ASR patrols until the end of the year.

Despite No. 180 Sqn having pipped No. 98 to the operational post by a few weeks – even with a routine ASR patrol – any rivalry created between the two units was healthy enough. Personnel were very conscious of the responsibility of proving a new type of aircraft in action, and at last, on 21 January 1943, the operational orders came through. But problems with the Mitchell's turret armament, its hydraulics, and other irritations, persisted during the working-up period of both squadrons. It was not uncommon for example, for one gun to suddenly 'pack up' after about a dozen rounds, while the remaining gun fired normally. In the face of such annoyances, the crews had still to develop a reliable set of tactics to use the American medium to best effect. Some early mishaps were to highlight the fact that 2 Group was still to some extent 'rewriting the book' vis-a-vis daylight medium bomber operations over Europe.

By late 1942 an outline operational plan existed to pave the way for an eventual invasion of continental Europe; the RAF and USAAF medium and light bomber force based in England would continue to attack targets in daylight. For the RAF, the old-style 'Circus' operation – when a handful of bombers with a massive fighter escort, intended primarily to entice German fighters into combat, penetrating enemy airspace as far as their range would allow – was largely replaced by a new tactical policy aimed at making much more effective use of modern bombers. A revitalized 2 Group would carry out precision 'Ramrod' attacks on important enemy installations, particularly factories and power stations, as well as airfields and the continental transport system in general.

Determining which was the safest altitude at which to operate the Mitchells posed some tough questions. A low-level target approach had proved effective with Blenheims and Bostons, although the hazards (albeit slightly reduced) from German flak and fighters were obvious. A 'Ramrod'-type attack, with the bombers heavily escorted all the way into and out of the target area, seemed most appropriate, and in time, the medium altitudes for

side the Ghent-Terneuzen canal in Holland. The Mitchells – each loaded with two 1,000lb and four 500lb MC bombs – made a low-level approach, and climbed for their bomb-run in the face of heavy flak: FL693/VO-M of No. 98 Sqn was brought down by this barrage, and P/O R.D. Woods and the other three members of his crew died in the crash.

made by Oblt Walter Leonhardt who, like his comrade, identified the enemy aircraft as Hudsons.

For the Mitchell crews it had been a sobering baptism of fire, and in particular for those of No. 180 Sqn: the loss of a commanding officer at this early stage inevitably cast a cloud over everyone. Hodder's replacement, Wg Cdr G.R. McGill, was

On-going technical troubles, including unreliable gun turret operation, delayed Mitchell bombing operations until early 1943, when Nos 98 and 180 Sqns hit their first continental targets. By the time this photo was taken in 1943, FL684/EV-S had flown three operations with No. 180 Sqn. Many similar photos were taken on Mitchell stations during press facility visits. IWM

which the Mitchell had been designed were found to be ideal. Initially however, an attempt was made to duplicate the relative success of earlier 2 Group operations, at low level.

January: Sad Debut

For its first Mitchell bombing raid in the afternoon of 22 January 1943, No. 180 Squadron fielded six of its own aircraft, and six belonging to No. 98 Sqn. The force was briefed to attack target No. Z.885, the Purfina and Sinclair oil facilities located along-

No. 180's CO, Wg Cdr C.C. Hodder, flying FL212/EV-A, was lost in this confrontation. Coming off the target his starboard engine had taken hits from flak; he managed to get clear of the area, but was then bounced by Fw 190s of JG 1. Uffz Hans Vorhauer of II. Gruppe shot the Mitchell down, killing all five members of this particular crew, which had one man more than normal aboard. The same German fighter unit also despatched the Mitchell flown by P/O W. H. Cappleman (FL678/EV-J), again with the loss of all four crew members. This latter may have represented the claim for a second bomber

conscious of the need to put a few more operations 'on the board' without delay, although these did not materialize for some weeks as No. 180 was not then fully operational due to the Mitchell's turret faults.

February Campaigns

By early February, ASR patrols were resumed by No. 180 Sqn. On one such sortie on the 27th, German fighters were responsible for the loss of another Mitchell II (FL672/EV-B): American pilot Sgt P.M. D. Marx, plus his crew of three, perished

Seen on 21 October 1943 after a recent raid on Flushing, No. 320 was the only Dutch-manned Mitchell squadron in the RAF. Missions to targets in the Netherlands were especially poignant, particularly for those crew members who were briefed to destroy targets in or near their home towns. IWM

when the Mitchell came down in the sea off the Dutch port of Ijmuiden.

After these early setbacks, both squadrons enjoyed a period when casualties from fighters were few; indeed in statistical terms, the rate of loss regarding this particular cause was remarkably low. This was largely because the bomber crews were perfecting the technique of adopting mutually protective, close formation boxes of six aircraft, and were ably backed up by a substantial fighter escort, usually of Spitfires, Typhoons or Mustangs – fortunately these had become an integral part of Fighter Command's planning.

The winter months had played havoc with bomber sorties, heavy cloud cover frequently compromising the amount of damage that could be inflicted on tactical targets. In the meantime the Mitchell squadrons continued to work on their gunnery problems, all the while flying more ASR sorties: between February and April 1943 No. 180 flew no fewer than ninety-five of these, while No. 98 completed at least forty, probably more.

March Operations

On 9 March 1943 a third Mitchell unit, No. 320 (Dutch) Squadron, began training at Foulsham. Funded by the Dutch government in exile, the squadron received its first Mk IIs on the 17th, although it was to be some time before combat operations could commence.

Exercise *Spartan* took place in March, the Mitchells of No. 98 Sqn participating in one of the largest tactical exercises of the war. During a busy month, the first two Mitchell Mk IIs (FR143 and FR149) for No. 320 Sqn arrived at Methwold in Norfolk on the 17th. Squadron personnel, many of whom wore the dark blue uniform and aircrew insignia of the Netherlands Navy, had arrived two days previously. These Mitchells were followed by a further sixty-two, all paid for by the Dutch government and made available to the RAF to equip the squadron.

At first glance, upwards of sixty bombers might seem a generous number of aircraft for a single squadron, which usually had a regular establishment of twelve to eighteen aircraft, with eight in reserve; but almost one hundred Mitchells were used by No. 320 during the course of wartime operations – when loss or damage in combat necessitated replacement, aircraft were borrowed from other units. Attrition resulted in only twenty-eight of the unit

A Mitchell that gained some fame in No. 320 Sqn was the Mk II 'Margriet', the aircraft that flew Prince Bernhard and Queen Juliana across the Atlantic on 25 October 1943. Named after the royal couple's daughter, FR142/NO-F was later shot down in error by a Mosquito. IWM

originals remaining in service at the end of the war.

Formation Flying

The Dutch unit stayed only a fortnight at Methwold before moving to Attlebridge near Norwich, where April and May were spent on conversion training. Given the theatre of war, new aircrew ignored the doctrine of mutual protection at their peril: like most bombers, a single Mitchell was highly vulnerable to German fighter attack. However, 2 Group knew that, in such a situation, aircraft in close formation had more than a fighting chance of survival, and that bombers in particular were safer in tight formations where their defensive guns could offer mutual protection – provided that the pilots were able to maintain station. Mitchell crews therefore practised such flying to perfection

Theoretically, a 'box' of aircraft could turn, climb and dive together without spreading out, losing speed or reducing the number of guns that could be brought to bear on attacking fighters. By multiplying the boxes it was possible to put a substan-

tial weight of bombs onto a target, even if each aircraft's individual load were modest. After all, ten bombs placed squarely on the target was worth a hundred near misses. It was to the lasting merit of the 2 Group Mitchell force that its squadrons put the theory into practice; moreover the crews were under no illusion that operating comparatively slow medium bombers in daylight against formidable, highly organized defences would be tantamount to a repeat of the near-suicidal early days of light bomber operations if their tactics were found wanting.

Not only would a high standard of formation flying achieve well concentrated bomb patterns, but in addition, heavy escort would deter all but the most determined enemy fighter attack. Increasing the number of aircraft also improved the degree of target destruction. Later on, when operating in two-wing strength of seventy-two or ninety-six aircraft, the Mitchell squadrons became a force to be reckoned with.

As was common with medium bombers operating in all war theatres, as the Allies steadily gained the upper hand, the main losses were not to fighters but to very efficient and largely unavoidable German flak. That said, evasive action often proved successful even when groundfire was the major hazard to operations.

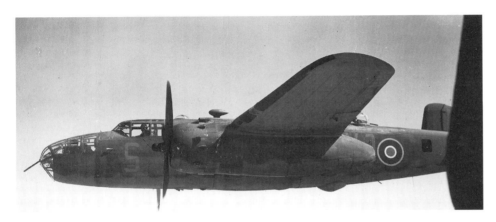

Constant practice brought close formation flying to a fine art in RAF Mitchell squadrons. Mk II VO-S of No. 98 Sqn has its portrait taken from the waist of a second Mitchell as the pilot eases it in. IWM

Fast, close-proximity take-offs and landings were another hallmark of Mitchell operations, as No. 180 Squadron demonstrates. Mk II FL707/EV-Z is 'tail-end Charlie' in this taxiing view. IWM

May Offensives

A resumption of Mitchell operations in May 1943 was punctuated by successes, losses, accidents and incidents as well as recalls due to weather – as on the 6th, when No. 180 Sqn attempted a six-aircraft attack on marshalling yards at Boulogne. The raid was recalled, as was a similar one against the same target on the 11th. Early in this month No. 180 Sqn lost one Mitchell inadvertently: on 7 May, Fg Off C.J.F.M. Pike landed Mk II (FL709) at Foulsham with a punctured port main-wheel tyre following a training flight. The pilot swung the Mitchell off the runway, and it was later the subject of a technical inspection: at first it was believed to be repairable, but ultimately it was declared that the damage sustained in the landing was such that the aircraft should be downgraded to 'instructional' status. As 4023M it therefore passed to No. 1 Air Armament School at Manby, where it remained until being struck off charge on 25 April 1946.

On 13 May a railway at Boulogne was targeted, and this attack brought disaster to a No. 98 Sqn Mitchell II (FL197): flown by P/O G.A. Calder, RCAF, the aircraft crashed into the sea off Hardelot Plage, SSW of the target town. Why exactly it came down is not known. Calder and one crew member perished, but two others were rescued and made PoWs.

On 26 May was Circus 298 to Caen, and during this raid Flt Sgt J.A. Hole of No. 98 Sqn was hit by flak over the continent. He managed to get back to Foulsham but was obliged to overshoot, and as he went round again the Mitchell (FL207) lost both engines at only 500ft (150m). It stalled and crashed at Hindolvesten in Norfolk, all the crew sustaining injuries in the crash.

Seven operations were completed by the end of May, including one partially carried out against Abbeville airfield on the 25th. Only five aircraft, out of twelve despatched, were able to bomb, which meant that this was a costly raid for No. 180. Flak claimed Flt Sgt Paterson's aircraft (FL211), and a second Mitchell (FL175), piloted by Sqn Ldr J.T. Hanafy, went down in the target area. The entire crews of both aircraft were lost.

Hotter pace

On 26 May Sgt J.K. Fulton of No. 180 Sqn – who had written off a Mitchell in April – took up a Mk II (FL696) for an air-firing training flight in the vicinity of Wells-next-the-Sea. But something must have gone badly wrong because the aircraft went into the sea, and all the crew were lost.

On the 31st, Nos 180 and 98 combined for a strike on a shipyard at Flushing, the last raid mounted by 2 Group under its original title. Of the fifty-four aircraft despatched to various targets, flak claimed one – Mitchell II (FL198) of No. 180 flown by Sgt A.L.H. Dobbie, who had to ditch off Clacton. Three of the crew were injured, as was Dobbie, but all were rescued. Sadly New Zealander Flt Sgt A.W. Wood, the wireless operator/air gunner, was trapped in the wreckage and died: as a result of this he gained the dubious distinction of being the last casualty in 2 Group while it was part of Bomber Command.

Embry takes over

With the impending establishment of the 2nd Tactical Air Force, 2 Group was temporarily absorbed by Fighter Command, and ceased to exist as a separate entity as an element of Bomber Command. A new C-in-C of the tactical bomber force, the dynamic AVM Basil Embry, took up his appointment, effective 1 June. He had the challenge of providing air support for the eventual Allied invasion of Europe, and set about his huge task with relish, even though his planning was disadvantaged by having to take into account the different performance characteristics of the four aircraft types in his command: Mosquitoes, Mitchells, Bostons and Venturas. Limited availability of aircraft prevented the deployment of each type in the numbers required, and although mixed formations had caused problems before, these had to continue, as many targets needed the maximum weight of bombs if they were to be destroyed or at least crippled for any appreciable time.

Up to that point No. 180 Sqn had flown 151 Mitchell sorties in nine operations, and carried out fourteen sea searches for the loss of four aircraft (2.6 per cent). No. 98 Sqn had logged seventy sorties in five raids and seven sea searches for the slightly higher percentage loss rate of two Mitchells (2.9 per cent).[1]

June

Mitchell operations in June had a disappointing start with an abortive bombing raid on a power station near Ghent. Flak took its toll, and several aircraft were lost from this, and subsequent combat sorties. For instance, on the 13th a formation of thirty Bf 109s appeared when Nos 98 and 180 Sqns were in the process of raiding Flushing, though the Spitfire escort came tearing in to protect the medium bombers. One RAF fighter shepherded a damaged Mitchell home through the enemy fighters.

On 12 June No. 320 began SAR flights: the unit's crews were considered operational, but they were all keenly anticipating the day their aircraft would be allowed to drop bombs in anger. But that milestone would not be reached until August, by which time the squadron CO, Cdr Overste Bakker, was very glad to be able to let his eager young patriots off the leash: few of them would have been unaware that their comrades in No. 18 (NEI) Sqn in Australia had by then been operational on Mitchells for six months.

July

Eight raids went 'on the board' for the Mitchell squadrons in July, which bombed such diverse locations as the Fokker works in Amsterdam, the rail installations at St Omer and the airfields at Brest, Merville, Tricqueville and Fort Rouge, with variable results. With the Mitchell force being expanded, No. 226 Sqn – which had formerly operated Bostons – was due to finish conversion to Mitchells in July. The unit went north to Drem to undertake a fighter affiliation course with the Spitfires of No. 340 (Free French) Sqn.

This turned out to be highly productive, if a little 'hairy' for the bomber crews as the French pilots enthusiastically played out the part of 'enemy' fighters. Their knife-edge passes through the formations gave the Mitchell gunners some very good practice in tracking and 'leading' high performance interceptors. Turret gunners henceforth became temporary captains in Mitchell crews as they directed the pilot in manoeuvring the aircraft during fighter attack. Turning into the fighter, maintaining altitude, keeping the aircraft steady, and above all calling out 'bogeys' as soon as they were spotted, became the cornerstones of survival. To avoid a 'stab in the back' a member of the leading crew in the formation had to crawl into the rear fuselage of his Mitchell to watch that potentially vulnerable quarter through the small perspex tail-cone.

The first operational flight by a Mitchell II in No. 226 Sqn colours was on 30 July, and ironically, the aircraft involved was lost to fighter attack. Setting out on an ASR patrol, Mk II (FV932/Q) – piloted by F/O R.M. Christie and with Arthur Eyton-Jones as navigator – flew across to the Dutch coast to try and locate some American airmen reported to be in a dinghy. Having found them, the Mitchell crew spent some time circling the spot, waiting for relief aircraft – but their humanitarian intentions went awry, because all the while they were circling they were transmitting a 'fix', the full danger of which was not realized at first – until the Mitchell suddenly had company in the shape of eight Me 410s, four of them formatting on each wing, according to Eyton-Jones. Evidently the Luftwaffe crews decided that the bomber – a type they had probably not previously encountered – was hostile, and proceeded to blast it out of the sky. Thus began a gruelling saga of survival at sea by the navigator and two other members of the crew.[2]

August

No. 320 Squadron flew its first sorties against an enemy target on 17 August, a short run to railway yards at Calais. Nos 98 and 180 Squadrons moved to Dunsfold in Surrey the following day, the change of location placing both units closer to their potential targets in northern France. Led by Wg Cdrs Phillips and McGill of Nos 98 and 180 respectively, the Mitchells arrived singly during the course of that day. Co-locating the Mitchell squadrons at Dunsfold was part of Operation *Starkey*, an attempt to fool the Germans into believing that an invasion of the continent was imminent. By bombing airfields the planners hoped that the Luftwaffe would send up fighters, which would then be destroyed by the RAF fighter escort.

The Dutchmen flew back to their homeland on the 20th, though this time it was to deliver bombs on a Dornier repair facility plant at Vlissingen adjacent to the shipyards on the Schelde estuary. The flak retaliated and one crew went down, but was rescued by a Walrus amphibian.

The first Mitchell operation from Dunsfold took place on 23 August: this was a raid by six aircraft from Nos 98 and 180 Sqns on St Omer, and it was carried out without loss. A week later, however, No. 180 lost a Mk II (FL190) to flak: on this occasion both units had again combined, to put two dozen aircraft over an ammunition dump located in the Forêt d'Eperleques.

It must be said that No. 320 Sqn crews were not overly happy about operating Mitchells from the grass runways at Attlebridge, and since beginning cross-Channel bombing sorties they had occasionally been able to use Methwold. Transfer of the unit to Lasham on 30 August was therefore a most popular move.

September

On 5 September another bomber unit, No. 305 (Ziemi Wielkolskiej) Sqn commanded by Maj Kazimierz Konopasek, was transferred into 2nd TAF and issued with Mitchell IIs at Swanton Morley. As part of 1 Group the Polish airmen had previously flown Wellingtons, and they spent a month or so on Mitchell conversion training, including formation flying, stall tests and single-engine handling.

On 8 September Nos 98, 180 and 320 Squadrons staged a combined operation to Boulogne, taking off at first light from Dunsfold in massed formation. The German gun positions at Boulogne were one of the final Operation *Starkey* targets – and this was one operation that most medium bomber crews were glad to put behind them, considering it to be a hair-brained, dangerous scheme dreamed up by a chair-borne strategist. As an invasion spoof it did not appear to have convinced the Germans, while the bombers made themselves

Tedder's Personal Mitchell

Outside Europe, RAF Mitchell operations on any scale were confined to PR activities in the Far East; however, several examples were flown on liaison duties in the Middle East, where North American field representative William C. Carr was responsible for providing a Mitchell for the use of Air Chief Marshal Sir Arthur Tedder, commanding all Allied air forces in that theatre. Legend has it that Carr directed the assembly of a single aircraft from at least twelve wrecks in US depots in North Africa. However unofficial this move might appear, it did not escape the eagle eye of the record keepers who logged B-25G-5 (42-65094) as a theatre transfer, although it never had an RAF serial.

Air Chief Marshall Tedder greeting another officer after having parked his B-25G on a steel plate dispersal. Just visible on the aircraft is the rank pennant on the nose and the plated-over orifice for the 75mm cannon barrel. This Mitchell, which had a modified tail-gun position, was later stripped of camouflage. After the war it was photographed at Shaibah, Iraq, where it was presumably scrapped. IWM

Sqn Ldr Bell-Irving (third from right) with two photographers and Mitchell air- and groundcrew members pictured on 29 July 1943. IWM

bait for Luftwaffe fighters. In fact, all that most Mitchell crews saw was not fighters but the flak, bursting ever closer to their aircraft.

Nevertheless, whatever the aircrews' view, *Starkey* was a qualified success in that von Runstedt believed (as intended) that an attempt would be made by fourteen British and Canadian divisions to establish a bridgehead either side of Boulogne between 8 and 14 September. Even though it never materialized, the German general remained convinced for months afterwards that an Allied invasion would ultimately be mounted in the Pas de Calais.

On 17 September Wg Cdr John Castle took over command of No. 180 Sqn, Wg Cdr McGill having finished his tour.

Few enemy fighters had ever been seen in the air during the *Starkey* operations – although this did not mean they were not there, as No. 98 Squadron found out to its cost during an attack on a synthetic paint plant at Lens on 21 September. It was one of the comparatively rare occasions when enemy fighters actually penetrated the Allied escort and got through to the Mitchells. Over St Pol about thirty FW 190s saw their chance and promptly shot

down Mk II (FL683/L), which dived into the ground near Hesdin with its entire crew.

Had the bomber crews been aware of the identity of the German fighter unit, they might have thanked their lucky stars to have escaped comparatively lightly – for the attack was led by none other than the Experten, Oblt 'Pips' Priller of JG 26: he destroyed FL683 for his 94th victory claim of the war. Among the targets of the other Jagdflieger was FL674/W: this aircraft had its hydraulics shot out, but survived. Also, cannon fire from Hptmn Hans Naumann's fighter damaged a third Mitchell (FV944) to such an extent that it had to be ditched in the Channel off Berck-sur-Mer. Fortunately ASR was on hand to rescue the crew.

Even now the problems with the Mitchell's armament had not been entirely eradicated, as was reflected in combat reports from this operation: some gunners complained that their defensive fire against the '190s was not as effective as it might have been, as they found difficulty in fully depressing the turret guns; this may have been due to trouble with the solenoids.

While enemy fighter attack remained a threat, the Mitchells were usually well covered by their escort, and this kept German

fighters – which were, in any event, showing some reduction in numbers – at bay.

Flak remained potentially deadly to the tight formations, particularly when they reached the 'straight and level' phase prior to release and droned over their targets at or above 10,000ft (3,000m). Consequently Mitchells frequently returned from operations with numerous holes made by shrapnel from exploding shells. Time and again they were repaired and returned to service – and in fact, despite the concentration of flak around some targets, actual losses remained well within normal attrition rates.

October

For the Dunsfold Mitchell units, part of October was taken up with night flying training – although during this month an attack was made on Brest aerodrome, another unpopular 'live bait' show apparently designed to draw the Luftwaffe into battle. On the down side, on the 25th No. 320 lost Cdr Bakker, whose Mk II (FR178/W) became a victim of the flak defending Lanveoc-Poulmic. Cdr H.V.B. Burgerhout took over leadership of the Dutch squadron. Less strenuous sorties were also laid on in October to give cadets from the local Air Training Corps air experience flights in the Mitchells.

November

Having been ordered to stand down from regular bombing operations, 2 Group prepared to issue a new target list within Operation *Crossbow*, the campaign against the V-weapons launching sites in and around the Pas de Calais area of northern France. The assault opened on 5 November 1943, and involved aircraft from the entire Mitchell force; their briefing assumed that the site was connected with the robot bombs. The participating Mitchells were: twenty-four from Nos 98 and 180 Sqns; fourteen from No. 226; six from No. 320; and four from No. 305. Bostons of Nos 88 and 107 Sqns were included in the force, although they were obliged to abort en route due to bad weather and because the aircraft carried no bombing aids.

The Gee-equipped Mitchells pressed on, covered by eighteen squadrons of Spitfires. First wave bombing led by Sqn Ldr Roderick K.F. Bell-Irving ('BI' to everyone who knew him) a flight commander in No. 180 Sqn, was accurate, 187 500lb HEs falling squarely on one of the excavation sites. A second wave under Wg Cdr C.E.R. Tait, CO of No. 226, missed the aiming point by some margin. The raid met with heavy flak and was not judged a success; however, a follow-up raid carried out three days later achieved a good bomb pattern.

Unbeknown to the Mitchell crews, medium-size bombs had to be very well aimed to shake the foundations of the massive Mimoyecques earthworks, for this was the location of Hitler's third V-weapon, a nest of long-range guns intended to bombard London. The so-called V3 was eventually knocked out before it could be used in anger, but by much heavier bombs than the Mitchells were capable of lifting. To reassure French locals, some aircraft on these early *Crossbow* sorties dropped leaflets explaining why Allied aircraft were suddenly bombing 'rural' areas of their country.

With twelve Mk IIs on strength, No. 305 Squadron's contribution to the Mimoyecques raid marked its Mitchell debut. Between this date and the 18th the Polish flyers attacked three more targets in France before joining No. 320 Sqn at Lasham, Hampshire. From there it flew one operation on 26 November – which turned out to be its last on Mitchells before conversion to Mosquitoes. Hampered by a lack of crews, No. 305 was able to fly only fifteen Mitchell II sorties, and in the process it lost two aircraft, one (FV941) to enemy action and one (FV911) in an accident.

Follow-up raids were common fare for the 2nd TAF medium bombers, and while these carried a degree of risk, the targets were invariably important. For instance on the 11th, No. 98 Sqn – again in company with No. 180 – flew a *Ramrod* to hit an important German headquarters located at Autinghen, a small village in the Pas de Calais. Then, on the 25th, both units were part of a large-scale 2 Group attack on the same target, which recorded no Mitchell losses, despite heavy flak. Allied intelligence had confirmed that the earthworks associated with the V-weapons were under the direction of a local HQ of the Todt Organization, and the raids on the village were an attempt to destroy it: in this they succeeded, for Autinghen was all but wiped out after the second heavy raid.

Noball sites occupied the bomb aimers of all Mitchell squadrons in November; for example on the 26th, the crews participated in a large-scale raid on the one at Martinvast. No. 180 Sqn led this attack – but the flak ranged in quickly and accurately enough to shoot down three aircraft. However, there could be no let-up in pounding such high priority targets, and the RAF tactical bombers continued to make their contribution to what grew to an enormous tonnage of high explosive dropped on the V-1 assembly, sighting and firing operations spread around the woods and fields of France. But the effort was felt to be justified in that a successful flying bomb offensive could have bought the Germans a significant breathing space, and possibly

disrupted – or at worst, wrecked – the preparations for D-Day, still some six months away.

December

Inevitably as winter deepened the weather began to have an adverse effect on the anti-V1 offensive, as well as other tactical bombing operations – but in the last half of 1943 the rejuvenated 2nd TAF squadrons had been largely successful in damaging, if not destroying, a range of enemy production facilities, also in disrupting power generation, making life generally unpleasant for the Luftwaffe, and harassing transportation over a broad sweep of north-western France.

The RAF Mitchell units, despite their unavoidably delayed entry into combat, were proving very effective. Able to carry a greater load than the command's two other American medium bombers, the tough and reliable medium was a firm favourite with the crews who flew it, and at high-command level it was judged to be a suitable replacement for both the Boston and Ventura. In the interests of standardization it was always preferable for such a force to operate with the minimum number of aircraft types, a goal that would be largely achieved in late 1944. And the experienced Mitchell crews, continually demonstrating their very high level of efficiency, would soon operate independently, without need of a fighter escort.

Although based mainly in the UK, Mitchells in RAF markings got around the world. This unarmed Mk II at Foggia Main in Italy on 5 December 1943 has a pennant denoting either an Air Chief Marshal or Air Vice Marshal (both were similar) on the nose; however, the serial number of 'T' cannot be deciphered. H. Levy

CHAPTER ELEVEN

Mitchells over Burma

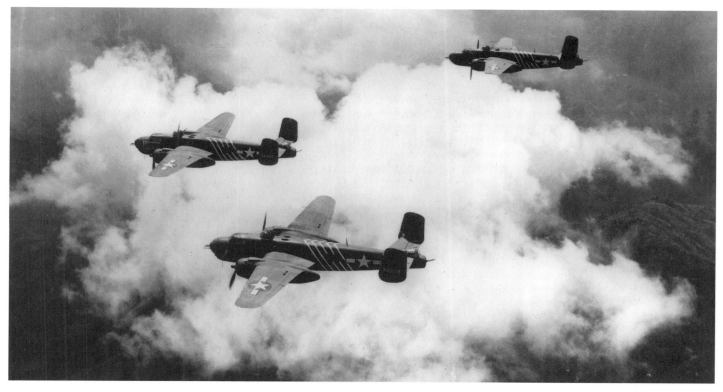

Air Commando trio of B-25H-1s with their distinctive five white diagonal fuselage stripes. These 'single pilot' B-25s were flown much like fighter bombers during the most hectic period of support for Chindit operations. USAF

USAAF B-25s made their combat debut over Burma as part of the specialized air support unit for Orde Wingate's long range penetration (LRP) force which became famous as the Chindits. At the Quadrant conference in Quebec in August 1943, Wingate made known his intention to lead another guerrilla expedition behind Japanese lines in 1944. The first deployment of his LRP force in 1943 had been able to inflict losses on the enemy but at the cost of the inevitable Allied casualties. The worst aspect had been the fact that there had been no way to evacuate the wounded, some of whom had had to be abandoned to their fate. Wingate believed that any new operation would be considerably helped by

the availability of light planes to evacuate wounded. Gen H.H. Arnold not only enthusiastically backed Wingate's plans, but broadened the basic concept of aerial casualty evacuation into that of an independent armed air task force, the first of its type in military history.

'Hap' Arnold believed that by flying combat missions as well as supporting Wingate's columns in their forays behind enemy lines, he would put the CBI theatre on the map, offer increased hope to the beleaguered Chinese, and speed the defeat of the Japanese. Exceptional, well-qualified officers were appointed to lead each air section of the force that, in addition to the L-1 and L-5 'grasshoppers', would

deploy a fighter section of thirty P-51A Mustangs, and a medium bomber section with twelve B-25H Mitchells. Transports and gliders would be made available, to insert a sizable force behind enemy lines.

With the provisional designation of 'Project 9', this innovative plan was headed by Maj Philip G. Cochrane and Lt Col John R. Alison. When it was decided that the unit would include medium bombers, none other than Lt Col Robert T. Smith was chosen to lead it. 'Tadpole' Smith – or simply 'R.T.', as he was known – was an American Volunteer Group veteran with considerable front line experience of a small, self-reliant force, similar to that now proposed for the northern Burma front. He was given virtual carte blanche to select crews for the bomber section, his career having included enough P-38 flight time to provide him with twin-engine experience. The air component of Project 9 was intended to be a self-sufficient force able to fly combat missions without being subject to burdensome military bureaucracy or the AAF chain of command. Flexibility was the keynote, the organization being run on lines similar to those of the Flying Tigers – but, as one observer put it – with more discipline!

Putting fighter pilots into the cockpits of B-25s fostered a 'can-do' spirit which the organization required. With its single pilot seat plus four-man crew – navigator-bombardier, turret gunner/engineer, radioman /waist gunner and tail gunner – the B-25H became an ideal close support aircraft in Burma. Pilots became skilled in using the 75mm cannon with a high degree of accuracy against ground targets, many of which were flimsy, native-built structures unable to withstand the impact of heavy shells. The

first 300 B-25Hs (up to H-5 43-4405) had only one pair of package guns on the starboard side of the fuselage, and it was from the original batch of B-25H-1s that the first twelve aircraft were delivered.

By November the majority of the unit personnel were in Karachi awaiting their aircraft, which were shipped to India by sea. Smith chose to lead the first few missions from the cockpit of a B-25H. Intensive training began in December, the month the air support project gained a new designation, that of the 5318th Provisional Unit (Air).

Enough B-25Hs had arrived in Karachi by 7 January 1944 to get the unit operational, and early in February the 5318th moved to a forward operating base at Hailakandi in the tea-growing region of Assam. With the Mitchells safely out of sight on jungle dispersals adjacent to native bashas (huts), the crews made themselves at home in preparation for the first bomber mission. Hailakandi's primitive living conditions, limited facilities

and poor food were aptly summed up by that time-honoured American word 'rugged'; and in line with the 'self sufficiency' philosophy, each B-25 crew also carried out their own arming and bombing-up. They were provided with the means to do so by the unit armament officer, Capt Andrew Postlewait, and it was not unusual to see boxes of fragmentation bombs, .50cal ammunition, and tubed 75mm cannon rounds stacked around each dispersal. With its twelve 0.5in guns, the cannon, and a 3,000lb (1,360kg) bomb load, the B-25H-1 was to become a formidable weapon in the hands of the 5318th.

To save time, a system was devised whereby aircraft were usually loaded the day before a mission was due to be flown, or after the last sorties of the day had landed. That was fine if the ordnance combination (typically six 500lb GP bombs, or a dozen frag or incendiary clusters) loaded was not changed because the type of target had changed. If a new target had been selected, the crews were faced with the chore of

Famous fivesome of 1st Air Commando B-25H-1s led by 'Barbie III' and 'Dolly'. These Mitchells lacked package guns on the port side. USAF

unloading and reloading before they could take off – hardly a popular task.

As delivered, the B-25Hs assigned to the 5318th Provisional were in standard USAAF camouflage, but they soon adopted what became an unmistakable unit marking in the form of five white diagonal stripes around the rear fuselage. These stripes were carried by Mustangs, L-5s and C-47s, though the B-25s later had theirs changed to dark blue so as to contrast more effectively with their natural metal finish when factory camouflage paint was deleted from Army combat aircraft after October 1943. Other air commando formations were subsequently formed, but the use of the B-25 was restricted to the original unit.

Combat Debut

Mitchell operations by the 5318th commenced on 12 February after a B-25H flew to Imphal to pick up Wingate, who wanted to observe targets – actual and potential – from the air. The unit flew what was primarily a reconnaissance mission to Katha in Burma, but also attacked a section of railway with 75mm cannon fire. The result was a bridge destroyed and a warehouse that lost its roof, swept away by cannon fire from the Mitchell flown by Maj Smith – who admitted that he was actually aiming at a switching point some distance in front of it.

With an average flight time exceeding two hours from their base, the Mitchells flew armed photo-recon missions throughout February, crews attacking numerous targets of opportunity including trains during that initial period of operations. Skip bombing and strafing techniques were also perfected, combat reports reflecting a welcome lack of enemy air opposition and the general inaccuracy of small arms fire on numerous sorties. Combat mission No. 16 was the first undertaken at night, primarily to harass Japanese troops, destroy equipment and deny them sleep.

Invasion

Operation *Thursday* was the name given to the invasion of Burma by Wingate's glider-borne force; it took place on 5 March at Okkyi, and was given the temporary cover name *Broadway*. Quickly organized for combat, the ground troops fanned out into the surrounding jungle. They received

---

B-25Hs known to have been used by the 5318th Provisional Unit/1st Air Commando Group

B-25H-1 43-4211/8 'Erotic Edna' (lost 29 Mar 44)
B-25H-1 43-4242 *
B-25H-1 43-4245?/ 'Jimmy'
B-25H-1 43-4271/6 'Dolly'
B-25H-1 43-4278/7 'Little Natural'
B-25H-1 43-4322/3 'Satan's Sister'
B-25H-1 43-4325/10 'Burma Baby' (lost 8 March 1944)
B-25H-1 43-4329/2 'Sweet Sue'
B-25H-1 43-4360/
B-25H-1 43-4380/1 'Barbie III'
B-25H-   43-???? 'Fongutongu'
B-25H-5 43-4472 'Dangerous Date'
B-25H-5 43-4553
B-25H-5 43-4561
B-25H-1 43-???? 'Barbie II'**
B-25H-10 43-9335 ?
B-25H-10 43-4966
B-25H-10 43-4974

* This was the replacement aircraft that flew Orde Wingate on his fatal sortie on 24 March 1944.

** The first 'Barbie' was a 1st ACG P-51A.

---

indirect support from the B-25s and P-51s, particularly by the bombing of Bhamo airfield on 7 March, where the JAAF was amassing aircraft. On the 8th the Mustangs attacked airfields during the hours of daylight, and that evening at 20:00hr the B-25s, flown by some of the fighter pilots including Smith and his deputy Maj Walter V. Radovich, carried out a moonlight strike on Inbanki and Shwebo; they landed back at their base by the light of flaming oildrums. Fuel stocks and twelve Japanese aircraft were claimed as destroyed by the bombing, the total for the day rising to forty-eight enemy aircraft – or 40 per cent of Japanese losses throughout the CBI during March.

Bomber and fighter action increased dramatically as the success of Operation *Thursday* became increasingly obvious; and still no Japanese ground opposition materialized, and gliders and transports carrying troop reinforcements and supplies of all kinds were able to establish a bridgehead without interference. Having built airstrips at Broadway and Chowringhee, the engineers continued their vital work while combat aircraft were busily engaged in keeping the enemy from infiltrating either location. Broadway lay some 200 miles (320km) behind Japanese lines and remained secure, although enemy activity around Chowringhee caused this base to be abandoned.

The B-25Hs continued to fly from Hailakandi on pre-briefed sorties, and also on what were later to be known as forward air control sorties, and gave able support to Wingate's ground forces, both by bombing and by photographing enemy strongpoints and transportation. Such was the turn-around speed of the PR sorties that Allied troops were able to order rechecks on targets before patrols were risked on potentially hazardous probes against the enemy, who might have quickly reinforced given areas – thus information more than a day old was not used unless the target could be verified. Behind the lines, the B-25Hs helped keep the enemy short of supplies by bombing and strafing the railways and destroying rolling stock and locomotives.

But the LRP force, now enjoying the benefit of its own air support, was unfortunately destined to be short-lived, at least in the form its colourful commander had devised. The unconventional warfare concept for which Orde Wingate had fought so tenaciously – and which proved to be such a source of danger to the Japanese – had always been doubted in many regular army circles, and shortly after the successful completion of *Thursday*, it received a fatal blow: on 24 March 1944, Wingate boarded a B-25H (43-4242) commanded by 1st Lt Brian F. Hodges of the 5318th at Broadway. Heading west for the HQ of the Third Indian Divn at Sylhet, the aircraft made an en route stop at Imphal. It took off again, but never reached its destination, for it apparently exploded and crashed in the Chin Hills, killing all on board: as well as Wingate and his adjutant, two war correspondents and all five members of the B-25 crew perished.

Considerable speculation surrounded the cause of the crash. Engine malfunction, weather conditions and sabotage were examined as far as was possible, but the position of the wreckage – incidentally reflecting a flight path in an easterly (i.e. wrong) direction – was very inaccessible. Hodges had not been able to fly his regular aircraft (B-25H-1 43-4329, named 'Sweet Sue') as this had been damaged shortly before the fateful flight carrying Wingate. Whether or not the condition of the replacement aircraft was a contributory cause of the crash is unknown – in fact no definite conclusion about the true cause was ever firmly established. However, it is most likely that the Mitchell succumbed to the severe weather in the area at that time. Electrical storms had prevented other aircraft from taking off until these had abated, and a sudden diversion to skirt a weather front might well have explained the apparent 'wrong' heading the aircraft had taken. Directed by 5318th pilot Lloyd L. Samp, a British search party found the crash scene; but little more than a wing section and a strut could be identified.

Maj Gen Walter D.A. Lentaigne took over the LRP force and, immediately after Wingate's loss, the 5318th became officially the 1st Air Commando Group. Furthermore, at the behest of SEAC C-in-C Mountbatten and William Slim, commander of the 14th Army, Lentaigne changed the nature of Chindit operations so they were used more as regular troops in assaults on strongpoints in force, rather than as Wingate's self-sustaining, mobile guerrilla columns.

As the monsoon struck Burma with its full force in May, the missions of the Air Commandos were severely curtailed and then stopped altogether. Torrential rains flooded Hailakandi to the point that no further B-25 missions could be flown after the 19th, and most of the aircrews pulled back to Asanol, India. During its final full month of operations in April 1944, the 1st Air Commando Group claimed thirty-five enemy aircraft destroyed, 135 bashas had been neutralized, as had eleven AA positions and forty-five barracks. In addition the unit had denied the enemy the use of several bridges, assorted rolling stock and ammunition dumps. During its short period in the theatre the unit's bombers and fighters had been instrumental in assisting the Chindits in creating havoc among Japanese Army units, and enabling regular Allied forces to go firmly onto the offensive against a weakened and demoralized adversary.

The day after the last sorties had been flown, on 20 May, the 1st ACG was awarded a Distinguished Unit Citation. The cost in terms of lost aircrew and aircraft was modest, considering the intensive nature of the missions and the operating conditions. The 1st ACG had received a number of replacement Mitchells, initially the H-5 model which introduced a full complement of package guns, followed by examples of the B-25H-10.

The monsoon now struck with its full fury, to wash out airfields alarmingly quickly. The weather further sapped the energy of the guerrilla groups still in the field, jungle warfare being highly debilitating at the best of times. Operation *Thursday* was finally completed in late May, just

before even the small Burma landing strips had to be abandoned.

In supporting Wingate's daring and unconventional methods of warfare, the 1st ACG had had a highly detrimental effect on enemy morale, quite apart from the losses it inflicted in terms of men and material. During the monsoon season Air Commando B-25 crews were thinned out as tour-expired men returned home, their aircraft remaining behind to be thoroughly overhauled and assessed as to their fitness for further combat. Cochrane, Smith and Radovich were among the pilots who returned home, and for some months British and US views on the future conduct of the war in Burma were at virtual loggerheads.

Still fired with enthusiasm for the independent air support unit, Hap Arnold was prepared to divert substantial numbers of aircraft to equip an expanded air commando force. But this was largely vetoed by the British high command, which remained wedded to the notion that air units had to be subordinated into a recognized command structure. In late 1944 a compromise led to a regenerated air commando force becoming part of the Tenth Air Force, in which several B-25s constituted a 'bomber, night intruder section' under the command of Capt Edward 'Sam' Wagner.

Although the assault element of the air commando concept built around B-25s had proven to be extremely sound, the availability of more effective fighter bombers such as the P-47 showed that this role could be handled more economically by single-seaters. Thus by the time the 1st ACG embarked on its second combat phase in the autumn of 1944, the original P-51As had given way to P-47Ds, and the separate B-25 bomber element had been reduced – but the value of the Mitchell as a combat aircraft was acknowledged to the extent that it not only remained, but took on the intruder role.

New command

Eastern Air Command had been established on 15 December 1943, by which time the Allies in Burma were in a position to seriously threaten the Japanese hold on the country for the first time since 1941. The country was an integral part of the AAF's CBI theatre and the British South-East Asia Command, and a significant degree of inter-service co-operation developed between the Americans and the RAF while Burma remained contested. On 18 December 1943 the 3rd Tactical Air Force had been formed as a subordinate command of

The nomadic 341st Bomb Group split its squadrons between two air forces in Burma and China for much of the war. This 22nd Squadron B-25H named 'Marion' is flying over the chequerboard paddyfields of China. USAF

EAC with headquarters at Comilla under AM Sir John Baldwin.

Defence of the Hump route was primarily the responsibility of 3rd TAF, whose operations had contained the Japanese by the spring of 1944. Although the enemy had some success in January, it was facing a serious lack of reinforcements and material, and the number of aircraft available to intercept Allied bombers also fell as units were posted away to bolster the fighting in the central Pacific.

To support a final attempt by their ground troops to capture Imphal, the JAAF sent reinforcements to occupy forward airfields in central Burma. But EAC reacted swiftly and neutralized many aircraft on the ground. Further reinforcement of the region availed the Japanese little, and it was soon clear that their main focus had shifted away from Burma.

By January 1944 Mitchells were well represented in General Davidson's Strategic Air Force. With its HQ at Belvedere Palace, Calcutta, SAF was a mix of RAF Wings and USAAF groups, the latter including the 341st Bomb Group with a strength of thirty-seven aircraft. But the US was having to divide its available forces between Burma and China, and before the end of that month the bulk of the 341st had had to be transferred across the Himalayas. Left behind in Burma was the group's 490th BS with sixteen B-25s.

A crew of the 341st Group pose with their aircraft on a Chinese airfield where, despite conditions generously described as primitive, the group fought its tough war to the end. This B-25J has the prominent shell-collector chute fitted to prevent spent brass striking the underside of the aircraft. USAF

Burma Bridge Busters

Despite reduced aircraft strength, the remaining crews of the 341st Bomb Group gave a good account of themselves against a plethora of enemy targets in Burma. The Japanese moved considerable quantities of material by sea, but many vessels were beyond the range of medium bombers and could not be directly attacked. An aerial mining campaign, mainly by AAF heavy bombers and RAF Wellingtons, was effective in blockading ports and inland seas – and interdiction of railways became something of a specialty with B-25 crews. As with most extensive national railway systems, Burma's tracks crossed numerous bridges (over 300 of them) which became prime targets for the low-flying mediums. The main line linking Burma with Siam included a section 420 miles (675km) long between Bangkok and Pegu, and breaking it effectively severed the link between the two countries.

New Weapons

In war, certain basic ideas often bring success out of all proportion to their simplicity, and one such, very widely deployed against the Burmese railways system, was the 'spike bomb'. This was a standard 500lb GP bomb fitted with a tapered nose section that enabled it to dig into the track bed and cause maximum blast damage to rails and sleepers. The 490th Squadron became very adept at repeatedly cutting the railways at important points using spike bombs. Neither did the crews overlook the rolling stock and locomotives that carried enemy supplies of all kinds – increasingly so as river traffic was made gradually more costly through air attack. A war of stealth developed, the Japanese making stringent efforts to hide their locomotives from aerial observation, while the Allies became extremely adept at spotting 'hides' built to protect enemy trains.

Mitchells from Italy

During March the small B-25 force in SAF was augmented by the arrival of the 12th Bomb Group; eventually this boosted the number of in-theatre Mitchells to eighty-five, higher than it had ever been before. The Earthquakers had left behind a distinguished combat record in the Middle East. They arrived in Bombay on 12 March, and personnel appreciated the fact that they could now live in bashas rather than the tents they had endured on desert landing grounds. The group had generally used early model B-25Bs and Cs in a conventional medium bombing role in North Africa; however, when it became part of the Tenth Air Force in Burma, it took delivery of new H and J models.

These cannon-armed Mitchells arrived as from 1 April 1944 and created much interest, as few of the new personnel had any previous experience of them. But they came to appreciate that where German

(Top) When the 12th Bomb Group transferred to the CBI early in 1944 the group's 82nd Bomb Squadron had B-25H-10 'Bones' – the 1,000th and last H model built – on its roster. Signed with NAA employee names, it had tail number 45. H. Levy

(Above) As well a a mix of B-25 models, the Earthquakers flew camouflaged and NMF aircraft. One of the latter in the 82nd Squadron, gleaming in the Burmese sun in 1944, was named 'Blazin' Betty'. Crow

'Betty' in all her glory. A consistent style indicates that these popular paintings were done by the same artist – who must have been busy, as most B-25s in the group were similarly personalized. Crow

defences had made low-level 'buzz' bomb-ing and strafing all but prohibitive in the desert, the Japanese had far fewer AA guns, which made this type of attack much more productive in the CBI. Deployment of the B-25H brought con-siderable success, pilots honing their technique to the point where they could hit with cannon fire targets as small as a single truck. Both the 75mm cannon and the nose machine guns were boresighted at 1,000yd (900m), and a typical pass would see three cannon rounds fired at 1,500, 1,000 and 500yd (1,400, 900 and 460m) out, the pilot aiming with the optical gunsight. Each cannon round was interspersed with machine-gun bursts, due allowance being made for the differ-ent range of each type of gun, and the degree of turbulence. Attack runs would be initiated at 200 to 250mph (320 to 400km/h), with the pull-out often being at 'zero feet'.

Spring/Summer 1944

April

The Earthquakers made their combat debut over Burma on 16 April by attacking Japan-ese storage dumps at Mongaung. Crews who had believed that North African desert storms were hazardous were shown that the weather over Burma could be even deadlier,

(*Above*) Sections of the 12th Group, with a B-25J and an H working together, could bring a devastating rain of ruin on most Burmese targets – a deadly combination of machine-gun bullets, cannon shells, HE, incendiaries and parafrag bombs usually did the trick. Here, aircraft of the 81st BS are operating in this way. Levy

Servicing scene, probably at Fenny, India, with B-25H-5 (43-4470) 'Paper Doll' of the 82nd being tanked up from a bowser which has its own 'nose art'. Crow

when one B-25 disappeared without trace when it flew into a thunderhead. By then the pivotal battle for Imphal was taking place, and Earthquaker Mitchells were called upon to fly ammunition into British-held airstrips behind enemy lines.

On the 18th the 12th Bomb Group flew its first spike bomb mission. Liberally sprinkling the bombs across the rail lines linking Sagaing and Shwebo, the B-25s released 144 bombs, the crews claiming twenty-five direct hits.

(Above) B-25J 'Milk Run' leads 'Paper Doll', another 82nd BS aircraft in a typical model mix in the 12th Group. Crow

Close-up of the quite substantial 'doll' which graced B-25H No. 37 of the 82nd BS. Crow

bomber crews. Lying about 50 miles (80km) north of Chittagong on the Bay of Bengal, Comilla was to be the Earthquakers' base for the duration of the war.

July

In July 1944 the Earthquakers moved into Comilla, the group's aircraft also operating from Feni. The first mission out of the latter airfield was flown on 23 July, the group attacking Myitkyina in support of Merrill's Marauders, the US force commanded by Stillwell and patterned on the lines of the Chindits. Stillwell cabled that he was well pleased with the tactical bombing efforts. For the 12th, these and subsequent missions over Burma saw the gradual replacement of standard medium altitude attacks in favour of 'zero feet' bombing and strafing, as demanded by the various targets, many of which the Japanese had camouflaged. On occasions pattern bombing was used, the group responding to the prevailing tactical situation as dictated by the 14th Army's visual command posts

May

As the monsoon hit Burma, air operations were reduced in scope and number until flying weather improved; but neither air nor ground activity stopped completely, as the Allies knew that only by keeping up the pressure would the Japanese be defeated quickly. Flying in monsoon conditions was never pleasant, but the enemy was to be given no respite. All previous monsoon seasons had seen a slowdown in Allied air operations, handing the Japanese a breathing space.

June

During June the 12th moved base to Madhiganj and Pandaveshwar in order better to support the advance of the ground troops. En route refuelling stops were made at Comilla, a base that would soon become much more familiar to the US medium

(VCPs) which vectored the B-25s onto their targets.

Missions back up into northern Burma and to targets along the Burma Road, which snaked into China, often proved to be on the limit of the B-25's endurance, crews frequently landing at Feni with the red 20min 'fuel low' light burning too brightly for comfort.

August

Despite the low number of Japanese AA guns to oppose its sorties, the 12th inevitably sustained casualties. On 13 August the CO of the 81st BS, Maj Warren W. Sutton, was shot down by groundfire

back, their air support recorded an almost routine lack of enemy air opposition. During the autumn, US heavy bombers flew an increasing number of fuel supply missions, while the B-25s interspersed their more normal air support missions by laying parachute mines in the Chindwin, often in company with RAF Wellingtons.

Allied success on the ground pointed the way towards the final ejection of the Japanese Army from all Burmese territory, and concurrent with the November 1944 launching of Operation *Capital*, the penultimate drive to liberate Burma, the 1st Air Commando Group's B-25 Night Intruder section flew its first mission. The fighter section was made up of the 5th

1945. In that time the crews of Maj Wagner's small unit of four B-25Hs carried out a number of sorties against the Burmese rail network. When natural moonlight failed to give enough light to attack trains, M-8 flares were released. From a drop height of 1,500ft (460m) the flares burned for several minutes, usually time enough for a B-25 to make two passes with cannon and machine guns.

Nine sorties were accomplished in November, and the success of these led to three more Mitchells being allocated to the unit, bringing the total to seven. All assigned B-25Hs were apparently in natural metal finish rather than camouflage, despite the nocturnal nature of the work,

When the 1st Air Commando Group was reorganized in 1944 it generally dispensed with B-25s in favour of more economical fighter bombers – apart from a handful of H models that formed Sam Wagner's Night Intruder section, most of which is represented here. USAF

while carrying out a low-level attack on a railway bridge near Kanbalu.

By mid-summer 1944 the 12th was a virtually new group in terms of personnel, both air and ground, as many of the original members had rotated home. New crews brought their aircraft with them from the US via the southern ferry route, which took in Arabia, Iran and India.

Autumn/Winter 1944

September–November

As the ground forces continued their offensive operations to roll the Japanese

and 6th Fighter Squadrons equipped with P-47s, and handled a high number of daylight sorties, many of them against railway targets. The 5th FS had the primary task of medium bomber escort, which they carried out mostly for units other than the 1st ACG's bomber section, whose daytime activities had been curtailed.

The Japanese became adept at moving supplies by night, and it was in denying them the comparative safety of operating under cover of darkness that the 1st ACG's night intruder B-25s came into their own. The first mission was flown on 23 November, the first of a period of moonlit nights that lasted until 3 January

the five blue Air Commando identification stripes usually being applied to the fuselage.

Capital became *Extended Capital* as Slim's 14th Army relentlessly pushed the Japanese out of their jungle redoubts; with Allied troops across the Chindwin, the Imperial Army fell back to regroup, its intention being to heavily defend central Burma after the Allies had crossed the Irrawaddy. Slim's airpower was the key to curtailing this plan and, without official approval, he prepared to strike. But when a Japanese offensive in China resulted in the loss of 14th AAF bases and threatened the Hump route, more than 25,000 Chinese troops were pulled out of Burma, putting even greater responsibility onto the airmen to even things up for the troops on the ground.

December

The uncontested securing of the airfield on Akyab Island on 12 December greatly aided air support to a ground advance into the Arakan, a campaign that continued into the New Year. A period of moonlight from 23 December to 3 January 1945 was exploited to the full by the B-25s of Wagner's Night Intruder Section.

Winter/Spring 1945

January

Continuing to operate out of the main 1st ACG base at Asanol, the B-25s attacked troops, locomotives, supplies and bridges. Enemy gun positions were also destroyed, to reduce the enemy's bolstered AA defence of the vital bridges. The 75mm cannon in the B-25Hs were well able to deal with such targets, although the Japanese gunners quickly realized that tracer rounds gave away their positions, and promptly stopped using them. Without visible tracers to pinpoint the guns, the mediums often found themselves suddenly flying through bursting shells. During the last weeks of January, six B-25s sustained damage, though none of it was fatal.

Air Commando B-25s also indulged in 'loco busting'. These attacks were usually initiated from 300 to 500ft (90 to 150m), and crews reported that the Japanese train drivers generally saw the aircraft at about the same time as the Americans spotted them. Once the train had been stopped by a carefully placed bomb or two, the aircraft came in broadside and blazed away with all guns, the turret and tail gunners having their turn last, as the pilot pulled up in a steep banking turn. Rarely more than three passes were needed to reduce the train to a steam-wreathed wreck, and ruined equipment all along its length.

Thirty-six B-25 sorties were flown in the last ten days of January, an effort that resulted in the destruction of 15 locomotives, 255 vehicles, 128 items of rolling stock and a single small boat.

Operation *Multivite* was the outcome of the ground plan to ultimately secure Meiktila, the hub of Japanese operations throughout Burma. To this end the 1st

Provisional Fighter Group was formed in late January, in which the B-25s of the Night Intruder Section, the P-47s of the 5th and 6th Squadrons and the P-51s of the 2nd ACS were brought together under a single command.

February

The 1st PFG was deemed to be operational by 11 February, by which time it had moved base to Hay in eastern India, close to the Bay of Bengal and Cox's Bazaar, the forward base for the 2nd ACG.

By 13 February a beach-head had been established on the eastern bank of the Irrawaddy and, to keep the enemy guessing, the 1st PFG made diversionary raids. Slim had chosen the least likely point to cross, and this completely fooled the Japanese – until British troops were caught in mid-stream at dawn. The enemy reacted with heavy fire, although their efforts were inhibited by three Commando UC-64 Norsemen ploughing up and down the river above the cloud cover. The raucous sound of their engines unnerved the enemy and masked the sound of approaching tanks and boats.

Then at 06:35 the unarmed Norsemen were suddenly replaced by three Night Intruder B-25s that marked Japanese positions with smoke before attacking the targets with cannon fire and frag clusters. Enemy guns were quickly silenced after they had fired a few ineffectual rounds. P-47s and P-51s established a continual 'cab rank' patrol over the Irrawaddy crossing while the B-25s and other fighters of the unit ranged out south of the river, where the pilots found plenty of targets.

March

With the British capture of Meiktila on 3 March, the road to Mandalay was then blocked by the centuries-old Fort Dufferin. With its massive moated walls, the fort would have been a tough proposition for the ground troops, and to prevent needless casualties the Earthquakers were employed to soften it up. Their opening attack was on the 21st, when four aircraft flew at 200ft (60m) and dropped 2,000lb bombs, breaching the north wall in two places. In the follow-up attack the bombs dislodged the Japanese gun emplacements, thereby curtailing the deadly crossfire that had stopped friendly troops from fording the moat. After the aerial

bombardment they met little Japanese resistance. Between 11 February and 5 March the 1st ACG B-25Hs had flown fifty-two sorties.

Bridges continued to be familiar targets during the last months of the war, the 12th Group making life difficult for the retreating and often starving Japanese who had their supply system either destroyed or disrupted to the point where further resistance was clearly futile. But there was no question of surrender, and the low-flying B-25s maintained the pressure, harassing the enemy wherever he was found.

April

On 4 April 1945 the Toungoo road bridge across the Sittang finally succumbed to bombs aimed by aircraft of the Battering Rams (81st BS). A long-time nemesis of the Earthquakers, this bridge had withstood tons of high explosive aimed by AAF and British aircraft, and it was fitting that the group CO, Maj Samual C. Galbreath, was credited with dropping the four bombs that finally removed the centre span. Just before darkness fell Galbreath led the attack in and marked the target by dropping an incendiary made from a 55gal (250l) oildrum. Over the next few days the Tornado Squadron (434th BS) also made its mark in this round of 'bridge busting', as did the Bulldogs (82nd BS). At the end of the week, having deployed only small numbers of aircraft on each raid, the 12th had accounted for twenty-five road and rail bridges.

Flying from Meiktila, Meidavale and Magwe in central Burma by late April, the 12th began to realize that its interdiction campaign might have been almost too successful. With most road and rail links smashed, all the group's supplies, including fuel, bombs and ammunition, had to be flown over the Chin Hills from Feni. Orders therefore went out to cease the bombing of bridges that could be used by the Allies.

The war was now drawing to its inevitable conclusion. With the RAF having largely taken over air support sorties prior to entering Rangoon early in May, the 1st Air Commando Group disbanded its Night Intruder Section. In April Wagner had consigned the majority of the remaining B-25s to a depot in Bangalore, although one B-25H and a single J model remained with the 1st ACG headquarters as late as 23 September 1945.

CHAPTER TWELVE

RAF Mitchells – Going the Distance

Winter/Spring 1944

By 1 January 1944 the four RAF Mitchell squadrons had become an integral part of 2nd TAF's striking power. On 16 January the Group HQ moved to Mongewell Park in Berkshire, when the 2nd TAF comprised four bomber wings: 137, 138, 139 and 140. The Mitchell squadrons were concentrated in 137 (No. 226) and 139 Wings (Nos 98, 180 and 320 Sqns).

No. 180 Sqn opened the year with a twelve-aircraft *Ramrod* to a *Noball* site at Yvrench on 4 January. As was usual, the bombing soon blanketed the site in dense smoke so crews had to await the PR photos to know definite results. The Germans had realized that the Allies were only too aware of the danger their V1 represented, and had surrounded the launching sites with light, medium and heavy flak batteries. Their efforts served to keep aircrews alert, although in the case of the Mitchell squadrons, bombing patterns were usually kept tight and well timed so that the crews were exposed to gunfire over the target area for the shortest possible time.

February was a relatively quiet month due to bad weather, but *Ramrod 598* went ahead on the 28th. Nos 226 and 320 Sqns, escorted by Typhoons, attracted flak in the target area at Moyenneville and two Mitchells were badly damaged, with crew fatalities when one ditched and the other crash-landed.

March

No. 180 Sqn relinquished Sqn Ldr Bell-Irving early in March, this unit's loss being No. 98's gain when he took over from Wg Cdr A.M. Phillips. Improving weather meant that on the 18th the new CO was able to lead the squadron to Domurten Pontheib; but despite clear conditions and meagre flak, on this occasion, the bombs missed.

(Above) A Dutch crew of No. 320 Sqn consulting their maps before another sortie in March 1944. IWM

During lulls in operations No. 180 Squadron gave air experience flights in its Mitchells to a number of ATC cadets, one of whom is having his straps checked. IWM

On 26 March a heavy raid was planned, involving Mitchells and several hundred 9th AAF B-26s, with the aim of reducing the German S-boat fleet based at Ijmuiden. Two S-boats were destroyed in the attack, but seven Mitchells sustained damage as the flak reacted viciously.

April

In April, No. 180 Sqn was sent on a two-week bombing course to Swanton Morley, beginning on the 12th, the object being to refine bombing accuracy in preparation for the invasion of Europe. To avoid unnecessary Allied casualties on the ground, the bomber crews were given

the pilot, Jopie Mulder, shouted for the crew to bail out. The navigator did so, but the gunners quickly reminded Mulder that he had forgotten his parachute when he changed to the spare aircraft. With little choice but to try for a forced landing, the aircraft came down northeast of Headcorn in Kent. The crew survived, but 'Margriet' was a write-off, although it emerged later that the offending Mosquito pilot swore his victim had been a Dornier.

A small but significant RAF Mitchell unit, 1483 (Bomber Gunnery) Flight commanded latterly by Sqn Ldr F.E. Frayn, disbanded at West Raynham on 1 April after a year's existence. First line squadrons had

ranging as far afield as Belgium to strike targets while continually attacking *Noball* sites and carrying out some night sorties. Intensive training for nocturnal bombing – which was to occupy the squadron's Mitchells for some time to come – had begun on the 27th, resulting in another temporary stand-down from regular day operations.

Then on 8 May, Wg Cdr Bell-Irving was shot down and killed. He had led an attack on a *Noball* site at Bois Coquerel that evening and at the Mitchells' bombing height of 13,000ft (3,960m) the flak had been heavy and accurate. His machine took a direct hit in the nose, which sent it spinning down to crash. No parachutes were seen.

Bomb trailers go out to waiting Mitchells of No. 320 Sqn. Most, if not all the unit's Mitchells, had the small House of Orange triangle on each side of the nose in appropriate orange with black outline. IWM

precise co-ordinates to follow. Marshalling yard raids also occupied the unit during this period.

On 26 April, No. 320 Sqn was obliged to record the demise of Mitchell Mk II FR142/F. Named 'Margriet', this was the unit's second allocated aircraft and the one that had flown HRH Prince Bernhard from the US to England. Its demise was the result of another 'misfortune of war': taking off as a replacement for a Mitchell that had gone u/s for an exercise known as *Bat's Eye at Dawn*, FR142 was attacked first by a Typhoon and then a Mosquito. Hit, and with both engines losing power,

demonstrably benefited from the work of this flight, which had moved to Swanton Morley on 1 December 1943. However, ongoing difficulties with the Mitchell's turrets had involved an intensive repair programme in conjunction with A&AEE and the squadrons.

Spring/Summer 1944

May

Wg Cdr R.W. Goodwin assumed command of No. 180 Sqn on 2 May 1944, the unit now

Command of No. 98 Sqn was given to Wg Cdr Christopher Paul during May, and he would see the unit through the D-Day period. Leadership then passed to Sqn Ldr Paynter in July.

June: Invasion!

Operation *Overlord* on 6 June was a vast undertaking, and all Allied squadrons participating in it had detailed orders for specific targets, timings and routes across the Channel. For the Mitchell force these were as follows: to attack static targets as a result of tactical information received by

Gee-H equipped aircraft, and to act as pathfinders to illuminate targets with flares or target indicators for non-Gee aircraft; to operate non-Gee aircraft individually, making closely co-ordinated attacks on static targets illuminated as described above; and to sortie independently in suitable weather and moonlight conditions to attack selected targets visually.

With some variation as dictated by local conditions, all these operations were flown by the Mitchell and Boston units over the course of the next few weeks and, certainly during the early stages of the invasion, they were all were at night. An early attack on 5/6 June used sixty Mitchells from all squadrons in forty-nine effective sorties: this deluge of high explosive plastered the villages of Villers Bocage and Falaise with 204 1,000lb bombs, including a bridge at Dives and a defile through Thury Harcourt village, the main objective being to block and destroy German vehicles attempting to reinforce the coastal defences. No. 180 Squadron's effort included bombing the Dives bridge and selected points at Villers Bocage and Falaise.

Seventy-plus ops were on the board by 12 June 1944 when 'Grumpy' had to be manhandled by the groundcrew with the help from an aircrew member who is 'pulling through' the propeller. This Mitchell Mk II (FL176/VO-B) of No. 98 Sqn eventually set a 2 Group record, with 125 sorties. IWM

(Below) A formation box of No. 180 Squadron's Mitchell IIs includes aircraft 'O', 'W', 'R', 'L', 'P' and 'Z'. IWM

On 7/8 June the target was railways, the Mitchells being briefed for troop detraining points at Villedieu, Vire and Flers. Mezidon was also bombed by both Mitchells and Bostons.

On the evening of 10 June a 'maximum effort' consisting of seventy-one Mitchells rained bombs on Chateau de La Caine, north-east of Thury Harcourt, the HQ of Gen von Geyr, area Panzer commander. The building was severely damaged, and the explosions killed a number of officers including Chief of Staff General Elder von Dawens. The results of this raid were disastrous for the enemy, and effectively prevented any organized reaction to the Allies by the Panzers for a few vital days.

As night fell, Nos, 98 and 226 dropped flares over the beach-head area and bombed St Sauvent and the rail junction at Le Haye. This was a pattern that the 2 Group squadrons repeated on following nights over the 2nd Army front.

By this time 2nd TAF had perfected its technique of bombing by boxes of six or twelve Mitchells, to the point where the squadrons were capable of hitting their targets hard, and had settled into a flexible pattern of bombing either visually or blind using Gee-H on a time-elapsed basis. For example, faced with ten-tenths cloud cover over the target, formations would be split, the lead box flying on for a predetermined period before turning and climbing through the 'clag'. The following boxes made their turns slightly earlier. By making a further turn above the overcast, all boxes regained formation prior to bombing, using the reliable British Mk XIV automatic sight. Preset for height, speed, wind and bomb load, the sight corrected any deviation without further input from the bomb aimer.

Good organization of the Mitchell wings extended to identifying boxes by colours – for example, yellow, silver, grey, blue and red were used by No. 320 Squadron. Linked to a number for each aircraft, this system enabled succinct identification over the R/T, and really came into its own when the squadrons were obliged to land under tight ground control, with many aircraft in the circuit at the same time.

The RAF's contribution to the success of *Overlord* included a massive airborne 'spoof fleet' that helped convince the Germans that the real attack would come in the Pas de Calais rather than Normandy. More modest in scope, but just as useful in terms of indirect support for the invasion, were special nocturnal sorties by Mitchells

When D-Day finally dawned, the RAF's Mitchell force was in the forefront of the Allied air effort. No. 320 was well represented, as this photo taken on 11 June shows. In the cockpit of Mk II FR201/NO-Z is the crew's canine mascot, 'Kip', who flew operationally on several occasions. IWM

of No. 226 Sqn. These had begun as early as the night of 1/2 June when a single aircraft took off from Hartford Bridge bound for France. In great secrecy and using the cover of a night 'nickelling' (leaflet) sortie, this aircraft was actually bound for a predetermined spot over open French countryside, where it would climb to 20,000ft (6,000m) and fly a 50-mile (80km) radius circle, seemingly to no obvious purpose. People on the ground, however, knew full well what the purpose was, because they were transmitting radio signals that were being 'read' by the Mitchell crew who were part of 'C' Flight of No. 226 Sqn.

The origins of this clandestine sortie lay with Supreme Headquarters, Allied Expeditionary Forces (SHAEF), which had during March established a network of agents in occupied France. They were to transmit important data to the Allies using a radio system that was largely undetectable by German mobile D/F sets installed in vans. In essence this 'quarter wave' relay method involved a normal voice transmission on a narrow vertical beam that spread out at altitude, allowing the aircraft's crew to monitor it clearly at any point of the orbiting circle.

No. 226's special flight came under the direct joint control of SHAEF, the squadron CO, Wg Cdr A.D. Mitchell and Gp Capt W.L.M. MacDonald, commanding 137 Wing. Each Mitchell crew in the flight included French radio operators who received the transmissions, two aircraft usually being despatched to contact two agents at a time. On return of the Mitchells to Hartford Bridge, the data was sent via despatch rider to London so that targets identified by the agents could be attacked without delay – usually later that same day.

Soon known as the 'Ginger' Mitchell Flight, this small unit existed until October 1944, by which time most targets in its operational area had been captured. The flight also operated over Holland, initially with disappointing results until it was realized that aircraft had to fly west–east right across the country rather than parallel with the Dutch coast, as before. The change brought an immediate improvement in the detection of ground transmissions.

Individual Mitchells operated by 'C' Flight of No. 226 recorded their sorties as small question marks in the style of the regular bomb log; one aircraft carried at least forty-one such marks. While their significance may have been lost on the casual observer, they masked the fact that, say, an A-4 (V2) rocket may have been destroyed before launching due to the unsung work of that particular medium bomber crew. To enhance the spoof, leaflets were actually carried on the first few missions and tossed out in bulk over France or the Channel, although this subterfuge was soon abandoned due to the lack of enemy reaction to the Ginger flights.

For No. 320 Sqn, 12 June 1944 was remembered as a special day because they were honoured by a visit from Queen Wilhelmina and Prince Bernhard. But during the royal visit the unit was ordered off for a mass attack on German positions in the Forêt de Grimbecq and St Laurent-de-Conde. Heavy flak greeted the incoming Mitchells: FR149 was mortally damaged and the aircraft went down in flames, and although the crew managed to bail out, it was behind enemy lines. Mk II FR191/NO-A, captained by F/O van de Wolf, was also hit by flak bursts at 10,000ft, but the crew had better luck. The Mitchell's nose was damaged and its starboard engine was wrecked, but it kept going and the pilot turned for England.

Inevitably the aircraft gradually lost altitude, and airspeed fell to 150mph (240km/h) due to drag from the windmilling starboard propeller which could not be feathered. Calling a Mayday, the captain maintained his course for England. When it was clear that the bomber could not reach an airfield it was decided to ditch near a naval convoy, and around 22:00hr the Mitchell went into the Channel. But the whole crew managed to get out of the aircraft, and were picked up by the destroyer HMS *Blankney*.

During the D-Day support period the Mitchell force remained primarily equipped with the Mk II, although several examples of the Mk III (equivalent to the B-25J) had been taken on charge during May. Not issued to 2 Group squadrons in any numbers until later in the year, the Mk III provoked more adverse criticism from British aircrew: in short, it was summed up as too heavy and too slow! Any additional weight was indeed a somewhat adverse factor in the type of close-formation flying the 2nd TAF crews had perfected with the earlier, lighter Mitchells, and a degree of re-planning had to take place, especially as the squadrons eventually had a mix of both marks.

The 2nd TAF effort for the whole of June 1944 amounted to 3,119 sorties for the loss

of thirty-one aircraft: fourteen Mitchells, fourteen Mosquitoes and three Bostons.

In mid-1944 Mitchell crews flew the same number of operations in a tour as their counterparts on Bostons, namely fifty, a figure introduced by 2 Group in 1943. The time equivalent was nine months' operational flying, whichever was completed first. Crews would then be 'rested' before undertaking a further thirty-five (second tour) sorties, or six months on a squadron; medical officers maintained a close watch on individuals to spot the first signs of battle fatigue.

Fully marked with recognition stripes for the *Overlord* period, Mitchell II FW214/EV-O of No. 180 Squadron tightens up the formation. Smith

July

On the night of 13/14 July a clash over France again involved not enemy aircraft but two on the same side. As related earlier, it had been appreciated that, under certain circumstances, the Mitchell could be mistaken for the Dornier Do 217, which it resembled in configuration, and with which it shared similar overall dimensions. RAF night fighter and intruder crews were briefed to be aware of this fact, and also that single Mitchells might be encountered at night; but on this occasion the crew involved pressed home their attack on a 'Dornier' that was in fact one of No. 226's 'Ginger' Mitchell Flight. Even after making four passes the Mosquito crew, belonging to

No. 100 (Bomber Support) Group, failed to recognize their adversary for what it was. Out of extreme exasperation the Mitchell crew returned fire as the Mosquito made yet another firing pass – and shot it down. Fortunately the Mosquito crew bailed out over friendly territory and lived to file a combat claim for a Do 217 'damaged'. In their turn the Mitchell crew claimed a Mosquito!

Such encounters were dangerous, and tragic if they resulted in death or injuries – but RAF Mitchell crews were certainly not the only flyers to suffer from the unwelcome attention of 'friendly' aircraft.

Despite comprehensive briefings and aircraft recognition lectures, the problem was never entirely solved.

Mitchell crews faced other unforeseen hazards. On 23 July, No. 98 Sqn experienced a mercifully rare occurrence when Mk II FV985 was destroyed by the premature detonation of its own bombs. The squadron was attacking Glos-Montfort at the time, and it was never established whether the loss was due to enemy action or faulty bomb fusing. A second Mitchell (FV931) suffered peripheral damage as a result of the explosion, and the pilot was obliged to crash-land at Tangmere in Kent on return. Later that same day No. 180 Sqn indulged in a little night intruding, losing one Mk II (FW118) in the process.

Clearly pleased at having completed their forty-second Mitchell sortie on 23 July 1944, this crew of No. 226 Squadron, then at Hartford Bridge, flew Mk II NQ-X – which was almost certainly FW110. IWM

(Above) Despite frequent aircraft recognition lectures on operational airfields, a number of Mitchells were mistaken for Dornier Do 217s and attacked by Allied aircraft. During Operation *Overlord*, AEAF stripes helped to emphasize that RAF Mitchells were 'friendly'. This Mk II of No. 98 Squadron proves the point. IWM

The remaining members of the crew of NQ-X of No. 226 Sqn walk from their aircraft after the same July sortie. By that time RAF Mitchells had generally gone back on regular daylight operations after their nocturnal flights during the immediate invasion period. IWM

August

The crescendo of Allied tactical bombing over the continent in daylight dropped off significantly at night; giving the enemy such a respite was counter-productive and both the RAF and USAAF medium bomber squadrons took steps to redress this. Consequently, night flare sorties added another variation to regular bombing operations by Mitchells. Each machine carried a stock of M-8 flares to illuminate targets for single aircraft or small formations to bomb.

bad weather increasingly intervened to reduce operations. September saw the Mitchell force returning to daylight operations – though on many days there were only 'blind' bombing conditions.

On the 17th, support for the Arnhem operation involved forty-eight Mitchells of 137 and 139 Wings: they participated in bombing three German barracks in the area, although cloud cover at 6,000 to 9,000ft (1,800 to 2,700m) prevented this being very effective. On the 25th, No. 98 Sqn lost Mk IIs FW194 and FW211 to FW

Belgium to make Melsbroek, alias B-58, its new base.

On 14 October No. 226 Sqn had joined two Boston squadrons to begin a demanding series of raids on bridges, and these operations continued for some time. Small and usually very well defended, bridges were vital to enemy movement and could be hard to knock down through aerial bombing. Those over the rivers Maas and Ijssel at Zutphen and Deventer opened this phase of operations for 2 Group. From the continental bases the target list was widened to take

Following the advance of the ground forces, the RAF Mitchell force used bases on the continent. No. 180 Sqn went to Melsbroek, from whence it operated older Mk IIs alongside replacement Mk IIIs. This photo shows that in many cases AEAF stripes were simply left on; however, they were not often applied to the newer B-25J equivalents. P. Jarrett

Such attacks, sometimes limited in material damage, were psychologically advantageous. That these sorties could be as dangerous as daylight ops was shown on 19 August when No 226 Sqn drew a night flare dropping mission from which Mitchell II (FW216) failed to return.

Autumn/Winter 1944

September

The speed of the Allied advance was such that the Mitchells were increasingly hard put to reach the front line and offer direct support, so for a time 2 Group concentrated on pockets of enemy resistance along the French coast. No. 98 Sqn remained on the ground between 2 and 8 September pending a move to the continent, though

190 attack while attempting to knock out enemy gun positions around Arnhem.

The following day was a landmark for 2 Group: the first raid on Germany itself. Of the participating squadrons, No. 226 did well to place bombs squarely on a road and rail bridge at Cleve. Other German targets had been bombed before the month was out, but they mostly entailed long, dangerous flights, and there was now an acute need for the Mitchell and Boston squadrons to be based nearer to Reich territory.

Forward Bases in October

After several more operations from England during the first weeks of October, the 2 Group mediums did make the move to the continent. B-50 Vitry-en-Artois became home to the squadrons of 137 Wing, while on the 19th, 139 Wing left England for

in bridge spans at Hedel, Roermond and Venlo. Repeat attacks to prevent lasting repairs were frequently necessary.

November

Bridges remained the priority targets for the RAF mediums, but for more than half of November the weather made effective operations impossible; furthermore, those that *were* flown met with only limited success, as about 50 per cent of the day sorties actually despatched by 2 Group had to be aborted. Bridges continued to occupy the medium bombers, but their task was frustrating because although these raids caused substantial damage, they were soon repaired, as the crossings were vital to the German supply situation. Nos 98 and 180 also experienced another hazard due to bad visibility: collision. On 11 November, Mitchell Mk II

FW228 of No. 180 collided with another Mk II (FW201/C) of its sister squadron, the former coming off worst and crashing with its entire crew. The No. 98 Sqn aircraft was damaged but repairable.

Disaster also struck No. 226 before the month was out, when Sqn Ldr G. Campbell and crew were lost on the 19th while leading an attack on Venlo. And on the 26th, F/O Twining's Mk II (FW230/B) was hit by flak, which tore the aircraft in half.

December

Weather on the Western front deteriorated to the point where air operations were all but abandoned, and then stopped completely over many sectors. Snowed over, iced up and fogged in, the vast air forces were pinned to their continental dispersals, which created an ideal situation for von Runstedt to launch a counter-offensive, beginning on the 16th. Conditions were hardly much better in England, as the cold front brought some of the worse weather for decades.

Seizing their chance and stabbing at a thinly spread US defence line across the Ardennes, German tanks were seen in force for the first time in months as they swept westwards with little initial opposition. Normally such daylight operations would have been tantamount to suicide for the Panzer crews, but now there was little to stop them. Hazardous Allied reconnaissance sorties provided a rudimentary picture of the advance and, employing Gee-H blind bombing, some medium bomber sorties were mounted in an attempt to disrupt the advance. On 22 December No. 180's Mitchells carried out a Gee-H attack on a reported troop concentration at Henebach, but without the crews being able to observe results. The following day the Mitchells went against Schmidtheim where they *could* see the target – and where the flak crews could unfortunately see them!

The ground situation remained tense as the Christmas of 1944 approached. During December, No. 98 Sqn became the first in 2nd TAF to receive Mitchell Mk IIIs to augment its Mk IIs. Then on the 24th the terrible weather suddenly cleared, and in bright sunshine the Allied air forces were unleashed against von Runstedt's offensive. No. 226 Sqn's escort clashed with Luftwaffe fighters, which were up in force, though on that occasion a running fight with Bf 109s ended inconclusively.

Winter/Spring 1945

January

The early hours of 1 January 1945 were shattered on Allied airfields across Holland and Belgium as the Luftwaffe fighter force executed Operation *Bodenplatte*. Catching many RAF and USAAF aircraft on the ground, the mass strafing attack included Melsbroek – although the results for the Jadgflieger were not so spectacular here, as the three resident Mitchell squadrons had taken off early.

On the ground, the fighters of JG 27 and JG 54 sprayed fire in the general direction of the 139 Wing dispersal area, and managed to damage beyond repair three Mitchells from No. 180 Sqn and one from No. 98. Two Mitchells of No. 416 ARF were also destroyed. RAF records put the number of Mitchells damaged at Melsbroek as high as twelve, and there was also a single personnel casualty here.

It was probably the smoke from burning Harrows of No. 271 Sqn that confirmed the enemy raid on Melsbroek to crews of Nos. 98, 180 and 320 Squadrons as they returned from an early morning operation to bomb a Belgian communications centre at Dasburg. Being out on a raid meant of course that the bulk of the units' aircraft had escaped being exposed to the Luftwaffe attack, although the crews had an indication from ground control that something was up. Having circled for some ten minutes at the rendezvous point, the Mitchell bombing leader broke radio silence, which was only done in dire emergency. Asking about their fighter escort, he was told that none was available that morning, and that it was his decision as leader whether to continue with the operation or to return to base. He affirmed that they would 'press on', upon which the controller advised the bomber crews to 'Watch out for fighters'. This warning proved prophetic, and on return the force was diverted to Epinoy for a few hours while Melsbroek was cleared up.

Mitchell operations were therefore only marginally hampered by *Bodenplatte*, and continued thereafter without crews having to wait for replacement aircraft, as some squadrons were obliged to do after the largely futile enemy air attack. In common with the rest of the Allied tactical air forces, the improving January weather enabled the Mitchell force to contribute to the all-out effort to destroy the rem-

nants of von Runstedt's winter offensive. Thus the Battle of the Bulge ran out of steam and almost everything else as air-power finally wrecked any further chance of a renewed German offensive on the Western front.

As well as destroying vehicles and troops in the battle areas, the Allies devastated the German communications network far behind the front lines. Oil refineries, dumps and transport centres were among the targets for the 2nd TAF Mitchell force, which soon returned to what had become a familiar target list – the difference being that the targets were now inside Germany.

February

During this month the 2nd TAF Mitchells attacked a variety of targets from Dunkirk to the Rhine. A tough target, and one that had already been visited by the Mitchells, was the bridge at Daventer. Heavily defended by multiple flak batteries, it had defied previous attempts to knock it out, and on the 6th, Nos. 98 and 226 Sqns tried again. But the flak more than lived up to its grim reputation, a No. 98 Sqn Mitchell being shot down, and five from No. 226 being damaged so badly that none of them made it back to base, two crash-landing and three making emergency landings in Allied territory.

Bomb hang-ups were not to be taken lightly, and when this happened to the crew of a No. 180 Sqn Mitchell (FW248) over Belgium, all hands preferred to bail out. In fact such misfortune might have been predicted by superstitious members of the crew, since the date was the 13th.

On 22 February Operation *Clarion* was launched. Intended as a final, all-out one-day effort to deny the Germans their last transport links, it was a prelude to crossing the Rhine. Ambitious in scope, *Clarion* involved nearly 9,000 aircraft, striking targets across a quarter of a million square miles of Germany.

March

To facilitate the crossing of Germany's main river artery, 2nd TAF's mediums flew twenty-three operations north of the Ruhr during March, mainly against rail centres. Sadly, the major effort made on 3 March had tragic consequences. After the first A4 (V2) fell on England on 8 September 1944, a desperate hunt was made for any fixed installations – ground guidance radars, launching sites, storage depots and so forth – that could be bombed. Next to nothing was found until another PR coverage of the Hague on 26 February finally confirmed an A4 ready for launching from the Duindigt race-course area north-west of the city. RAF medium bombers were briefed to destroy this 'fixed site', plus a building suspected of being used for rocket storage.

All the Mitchell squadrons contributed to this raid, plus No. 342's Bostons, and all the personnel sent on it were acutely aware of the potential danger to Dutch civilians, none more so than those of No. 320 Sqn. For this reason the raid was under Gee-H direction – but during the target approach, some of the leaders of the Mitchell boxes switched to visual aiming. Bombing what they thought was the rocket store, many bombs actually fell wide by 500yd (450m), and more than 3,000 Dutch people were killed or injured by bombs falling on residential areas. This appalling casualty figure prompted 2nd TAF AOC-in-C, AM Sir Arthur Coningham, to veto any further medium bombing of the Hague.

Only after the war ended was it realized that the A4 needed no fixed launching sites or storage depots, since the Meiller-wagen transporters that moved the rockets around were almost impossible to detect, and so almost totally foiled Allied reconnaissance.

The French-manned No. 342 (Lorraine) Squadron was the sixth and last RAF squadron to operate Mitchells; however, by the spring of 1945 it had become the fifth, as No. 305 converted to Mosquitoes. On 30 March a mix of Mk IIs and IIIs began to arrive at No. 342's base at Vitry-en-Artois – and once again the initial reaction to the Mitchell was negative. The French airmen were expecting new Bostons, the type they had flown from that base since October 1944, and their opinion of the Mitchell was nicely expressed by their squadron operations book: 'Disaster has swooped down upon us!'

Unaware that the Douglas light bomber was soon to be phased out in both the RAF and USAAF, the Frenchmen understandably felt a little chagrined; but when combat operations resumed with Mitchells on 8 April following a short training period, the still-reluctant crews had to agree that they could now place twice the bombs on a target with the same number of aircraft. That much made plenty of sense!

April

That first operation saw only one Mitchell from No. 342 taking part; otherwise a raid on Sogel was a 137 Wing show made up of No. 226 Squadron's Mitchells and the French crews, flying their Bostons for the last time. The next few days were hectic for the Frenchmen: on 9 April No. 342 despatched twelve Mitchells to bomb German flak positions west of Zutphen, an operation aided considerably by the fact that the enemy gun crews did not open fire. Cloppenburg was attacked on 10 April, again by

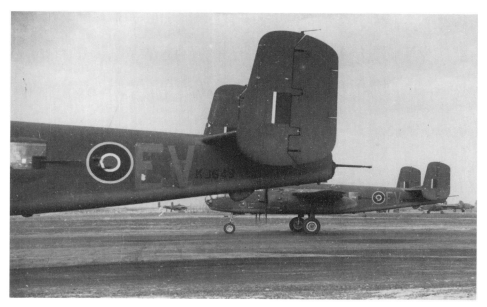

By 12 April 1945 when this photo was taken at Melsbroek, the Mk III was well represented in the Mitchell squadrons. Two of No. 180 Squadron's aircraft are taxiing out, led by KJ649. Flight/IWM

With some individuals wearing their all-purpose leather jerkins, a groundcrew of No. 226 Sqn pose for the camera in front of one of their charges, a Mitchell Mk III. Known as 'L – for Leather', the aircraft has a dark area showing where the package guns have been removed, ground strafing not being a regular activity for RAF Mitchells. E.R. Wright

Victor and vanquished. A Mk II Mitchell undergoing servicing on the Achmer flightline, while an abandoned Do 17 languishes in the background. IWM

twelve aircraft, with a second operation in the afternoon by six aircraft flying to the Monty area. Rotenburg was the target on the 11th, and on that day No. 342 experienced its first Mitchell casualty when Lt Dugot ran off the Vitry runway into a ditch. Although the aircraft, Mk III (KJ661), was wrecked, nobody on board was injured.

The ground war was now rushing to its crescendo, the Allied advance tending to leave the medium bombers with few remaining targets as these were overrun by Allied troops. Not until 17 April did the Lorraine flyers operate again, this mission to Oldenburg being the first (which was bombed blind) of two to that area on consecutive days.

The mission to Oldenburg on 18 April was eventful for the wrong reason: when Capitaine Guegden, leading the first box of six aircraft, opened his bomb doors, the load salvoed prematurely. Observing this, the rest of the box followed suit, which meant that the bombs landed 2,300ft (700m) away from where they were supposed to. Better results were obtained the next day when two boxes of Mitchells bombed a supply dump at Dunkirk.

A move to Holland was initiated by the squadron's ground echelon on 19 April, and on the 22nd the French aircrews, in three boxes of Mitchells, flew to Gilze-Rijen (B-77). There was little let-up in operations, however, for on 23 April No. 342 was briefed to attack enemy positions in the villages of Zeven and one lying south-east of Bremen. Targets in the Bremen area occupied the unit until the 25th,

after which the location was changed to a marshalling yard at Hamburg; this was bombed by twelve Mitchells each of Nos. 342 and 226 on the 26th. One Mitchell from No. 226 was reported missing. No. 320 marked 30 April as an historic day, for it was then that the squadron moved onto German soil, occupying Achmer (B-110).

Spring/Summer 1945

May

Weather prevented any sorties by No. 342 Sqn until the 1st, when with some difficulty it bombed an airfield at Lubeck which was all but hidden under 10/10ths cloud. A railway target at Itzehoe was hit on the 2nd by twelve aircraft, although again the results could not be readily be observed; other squadron Mitchells turned back en route to a similar target at Heide. And that proved to be the last mission of the war for No. 342 Sqn.

The 2 May date of the last operation of the French unit was shared by the four other RAF Mitchell squadrons, a tidy enough arrangement, entirely in keeping with the wartime 'precision' nature of their operations in north-west Europe. By the end of hostilities the 'Mitch' had indeed done its bit, none more so than Mk II (FL176/B) of No. 98 which chalked up 125 bombing sorties plus three ASR flights, while a second of the squadron's Mk IIs (FL186) had completed 122 plus five ASR flights. The record holder in No. 226 Sqn

was Mk II (FW111) with exactly 100 operations to its credit. This trio of '100 Club' members – otherwise composed of Lancasters, Halifaxes and Mosquitoes – was further proof of the aircraft's reliability. At least eleven other Mitchells are believed to have done fifty or more trips.

On the debit side, the RAF's Mitchell squadrons lost a combined total of eighty-five aircraft on operations. The build-up of Lend-Lease shipments to the UK had resulted in a wartime peak of 517 Mitchells on hand by December 1944; in May 1945 the inventory stood at 506 examples. The number of Mitchells officially struck off charge between May and December 1945 was 110, a process that continued after the war, as detailed in the final chapter.

June/July

England's crowded skies required extreme aircrew vigilance even in the early months of peace, but accidents continued to occur. Flying Mitchell Mk III (KJ673) over West Hendred in Berkshire on 11 July, a crew of 13 OTU was rammed from behind, apparently by a USAAF P-47. On this occasion the Mitchell managed to land safely, but at that stage of the war, shortly before it was probably due to be struck off RAF charge, the damage was not repaired. The identity of the P-47 has not been established; the 56th FG was the only US Thunderbolt group remaining in England at that time, but no loss was apparently recorded on that date, which would appear to indicate an aircraft on second-line duties.

CHAPTER THIRTEEN

Chinese Combat

Photographic Reconnaissance

During World War II the previously unanticipated need for photographic coverage of targets on a huge scale found most air forces wanting in respect of suitable aircraft. This meant that most of the combatants were initially forced to adapt standard service aircraft for PR work, pending the development of new types better suited to this exacting role. A compromise that proved very effective was to combine the mission of photographic reconnaissance with attack, a policy that made operational sense in that in some theatres it avoided the need for 'single role' PR aircraft, specialist aircrew and a ground support organization. The Pacific was a theatre where the US made widespread use of fighters and bombers in a PR role while maintaining an attack capability with a standard gun and bomb armament. In the case of the B-25, although the special photographic F-10 variant of the D model saw wartime service, the day-to-day tactical target intelligence requirements were adequately met by aircraft with no special equipment. The exploits of the 71st Tactical Recon Group, the 'Strafin' Saints', exemplified this dual role.

Not unusually for a reconnaissance outfit, the 71st was equipped with a variety of types, from medium bombers such as the B-25, and fighters including the P-38, P-39, P-40 and P-51, as well as liaison types. Since arriving in New Guinea in the autumn of 1943 the group's combat record had came to the attention of George Kenney and Fifth Bomber Command CO, Ennis C. Whitehead; when the time came to base medium bombers on the desolate island of Wakde, both men called for the 71st.

Having combined aerial photography with ground attack using standard B-25s, the squadron had begun operations on 23 November from Dobodura, New Guinea. In a move to rationalize the force, the bombers, fighters and liaison aircraft were grouped together in each of the four squadrons, and the 17th got the bombers.

By the spring of 1944 the US offensive in the Pacific was gathering momentum, and part of the plan to wrest territory from the Japanese was the invasion of Biak. Integral to any such advance was the provision of air support, and part of this particular move was to position the 17th and other units on Wakde, 180 miles (290km) to the west.

The Invasion of Biak

Tenaciously but hopelessly defended by the Japanese, the island presented the invading American troops with the grisly sight of numerous enemy dead. The corpses had only recently been bulldozed into communal graves when on 25 May the first B-25 rolled along a 6,500ft (2,000m) runway built by the 836th Engineer Aviation Battalion. Diehard Japanese snipers maintained a ragged fire around the strip which ran east-west, virtually the full length of the island. A putrid odour of death hung over the shattered island, which had absorbed so many rounds of naval gunfire and aerial bombs and had been heavily mortared and blasted by small arm rounds. Not for the first time, the AAF men saw at first hand how destructive their assault, combined with naval shelling, had been.

Knowing they would be there for some time (seventeen days as it transpired), the men made the best of things. They pitched tents and endured: rain almost every night, humidity levels off the barometer, and mosquitoes. Darkness also brought the Japanese Army Air Force, for Wakde was a plum target, crammed as it soon was with USAAF bombers and fighters poised to support MacArthur's Biak invasion. The proximity of Wakde, armed to the teeth with American airpower, gave the Japanese high command great cause for concern, for it had little choice but to defend Biak in an attempt to stem, if not prevent, the logical chain of US advance: the imperial warlords knew that if they lost Biak the Philippines would be threatened.

When US troops went ashore on Biak at Bosnek Village on 27 May, the ultimate prize was the three aerodromes on the island: denied the use of these, the enemy knew that its garrison on Palau would be in mortal danger of isolation. A showdown was coming, led by the Imperial Navy. On 2 June it launched a fleet covering force for 2,500 assault troops, destination Korim Bay, Biak.

Deploying the battleship *Fuso*, four cruisers, seven destroyers and support vessels, this fleet was potentially formidable and potentially well able to shield the landing force from American interference. But an erroneous report of US carriers sent the heavy ships back to port in the Philippines, leaving the destroyers to escort the amphibious forces. Little of this activity escaped the notice of Fifth Air Force headquarters, and on 4 June Kenney ordered a heavy bomber attack. But the B-24 crews noted that the enemy ships had changed course and were no longer heading for Biak, and the mediums were stood down – and a tragedy was in the making.

Believing that the Biak invasion had been abandoned, Kenney released his bombers for support sorties against Palau, while Adm Nimitz attacked the Marianas. Leaving the 17th Squadron on Wakde, other units pulled back to Hollandia and elsewhere.

Meanwhile the Japanese landed troops on Sarong, loaded 600 men onto the destroyers *Shikinami*, *Uranami* and *Shigaure*, and at midnight on 7 June set course north – for Biak. Despite being again attacked by heavies, this force steamed on unscathed. On Wakde the 17th was counting the cost of an enemy air raid on the night of the 5th/6th: six B-25s had been damaged, which meant that for any mission that materialized in the next few days it could muster just ten Mitchells.

On the morning of 8 June the squadron CO, Maj William Tennille Jr, addressed his men. He outlined the attack plan, detailed the bomb load that each B-25 would carry, and the order in which they should be dropped. There were no questions – but everyone was aware that they were on their own. Ten strafer Mitchells against three destroyers: those odds were not good. On the credit side, the B-25s would have an escort in the shape of P-38s from the crack 432nd and 433rd Fighter Squadrons. The Lightning pilots watched the B-25s take off; they would catch up with them before they reached the target area. Tennille led his force off into a darkening sky, and by 09:30 they were on their way.

An hour later the weather over Biak had developed into a severe front, with layers of cumulus and rain that cut visibility down to the absolute minimum. Weaving over the Mitchells, the Lightning elements temporarily lost contact with each other; once they had rejoined they led the bombers back towards the ships that were located some 35 miles (56km) north of Cape Waios (False Cape), en route to and west of Biak by more than 150 miles (240km).

Biak is Attacked

The attack was on. Tennille divided his force into two-plane elements and led the first in a power dive on the destroyers, moving now at flank speed in battle formation. Pilots mistook the larger destroyers as cruisers, but all present knew they had a fight on their hands. Enemy fighters from the 23rd Air Flotilla appeared to occupy the P-38s.

Boring in, the B-25s were met with 3in and 5in shells as well as AA fire. One aircraft flew straight through a waterspout thrown up by a shell, seemed to shudder under the sudden drenching, but flew on. Pilots chose their targets, firewalled the throttles, and opened the bomb doors – they handled the bomb release as the strafers carried no bombardier. There was little time for any other action before the destroyers, their gunfire lighting them up like Christmas trees, were almost in range of the Mitchells' forward guns. Tennille and his wingman, Lt Howard C. Wood, snapped at a ship – which promptly shot away one of Wood's wings. It spun in, and all the crew perished. Then it was the CO's turn. His strafing fire touched the enemy 'tin can' about the same moment that Japanese rounds hit the charging B-25. On fire, Tennille stuck to his course – but the aircraft was doomed. Eye-witnesses saw the wheels flop down seconds before the fuselage was engulfed in flames. Passing over his target, the major's B-25 became a

torch, which slowly rolled before plunging into the waves.

Nobody could confirm if Tennille had dropped his bombs, but Lt Glenn Pruitt, piloting 'Dragon Myasz', made sure: he pickled the load after raking a ship with .50cal fire, kicking the rudders to spread the impact. A 500-pounder hit the destroyer's bow, closely followed by other bombs dropped by Lt Al Wolfram.

So close did Lt Wesley Strawn's 'Miss Cue' come to a destroyer that the bomb never had a chance to skip off the water as intended: it just ploughed straight into the steel-plated hull side – with seconds to spare, Strawn had managed to get a malfunctioning bomb release to work. No such last-minute good fortune attended Lt Ronald Machnikowski, who suffered a close flak hit that jammed his bomb doors tight shut: with a perfect target in front of him he could do nothing about it.

1st Lt Fred Rimmer flying 'Little Stinker' had a different problem: his navigator, 1st Lt Morris Oberhand, had a leg blown off as the aircraft made its attack. Rimmer had little choice but to complete his strafing run, and only when he had come off the target could someone attend to Oberhand, whose leg was pumping blood.

Japanese shells also reached 'The Straggler', with Capt Sumner G. Lind at the controls: a fatal burst tore off a wing and, again, an entire Mitchell crew was lost.

But the attack had not finished. Opening the throttle until the engines raced far past redline speed, 1st Lt Archie Trantham dropped to zero feet and ran in, strafing all the way, leading his wingman 1st Lt Robert A. Beck, skipper of 'Sacramento Belle'. Both B-25s bombed, and their destroyer target was observed to be in dire straits: the tail gunners in each crew saw it slip quickly beneath the waves. Glenn Pruitt also had the satisfaction of seeing his destroyer settle, well ablaze.

When the last of the mediums had completed their attacks there were only three Japanese destroyers visible to the departing crews. On the down side, only seven Mitchells were left to return. Aboard 'Little Stinker' the crew did what they could for Oberhand, but the loss of so much blood and the onset of severe shock made it unlikely that the navigator would be able to survive the ordeal. Rimmer did get safely back to Wakde, but Oberhand died later in hospital. Sixty men had flown the mission: seventeen had either gone into the sea or had returned with fatal injuries.

The 17th Squadron grieved for its dead – but their sacrifice had helped prevent the invasion of Wakde by sinking the *Harusame*. In fact this was the only IJN destroyer actually to go down, contrary to the claims. However, in no way did this compromise the suicidal bravery of the B-25 crews of the 'Wreckoneers'. For the 17th RS this was their worst day. But the squadron went on to turn in a fine combat record, with many of its B-25s chalking up over 100 missions. One of the most reliable was B-25D (42-97293) 'Mitch the Witch', which flew more than 190.

By mid-1944 B-25Js equipped the unit, but as was common in most other theatres, the older Mitchells soldiered on. Based progressively on Biak, Tacloban, Mindoro, Luzon and Ie Shima, the squadron was one of only a handful of Fifth Air Force reconnaissance units to operate B-25s in any numbers, and received both US and Philippine unit citations for its prowess in combat.

Mitchell night fighters

North American's famous medium bomber certainly proved itself to be highly adaptable within months of its combat debut. But few in the design office at Inglewood would ever have called the Mitchell a night fighter – and to be fair, the single unit that operated it in this role thought of it more as a night intruder. That unit, the 418th Night Fighter Squadron, experienced at first-hand this particular pre-war gap in the Air Corps inventory – namely a chronic lack of aircraft able to fly effective combat missions during the hours of darkness. The B-25 was never intended as a night fighter *per se*, but represented an expedient measure to make up the shortage of more suitable aircraft.

In 1944 the 418th found itself based at Hollandia in New Guinea with just a handful of P-70s and P-38s to patrol a vast expanse of ocean and islands: basically, there simply were not enough available aircraft. The position hardly improved when night intruder missions were begun, their intention to take advantage of weak Japanese opposition. Such attacks were considered valuable, not only to destroy enemy equipment, but because their very presence over Japanese lines maintained the psychological element of surprise. 'Round the clock' missions also kept the enemy awake and thereby served to reduce his combat effectiveness.

The 418th was the first AAF night fighter unit to get into combat in the Pacific, but the use of B-25Hs as intruders was limited to a few sorties only. As most such units soon realized, the potent P-61 Black Widow took time to reach the various war theatres, and in the meantime something else had to be used. The 418th's B-25s were obtained in an in-theatre trade for P-70s – and incidentally, they became the first aircraft to bear the squadron's diagonal bar and star tail marking, made famous by the P-61.

China

Of all the Allied combatant powers in World War II, the US was the most desirous of perpetuating a pro-Western China; Britain, with its Far Eastern ambitions focused on Burma, showed little enthusiasm outside a desire to see Japan, the 'common enemy', removed from all conquered territories, and the restoration of the pre-war status quo. Nationalist leader Chaing Kai Shek's pleas to have something modern to fight with after the Japanese had decimated his armed forces finally bore fruit, but not before a considerable amount of political argument had taken place in Washington.

The saga of the 'stop gap measure' in the form of the American Volunteer Group is well enough known – but the AVG lacked offensive capability in the form of bombers. On 3 June 1942, towards the end of the Flying Tigers' service, six B-25Cs of the 11th Bomb Squadron of the 341st Group flew to China from India, to become the first US bombers to be based in that country. En route the Japanese airfield at Lashio was

(Above right) The impressive scoreboard of B-25C 'Mitch the Witch' of the 17th Reconnaissance Squadron, which probably completed 200 missions before the war ended. Goodrich

(Above) One of the primary recipients of Lend-Lease Mitchells, the Nationalist Chinese Air Force operated all main combat models including the C/D, this example carrying the tail number B31388. Jarrett

bombed – but then things started to go wrong. After one crew successfully beat off an enemy fighter attack, three aircraft flew into cloud-shrouded mountains, and a fourth ran out of fuel.

Six more B-25s were despatched and these, which had some Tokyo raid veterans among their crews, formed a nucleus to begin offensive operations. Even so, some of the early sorties over Hankow's docks and warehouses in July were reported as being a shambles by escorting P-40 pilots, who observed bombs falling on the wrong targets due to poor navigation. Things improved, however, as the 11th got into its stride.

The Chinese Air Task Force

Meanwhile on 4 July the AVG was stood down, though the danger of a void being created in the air defence of China was prevented by the creation of a joint organization known as the Chinese Air Task Force. The activation of the Tenth Air Force that very same day brought a command structure to the military air component in China, the 23rd Fighter Group and the B-25s of the 11th Bomb Squadron coming under its control. The CATF, with Brig Gen Claire I. Chennault in command, was itself a sub-command of the Tenth Air Force.

This force, modest as it was, had to operate within severe restrictions; but using bases at Kunming, Hengyang and Kweilin, the B-25s were able to bomb such locations as Hankow, the Japanese airfield at Nachang, and Canton. Small numbers of bombers – and sometimes only one – thus maintained enough pressure on the enemy throughout the summer of 1942 to disrupt ground operations and the flow of supplies.

Col Caleb V. Haynes commanded the CATF bombers, and on 15 July he led four B-25Cs to the docks at Hankow, their bombs setting fire to many of the port buildings. Back at Hengyang the Mitchells were refuelling when the air-raid alert obliged them to make for the emergency airstrip at Lingling. But when they were about 30 miles (50km) from this base a P-40 pilot mistakenly shot down one of them, although the crew managed to bail out.

These small-scale raids on Japanese bases in China were well co-ordinated, the B-25s usually having a three-element escort of P-40s. En route to the target one flight of fighters would form a top cover, typically 3,000ft (900m) above the bombers, with a second flight 1,000ft (300m) below, and a

third flight out on each flank. Over the target one flight of fighters would stay with the Mitchells until their bomb doors closed, while the other two swept the area seeking out targets of opportunity.

By mid-July the bombers were in need of major overhaul, and they were stood down from operations late in the month until early August. As well as being serviced, some armament modifications were made to these early model B-25s, including the addition of a 'wobble' gun to provide some tail defence. More guns were added to the nose, and the heavy ventral turrets were removed to increase overall speed, the Bendix device sometimes being replaced by two flexible 0.3in machine guns. Extra destructive capability was provided in the form of six 40lb (18kg) fragmentation bombs. Carried in the back of each B-25, these were released from the camera hatch on a signal from the pilot.

At times the medium bomber strength in China could be boosted by aircraft of the 22nd Squadron, sister unit to the 11th BS in the 341st Group based in India. On 25 October a force of twelve aircraft, again led by Haynes, bombed Hong Kong. Staging through Kweilin, the mediums and their P-40 escort were greeted by flak, although this did not prevent them hitting the docks, warehouses and the Kowloon

ferry terminal. But Japanese fighters took retaliatory action, and one badly damaged B-25 eventually went down, miles clear of the target area. That night the B-25s made a second visit to Hong Kong, while others attacked Canton.

Small-scale raids continued until the end of November. On the 27th, ten B-25s again hit Canton, the P-40 escort becoming involved in a large-scale air battle, and claiming to have downed twenty-one enemy aircraft. B-25 crews bombed two sizable freighters, their gunners claiming two fighters plus four 'probables'. The Japanese occasionally struck back at US airfields, although they caused relatively little damage as the Chinese early warning network invariably provided a timely warning. And if friendly fighters could intercept, the enemy usually took casualties. Supplies still trickled through to China at a very modest rate, bomber operations having to be held until enough fuel and ammunition could be marshalled for a force of any size. Hand-refuelling was the order of the day, a lengthy, laborious task as every gallon of fuel had to be strained to guard against rust getting into the tanks. Things continued in much the same way throughout the winter of 1942–43, the weather being another major factor in reducing the scale of air combat operations.

Boosting the strength of the medium bomber force in China were the B-25s of the 341st Bomb Group. This early example from the 22nd Bomb Squadron has a typical weatherbeaten finish. USAF

The Chinese-American Composite Wing

When the Fourteenth Air Force was established in March 1943, the CATF was absorbed and Hap Arnold and Claire Chennault agreed on the creation of a Chinese-American Composite Wing built around an initial allocation of forty bombers (B-25s) and eighty fighters (P-40s and P-51s) under the terms of Lend-Lease to China.

Formally activated on 31 July 1943, the Americans attached to the CACW helped train Chinese crews while flying combat missions. Both Chinese and American pilots and crews manned the medium bombers. American pilots and crews drawn from the 402nd BG were posted to the 1st BG (Provisional) and 3rd FG (Prov), which in turn provided crews for the 1st, 2nd, 3rd and 4th Bomb Squadrons of the CACW. The number of Chinese in the CACW grew apace, to the point where they soon outnumbered their American allies; but all-Chinese aircrews were in the minority until after the war had ended. Language was one of the major barriers to full crew integration – although the Chinese crewmen, many of whom had been drafted into an air force with meagre resources and had consequently received only the minimum of

Congratulations, probably before a welcome return home from China for one of these officers who are in front of a CACW B-25J named 'The Brat'. Part of the Chinese Air Force three-digit numbering system for the B-25 can be seen. Crow

(Below) Rough airfields, terrible weather and the Japanese combined to bring down a substantial number of Chinese Mitchells. This B-25J, No. 714 of the CACW, was good only for cannibalization – but such mishaps were a godsend to spares-starved groundcrews. Crow

'Lovely Louise II', with her fine set of teeth, was a CACW B-25H aircraft, No. 606. Crow

B-25H 'Loster Cherry' was flown by William 'Birdhouse' Bergin of the 1st Bomb Squadron, CACW. Lambert

were ex-11th BS ships which had seen better days. In the meantime a trickle of B-25s had reached China, so the medium bomber element of the Wing was able to organize itself to the point where the 1st and 2nd Bomb Squadrons were officially combat ready. B-25C and D models were the first on strength, with H and J models following over a period of time, China having been allocated a total of 131 Mitchells under Lend-Lease. All these aircraft bore the nationalist Chinese Kuomingtang insignia in blue and white.

On 4 November 1943 the 2nd BS at Erh-tong near Kweilin flew the first CACW combat mission, a sea sweep to Swatow Harbour, in company with the Mitchells of the 11th Squadron. Borrowing aircraft from the 341st Group was to be a fairly routine occurrence to 'make up the numbers' on missions.

As the target area of the first mission implies, the primary duty of the CACW was to keep the Japanese from taking full advantage of their sea and land supply routes. But they were far from beaten, and a dangerous situation unfolded in early 1944 when a three-pronged offensive by the Imperial Army swept aside Chinese opposition and soon threatened Fourteenth Air Force bases. With the object of securing their supply routes from Indo-China, the Japanese largely succeeded. It was to combat this singular late-war enemy offensive that most of the final CACW bomber sorties were flown. Missions were often modest in scope, one- or two-ship affairs and often just within the maximum range of the B-25.

Operating conditions in China, including disruptive base moves to stay ahead of advancing enemy troops, meant that a normal mission schedule was impossible. It also became usual for the B-25s to be stood down for days on end, some monthly mission totals failing to reach double figures.

Larger scale medium bomber raids were possible, however, if the strength of other AAF bomb groups could be called upon. On 29 February 1944 the CACW's 1st and 2nd Squadrons, plus the 11th, attacked railyards at Yochow. This was the largest raid to date, twenty CACW B-25s participating along with B-24s of the 308th Group. After the heavies had dropped their loads, the mediums went in low to finish off anything left, the crews noting with some satisfaction that enemy fighters appeared reluctant to attack the low-flying B-25s.

The CACW crews found the 75mm cannon of the B-25H to be an ideal

training, were enthusiastic about flying combat missions in modern American bombers.

But as others who had preceded them had realized, the US airmen assigned to the CACW soon appreciated why the Fourteenth Air Force was known as the most neglected military formation in the AAF. All its fuel and supplies had to be flown over the Hump or brought by surface and river transport. Airfield facilities were one degree above non-existent, accommodation was in much the same category, the food was terrible, promotions were rare to the point of non-existent, and the weather was generally appalling. Under such conditions the Japanese air forces often represented the least of the problems.

CACW beginnings were typically humble: under the command of Col John A. Hilger, Doolittle's second-in-command on the Tokyo raid, the Wing was based in eastern China, its initial equipment being six B-25s, two of which were flyable. All of them

(Above) Claire Chennault (second from left), long-time champion of American military aid for China, fought a long, personal war with Washington and it was a relief for the general to visit combat groups and forget politics for a time. In this view he poses with members of a 22nd Squadron crew in China. USAF

weapon for train busting, a mission that the unit drew increasingly as Japanese supplies poured into China. The flow of troops and material could be stemmed in a number of ways: at source in the railway marshalling yards; by destruction en route; or by breaking rail lines at vulnerable points such as bridges over rivers, forcing traffic to be re-routed and, most importantly, delaying it. Frustratingly, the CACW B-25 crews found difficulty in duplicating the success of their Tenth AAF counterparts in Burma

CACW's inventory included several B-25Hs, some of which were camouflaged. Nearest the camera is No. 718, with the insignia of what is believed to be the 21st Bomb Squadron ahead of it. Crow

strafing and parafragging everything in sight. One pass and they were gone, leaving twenty Japanese aircraft destroyed and others the worse for wear.

Invader Detachment

In order to prevent the Imperial Army from using river bridges, particularly those spanning the Yellow River, the CACW formed the so-called Invader Detachment. In February 1944, four B-25Hs moved to a forward base at Hsian, which was closer to the river, the idea being to fly bridge- and track-busting missions in company with P-51s. Numerous combinations of bomb and cannon strike resulted in a degree of success against bridges (always difficult to put permanently out of action), although the enemy always seemed capable of effecting repairs frustratingly quickly by employing large numbers of local Chinese labourers.

On balance, however, Invader Detachment was deemed not to have been an outstanding success owing to the small number of B-25s involved, several losses, and the damage that most of the aircraft sustained. And the Yellow River was a significant distance away from Hsian, so such missions ate deeply into precious fuel stocks. In any event, the chances of successfully dropping bridge spans slimmed in relation to the number of guns the Japanese deployed to defend them.

In total the 1st BS flew 154 missions during its existence, and while at the end of the war it had several B-25Js armed with rockets plus the full strafing gunnery suite, the problems it faced persisted. Of these, the distances it had to fly to engage the enemy were probably the most challenging, as was the terrain, the weather and a general lack of supplies – although this situation improved marginally in 1945.

Having begun in 1937, the war in China dragged on until August 1945, with the Japanese Army saving some face, not to mention thousands of troops, by avoiding the kind of pitched battles with the Chinese that bled it white against American forces in the Pacific. But it had lost air superiority, and this was ultimately to cost it dear in terms of supplies, troops and shipping. As far as the AAF was concerned, the war in China simply petered out; whilst bridges, particularly those spanning the Yellow River, were useful to the Chinese armies. For them, another war had already begun, even before this one ended, a civil war on a scale that was to shake the world.

Another variation on increased B-25 armament is this C or D of the 22nd BS, with four machine guns spaced wider than usual. The streamer tells its own story. USAF

(Below) Chinese and American B-25s operated together during the war with Japan. When it was over the Chinese faced a civil war which doomed the Nationalist regime on the mainland. These B-25Js include B.31306 on the left. Jarrett

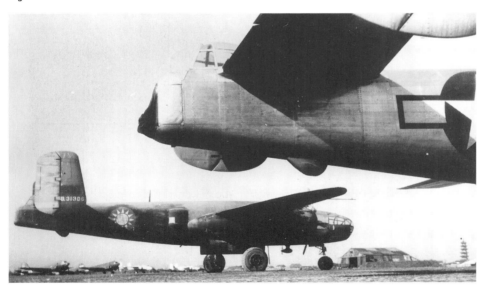

in using spike bombs against railways. Only a few missions were flown by the B-25s loaded with these munitions, and although there was little wrong with the delivery technique, it was suspected that the stocks of 'old' bombs supplied to the Fourteenth were unreliable. More than one frustrated crew obtained hits with delayed-action spike bombs, only to realize that they had not detonated even after the time delay had expired.

Fourteenth AAF medium bomber missions continued in much the same vein, all such sorties being flown by B-25s, with Liberators constituting the heavy element in China throughout the war. The AAF often held the initiative of surprise, and on 4 March Lt Col Joseph B. Wells, 11th BS CO, led a daring attack on Kuingshan aerodrome on Hainan Island. Achieving total surprise, his six B-25s cheekily charged straight down the runway, in line abreast,

CHAPTER FOURTEEN

Victory in Italy

With the progressive withdrawal of the Afrika Korps from its main combat areas in North Africa, and the loss of its air support when the Luftwaffe progressively abandoned its Mediterranean island bases, Italy had no option but to surrender in September 1943. Inevitably this brought the Allied hope that the war in southern Europe would be at an end; but this was not to be. Despite the fact that Hitler had always regarded the Middle East as a secondary theatre of war, he could see the threat posed to Austria and the Reich if all of Italy fell rapidly into Allied hands. He therefore decided to take over the country from his fatally weakened Fascist ally and continue the fight.

In allegiance Italians found themselves split between the Western Allies and their erstwhile German comrades in arms; but whatever their loyalty, they were all but powerless to stop the occupation of their country. Many of them knew that Italy's terrain could make even a major Allied campaign to secure the whole country very hard, particularly if it were defended by a determined adversary – and so it was to prove. Although the Desert Air Force and the Twelfth AAF were then powerful enough to deal with German forces in tactical battlefield support terms, Allied troops made painfully slow progress, hampered by the terrain as much as the enemy, C-in-C Albert Kesselring having established a number of fortified lines which effectively divided up the country to provide more easily defensible sectors.

Allied air units were hampered less and less by the Luftwaffe as their units were progressively pulled out of Italy, to leave the air defence of the country centred on a northerly enclave. There the fighters of the pro-Fascist Aeronautica Nazionale Republicana (ANR) posed the largest threat. But with the might of the Fifteenth Air Force ranging out to strike at industrial centres in Germany and Austria, the tactical bombing campaign in Italy concentrated on cutting off the enemy's vital supplies. For the Twelfth Air

Force medium bomber groups their toughest campaign was about to begin.

The 57th Bomb Wing eventually took the nickname 'Bridge Busters', and this was no fanciful title dreamed up by a publicity man: as time passed they perfected the exacting technique of destroying single-span bridges, which looked like thin strands of rope from 10,000ft (3,000m). The USAAF official history called the 310th, 321st and 340th Groups 'specialists' in this kind of aerial demolition, and cited figures to prove the point. In 1943 it was estimated that on average it had taken 196 tons of bombs to destroy a bridge, a figure that translated to sixty-three sorties, with each aircraft dropping 3,000lb (1,360kg) of bombs for one direct hit – but by the end of May 1944 these figures had dropped to one direct hit every twenty sorties, or 60 tons of bombs per bridge – three times better than before.

Ride of a Lifetime

On a cold, wet winter's day a young second lieutenant pilot in the 321st Group, based above Foggia during the miserable winter of 1943/44, was ordered to accompany General Robert Knapp, then 57th BW commander, as co-pilot on a run to Naples. The weather was windy, with snow and sleet, but it was a trip that was to prove to the sceptical lieutenant just how skilful was the general in his handling of a B-25.

When the lieutenant jumped aboard the B-25 it was already ticking over, the general eager to go. Occupying the right-hand seat, he watched as Knapp poured power to the left engine, whereupon the B-25 began slipping and sliding onto the taxiway, ploughing through the mud. Waiving a normal run-up due to the amount of mud under their wheels, Knapp blasted the B-25 onto the runway, ice forming on the windscreen as it picked up speed – this particular aircraft had no de-icer boots, which did nothing for the lieutenant's peace of mind. He had never

flown in such conditions. Was the pilot up to it, he wondered? Knapp appeared quite ancient to the twenty-three-year-old lieutenant, the general having served in World War I.

Pulling off when about a third of the runway had passed under his wheels, General Knapp's companion was horrified to see a big, blank nothing ahead and to the side: they had plunged straight into a snowstorm. The co-pilot, who also felt the B-25's airspeed to be just about marginal, could only sit there as the bomber climbed through the cloud layer to break into sunlight at 16,000ft (5,000m). Knapp flew along for a few minutes, above the mountains that separate Foggia from Naples before spotting what he was looking for – a literal hole in the clouds. Without warning he chopped the throttles to idle, banked sharp left, and shoved the nose down at what the co-pilot thought was a very steep angle. The B-25 spiralled down through the gap in the cloud, with the ground, amazingly, showing up at the bottom of it.

By this time the B-25's engine temperature gauges were falling fast, way 'out of the green'. Alerted to this fact, the pilot merely nodded. Picking up speed to 300mph (480km/h) with power still off, the Mitchell did a steep left roll and levelled off at around 300ft (90m). Knapp's goal was the 340th Group's base at Pompeii near the active volcano Mount Vesuvius – which was dead ahead. Flying now at 200mph (320km/h), the pilot called, 'Gear down'.

The lieutenant didn't think this at all wise: they were going too fast. 'Put the gear down, lieutenant!' came the firm reply. Orders are orders, and the youngster had little choice but to comply. The bomber shuddered and shook as its wheels dropped into the slipstream. On the downwind leg the IAS was 175mph (280km/h). 'Full flaps', said Knapp. Again the co-pilot was horrified, but without a word of protest he obeyed the order. The B-25 protested further at this indignity, its airspeed still falling. They were at 100ft (30m), and

The Mediterranean theatre produced many crack crews and veteran B-25s with impressive records of reliable service. 'Booger', a B-25C-1 (41-13175), was flown by Lt William N. McGee when this photo was taken after its forty-second mission, although several crews tended to fly individual B-25s. Three enemy aircraft and two ships sunk were part of the scoreboard. R.L. Ward

Knapp suddenly started to nod up and down – and almost instantaneously the lieutenant realized that this was because he was alternately 'reading' the runway and the instruments through bi-focal glasses!

As the B-25 crossed the runway threshold some 30ft (9m) up, it was still held in a bank. Then the 'old man' merely rolled out of the turn and almost simultaneously the lieutenant felt the tyres touch the runway in the smoothest landing he had ever experienced. He automatically opened the cowl flaps and raised the wing flaps, eyeing Robert Knapp with a new respect – there were few men he knew who could fly a B-25 like a Piper Cub. For him, the flight had been an unforgettable tribute to man and machine.

Winter/Spring Offensives

With the winter weather still doing its worst down in 'sunny Italy', the 57th Wing was ordered to begin Operation *Strangle*: this was aimed at stopping the flow of enemy supplies into central and northern Italy from Austria, as its name aptly implied. It entailed numerous medium-altitude bomb-hauling missions, to knock out road and rail bridges, viaducts and tunnels, and to create as many breaks in rail tracks and roads as possible. It would have been a long campaign even if all the targets had required just one visit, but the Germans became so highly skilled at repair, and at skirting around damaged bridges and roads, that repeat missions were frequently

necessary. And of course the enemy knew exactly where their transport links were most vulnerable to bombing, and increased flak defences accordingly. With the ANR facing numerous logistical and deployment problems in fielding enough fighters to counter Allied airpower over Italy, the flak arm gradually became the first line of defence for these vital targets.

An anonymous USAAF Mitchell of the 57th Bomb Wing over a target typical of the Mediterranean theatre where hundreds of rail, road and waterway crossings were bombed to deny the enemy supplies of all kinds. IWM

A Natural Disaster

On 15 March 1944 Col Willis F. Chapman took over the 340th Group, and from then on his B-25s were mainly engaged on close support and bridge-busting. At the time, air attacks were being made on the town of Cassino in an attempt to clear occupying German forces from within it: the town was dominated by Monastery Hill, and this stronghold was holding up the Allied advance. The 340th hit the monastery on 15 March. But two days later disaster from an unexpected quarter struck the group. To remain within range of their targets the medium bomber squadrons moved base as necessary, and by March all four constituent units of the 340th were based at Pompeii airfield. And then, on the night of the 17th/18th, Mount Vesuvius erupted. Pilots frantically donned padded suits and steel helmets in an attempt to fly the B-25s away, but they were forced to take cover instead.

The morning after, the scene was quite incredible – it was as though the group's aircraft had suffered the worst flak damage experienced by any unit in any conflict. But the holes in the 340th's B-25s were made by no human action: here, white-hot rocks and showers of molten lava had dented metal and ripped through flimsy fabric control surfaces with impunity. Also fine, volcanic grey ash coated every aircraft on the field, each one of which was up to its axles in the stuff. Worse, ash had penetrated every panel, intake and opening on most of the B-25s, so that all the eighty-nine aircraft on Pompeii airfield at the time were rendered virtually useless. Moreover, the Vesuvius bombardment did not die down completely for three days, the volcano continuing to rumble and spew out debris.

NAA's technical representative Jack Watson, another of the 'plane doctors', was on hand to take this immense job in hand. A makeshift road was built, and the B-25s were towed by tractors to an overhaul base where Watson helped the groundcrews salvage as many spare parts as possible. But there were few complete aircraft anywhere near ready to fly.

With the loss of its entire complement of B-25s, the 340th had little choice but to obtain new aircraft. When these arrived it moved to Cervione on Corsica, and met the mission schedule of attacks on targets on the Gustav Line.

Setback for the 340th Bomb Group

Things went much as planned until 13 May, when Col Chapman received another severe test of his leadership. In the early hours of the morning, the Luftwaffe carried out a devastating raid on the 340th Bomb Group. By the light of brilliant white flares, and scattering *Duppel* in order to hide their presence to Allied radar, Ju 88s, Do 217s (possibly from LG 1 and III./KG 100 respectively) and fighters bombed and strafed Cervione for an hour and a half, scattering SD-2 anti-personnel bombs throughout the various areas occupied by the group's squadrons.

The fuel dump received a direct hit, and men were cut down by the detonation of fragmentation bombs set to explode some 15ft (4.5m) above the ground. The 489th BS was hardest hit, with the highest num-

A great exponent of precision bombing by mediums, the 340th Bomb Group was overtaken by disaster three times (once in the US) but soldiered on, deploying its B-25Js (43-27487 of the 486th BS is shown) against hundreds of difficult targets as the Germans defended Italy to the last.

The second misfortune to strike the 340th was caused by Mt Vesuvius, which erupted and effectively grounded all B-25s on nearby Pompeii airfield. The fallout appeared to have given each Mitchell a strange new colour scheme as volcanic ash had coated them all, including this J model of the 489th Bomb Squadron. Crow

ber of personnel casualties, fifteen being killed and ninety-two injured. Only about fifteen B-25s completely escaped the carnage. Eight Mitchells were destroyed, and so many others were punctured by fragments that they were pronounced unfit to fly without major overhaul. Thus for the second time in less than two months, the 340th had been all but wiped out.

There were many questions: did a radio broadcast by 'Axis Sally' warn the group before the raid, as the rumour mill suggested? How and why was the 340th singled out? Why did Allied AA batteries fail to shoot down any of the raiders? How had an earlier air attack on the nearby RAF airfield at Poretta not served as a warning? There were few definite answers.

Spring/Summer Action

The 340th had no choice but to obtain more B-25s and get back into action as soon as possible – that alone would prove to the Germans that their raid had failed to remove the group from combat if, as was suggested, the Luftwaffe had tried to destroy a unit renowned for its bombing accuracy. By a small miracle the 340th managed to mount a mission in the afternoon of the 13th, sending eighteen B-25s to bomb a railway tunnel at Itri in northern Italy. The next day, using aircraft borrowed from the 310th and 321st Groups, plus several new arrivals, it flew the next mission as briefed, attacking various points on the rail network north-northwest of Rome.

Some considered that the enemy air raid held a hidden bonus: Marshall LaRue, a gunner in the 486th Squadron, welcomed the arrival of the replacement aircraft, and his comments regarding their revised armament configuration show why:

We were endowed with beautiful, new B-25Js; silvery, shiny and sleek as a Las Vegas showgirl.

[They] were a vast improvement over the old open-tailed models and [were] enhanced with a first class, gunner's dream. That little cubicle on the south end comprised an adjustable bike seat, a heated suit receptacle and control and two chattering Bell-turret controlled 'fifty' calibers. Truly a gunner's delight!

In the early days the 340th would apply camouflage paint to newly delivered B-25Js in natural metal finish; it was then discovered that painting compromised air speed, so they dropped the practice in order to (marginally) improve performance. After the German air raid, however, they repainted new aircraft immediately they were received, though only the upper surfaces were treated, the side and lower areas being left in NMF.

June: The Worst Mission

All groups routinely suffered damage from the attention of German flak, and 22 June proved a bad day for the 310th BG, in fact the worst of the war in terms of aircraft lost. Four missions were flown, and all of them drew accurate flak. The first was a three-ship 'nickeling' or leaflet raid on German troops, which drew no crew casualties although the enemy gunners put holes in several of the B-25s. Most participants felt these sorties to be a complete waste of time as they carried similar risks to combat missions, but with little to hit back with.

The next three missions for the 310th were scheduled unusually late in the day, which meant that any aircraft that was delayed would have to land at about 20:00hr, when it was virtually dark. All raids involved eighteen B-25s from all four squadrons.

The first target was the northern bridge at Vernio, and involved twelve aircraft from the 380th Squadron and six from the 379th. All carried 500lb bombs, and the time over target was approximately 1hr 40min flying time from base. Take-off and form-up was a well practised routine, the group having done this umpteen times before.

Hardly had the Vernio mission departed before twelve aircraft of the 428th Squadron were lifting off, bound for Leghorn Harbour

A pair of B-25Js of the 445th BS, 321st Group pull off their Italian target in 1944 with Pete Webb piloting No. 13 and John Doe No. 09. When the 12th left the MTO, similar large tail numbers were adopted by the group, which replaced its earlier Roman numeral identification system. Lambert

and the enemy shipping reported there. Three aircraft from the 380th and 381st Squadrons completed this force, which would fly for about 200 miles (320km) to hit a strategically important viaduct. In the event the 380th-led force was knocked about by the flak but there were no crew

scattered bunches, red flares arcing across the sky to warn of wounded men aboard. Flak near Florence, Castelfirentine, Volterra and Castiglioncello, as well as round the target, had chewed these aircraft to pieces; one B-25 had been hit over Florence and all crewmen had bailed out, while others

been damaged. Three were total losses. However, it later appeared that this bad luck was all compressed into one day, as the next seven missions flown by the 310th carried the report 'No flak, no fighters'. The men could hardly believe it.

Operation Mallory Major

On 11 July 1944 the Twelfth Air Force medium bombers were briefed for Operation *Mallory Major*, aimed at destroying all twenty-three of the bridges over the Po River; thirteen of these were assigned to the B-25s of the 57th Wing, and ten to the B-26s of the 42nd. All spans lay largely between Turin in the west and the Adriatic to the east, with Florence and Genoa to the south. Eleven were permanent structures, the other twelve consisting of pontoons, carrying both single- and double-track rail lines for electric or steam traffic – although these details really made little difference to the US aircrews, who aimed to hit them all in a concentrated campaign starting on the 12th and lasting until the 27th. The campaign did much to isolate the German Army in northern Italy though, as usual, repairs were often effected surprisingly quickly, necessitating repeat raids to keep lines blocked and bridges permanently down.

Shipping Targets

As a small break in the bridge-busting routine, the 321st drew a special shipping target on 18 August: thirty-six crews went to Toulon on the unit's 299th mission to sink a warship that had already been sunk. This was the 26,500 ton French Navy battleship *Strasbourg*, scuttled in November 1942 but later salvaged by the Italians. In mid-1944 she was being used to shell the Allied invasion beaches in the south of France following Operation *Dragoon*. Toulon was very well defended by flak, and the initial reaction by headquarters was that this was a job for heavier bombers. But the B-25s flew the mission, led by Capt Robert H. Neumann, and they silenced the battleship and a cruiser moored behind her, despite flak bracketing the formation and causing some casualties and airframe damage. There were no aircraft losses.

Grisly scenes like this occasionally greeted groundcrews on B-25 bases during the war. With a fighter on its tail, the Mitchell rear gunner had little chance if cannon shells found their mark first. A direct flak hit also created this kind of mess, from which some gunners managed to bail out. Further details of this 5 July 1944 incident are unknown. IWM

injuries, which everyone agreed was little short of a miracle. The bombs had burst accurately on rail tracks between a tunnel and the target viaduct.

Last back were the B-25 crews who had drawn Vernio as their target. They had the worst of it, and the Mitchells came back in

landed with engines out and hydraulics shot away. Three aircraft were also missing from the Leghorn Harbour group.

The day's operations resulted in much work for the sheet-metal specialist groundcrews, as thirty-eight of the fifty-seven B-25s involved in the raids had

On 23 September the 340th was also briefed for a shipping target, this time in La Spezia harbour, specifically the Italian cruiser *Taranto*. Allied intelligence had

(Above) Coming off an Italian target on 4 August 1944, a B-25J (43-27504) of the 488th Bomb Sqn, 340th BG shows the declining practice of applying nose art to late replacement aircraft. IWM

Using the Norden or Sperry sight, US bombardiers had a reliable aid to identifying their target prior to release point, many functions being automatic. These B-25Js were either 321st or 340th Group aircraft over a target in Italy. USAF

been informed that the Germans intended to tow the ship to the harbour entrance and sink her as a blockship. Harbours likely to be used by Allied forces in the future were not heavily bombed if this was avoidable, so that the time taken to clear up would be kept to a minimum. Consequently, the B-25 crews were briefed to sink the *Taranto* in her present position, away from the entrance, before she could be moved. The 340th sent off twenty-four aircraft from Corsica: without an escort the Mitchells stormed the flak in tight formation, the first three boxes smothering the *Taranto* with bombs, leaving the fourth box with little to do. As anticipated, the cruiser settled and remained where she was until the Allies took the port. Thanks to the bombing accuracy of one of the crack Twelfth Air Force B-25 groups, there was far less clearance work to do when La Spezia was in Allied hands.

Autumn/Winter 1944

Late October was a frustrating time for the 319th Group. For eight days, from the 23rd to the 30th, there had been no scheduled missions due mainly to heavy rain. Brighter weather on the 28th had not changed the situation – or the rumours. And then on the 31st the confirmation came: on the following day the group would cease to be a Marauder outfit and would be equipped with the B-25.

In the view of some fiercely loyal B-26 crews, the only good thing the men could perceive about that decision was that missions were cancelled until 4 November, when four were put on the board. In the meantime, enough Mitchells had arrived in time for an eighteen-ship mission to be flown to the Piazzola rail bridge. The eastern approach of the Montebello bridge was smothered by bombs from sixteen Mitchells, while another eighteen crews drew the Ponte S. Pietro Bergumo rail bridge. On the latter raid all the bombs fell 'long' and missed the spans. However, better luck attended the seventeen bombardiers who aimed at the Orio Litta bridge, as an 'excellent' concentration was observed and two spans went down. Another eighteen missions, mostly to railway bridges, were flown up to 11 November before the 319th was stood down for a day.

Weather intervened again to reduce the effort the 319th could put in, but the missions of the rest of November and December helped to show that the B-25 was not the inferior aircraft the Marauder men had believed – not that that fact reduced their affection to the Martin bomber!

On 10 November the 319th was attacked by enemy fighters for the first time since becoming a B-25 outfit, and one B-25J was shot down as the group pulled off the bridge target at San Michele. Nevertheless, gunners in other ships claimed five Bf 109s.

The 319th was sending out formations of twenty-four B-25s on the late-year missions,

Like its sister B-25 units, the 12th Group moved to Sicily, then Italy to follow the war. Probably photographed while the group was based at Foggia, these Mitchells are from the 434th BS. via NAA

Last to fly B-25s in the MTO, the ex-Marauder-equipped 319th Group flew Mitchells for a few months before taking Invaders to the Pacific. Wearing its blue group tail marking and white battle number, a 438th BS B-25J drops its load during a mission during the short period in late 1944 that the unit flew Mitchells. H. Oyster

but the winter weather sometimes prevented a clear view of the targets, and this resulted in some indifferent bombing returns. On clear days the bombing was often very accurate. The 319th crews were not alone in experiencing such a variable pattern of results during this period of changeable conditions; and of course occasionally enemy defences also dictated the accuracy of bombing. Finally by September 1944 the overcast weather got so bad over Italy that MATAF set up two Loran stations in an effort to beat it and so improve bombing accuracy.

On 10 December the 310th flew the first Shoran medium bombing mission to Fidenza railway bridge. Shoran, alias AN/APS-3, functioned on a similar principle to Oboe in that equipment in the aircraft transmitted a constant stream of impulses to two ground stations. These retransmitted the signals back to the aircraft's radar, which was linked to a computer to calculate altitude, drift and distance, and provided a highly accurate fix for precision bombing through cloud. Four Shoran-equipped aircraft led four boxes of standard B-25s against the rail bridge, but this initial mission yielded disappointing results due mainly to altitude errors and a poor signal from one of the two ground stations used. Nevertheless the bomb pattern was excellent and the mistakes were soon corrected. On 14 December the group cut four spans of a rail bridge at Parma/West, and on the 15th the B-25s hit an ammunition dump at Bologna through 10/10 cloud, helping to prove the operational value of Shoran for medium bombers.

Those 319th Group aircrew who had never really come to terms with the B-25 didn't have long to wait before another change was implemented: on 31 December it was announced that they were heading home to convert to A-26s. Mission No. 493, the third attempted that day (the other two having been scrubbed due to bad weather), ensured that the 319th went out in typical style. Eighteen B-25Js released their loads over the Piazzola bridge and obtained excellent coverage, with no enemy opposition. All aircraft returned safely.

Finale in 1945

For an aircraft type to be considered an all-round success in combat it had ideally to demonstrate that it could still return to base even when it had sustained a considerable amount of battle damage. Numerous B-25s passed this stringent test, and the 340th BG had one such 'flying wreck' incident on 2 February 1945 when Lt W. B. Pelton flew only his fourth mission as a pilot. But that amount of experience, plus nineteen sorties as a B-25 co-pilot, proved enough for him to bring back slightly less of the aircraft than he took off with.

The target was a rail fill along the Adige River south of the Brenner, and on reaching it, Pelton made two bomb runs to check the wind, which was gusting at up to 60mph (100km/h) that day. With great difficulty in the teeth of well alerted flak, the target was finally lined up, and on the third attempt the aircraft released its load. The flak had begun on Pelton's second run-in, and as he turned off the target at 10,000ft (3,000m), another B-25 collided with him, probably the result of a freak wind gust. One of the other Mitchell's propellers tore into the tail of his machine before spinning down. Pelton found the B-25 hard to handle as he levelled off at 8,000ft (2,500m) and called for a damage check. Asking what was left of the rear of the bomber, one man called over the intercom: 'Nothing'.

This sobering confirmation prompted Pelton to coax the aircraft up to 13,000ft (4,000m) so that the crew could bail out: but nobody wanted to jump. Pelton therefore pointed the B-25 towards home, taking a route that avoided the worst of the known flak batteries. He was helped in the difficult job of holding the crippled B-25 steady by co-pilot F/O H.K. Shackelford, the two pilots working out a system of signals to co-ordinate their efforts. With the comfort of a fighter escort, the B-25 limped along until the group's base at Alesan came into view. With both pilots working the controls, the landing was the most difficult – at any moment they felt they would lose it. But the B-25 touched down on all three wheels, stayed down and ran true. Few onlookers had seen a better landing. 'I think that God was really the co-pilot,' said Shackelford.

When the crew looked at the tail they saw that the starboard vertical stabilizer was completely missing, as was most of the elevator where the other B-25's propeller had cut through it like a giant circular saw. The most sobering aspect of the sortie was that the tail gunner, who had occupied his position during the bomb run, was also missing, although no bloodstains were found in the compartment.

During the week of 14 February the 310th Group completed its 800th sortie, another attack on one of the Brenner Pass rail bridges. Six crews had good cause to remember the occasion. This was just one of the daily missions to the Brenner railway system, which extended for 147 miles (237km). It was, the AAF estimated, broken at some point by air attack every day in February 1945.

March

By March it had become increasingly clear that the German troops in Italy could not hold out much longer as the Twelfth AAF continued to pound their increasingly meagre lines of communication. Harassed constantly from the air, the Germans could pump flak shells into the sky at an incredible rate – but they knew that only a tiny proportion of the Allied bombers would be brought down. The rest would bomb and further decimate their supplies, their transport, and ultimately, their will to carry on a hopeless struggle.

Those same random shells brought down novice crews as well as those who were considered lucky, having survived a few-score missions. But it was a random shell that brought down Larry Kahl's 488th BS crew on 16 March while on their forty-eight mission, all aboard the B-25 being lost during a strike on a rail bridge at Brixlegg in Austria.

April

On the 16th a massive aerial bombardment was made on German positions facing Gen Mark Clark's Fifth Army. This shattering blow all but convinced Kesselring that his war had run its course as the Allied armies pushed relentlessly forward.

Finally on 29 April, it really was over in Italy, and all German forces remaining in the country surrendered on that day. Even so, as is the nature of many wars, not until most of their positions were overrun did the enemy concede defeat. Victory in Italy had proved once again that air superiority was the decisive factor. Given the difficult terrain and the at times painfully slow progress of the Allied armies, a lack of tactical air power could have been little short of disastrous. That airpower, provided in great measure by the bombers of the Twelfth Air Force, finally proved decisive.

CHAPTER FIFTEEN

Return to Japan

George Kenney's Papuan campaign had brought the Fifth Air Force a long way; climbing the New Guinea coastal 'step-ladder' via a dozen jungle airstrips, his combat groups had been instrumental in wearing down the Japanese to the point where any challenge to burgeoning US, Australian and New Zealand air superiority was, at best, extremely risky. A war of attrition on the ground had been all but won as the enemy's priorities were forced to shift, and to concentrate more on the security of the outer defence perimeter around the home islands. With all hope of further gains in New Guinea gone, their supplies cut off and regular reinforcements a thing of the past, isolated enemy units could only hold out, confident that Japan's war aims would eventually result in victory.

But from bases in northern New Guinea, Allied medium bombers could range out to such locations as the island of Biak and pose a significant threat to increasingly vital seaborne traffic.

Autumn/Winter 1944

October: Return to the Philippines

When the US invaded the Philippines in October, FEAF B-25s provided initial support with anti-shipping operations against warships and transports in the Sulu Sea during the last weeks of that month. With the vast air-sea battles raging off Samur and Leyte Gulf, medium bomber units awaited their turn to move to forward airfields, given their somewhat limited range over such large areas of ocean.

On 31 October, the 28th Composite Group sent four B-25s to attack a target in Japan proper, a cannery at Tomari Cape; but this mission resulted in an unexpected experience for one Mitchell crew: as had once happened to one of the Tokyo raiders in April 1942, they had to make a forced landing in Russia, and as before, the ever-suspicious Soviets interned the American flyers.

(Top) Pacific theatre armourers replenishing the eight-gun nose of a B-25J. The barrels provided a convenient rack for the ammunition track sections, which were clipped into place. J. Stanaway

(Above) When ammunition replenishment is complete, this B-25 will be ready for another mission. The unit is not positively identified, although the small tail number (right) may indicate the 341st BG. J. Stanaway

November/December

FEAF P-38s were based at Tacloban on Leyte from late October, while several of the 28th Group's B-25s hit Torishima Island and Hayakegawa in Japan during November 1944. Geographically speaking, these were the first B-25s over the Japanese home islands since April 1942, although the active areas of Kyushu counted more – hence the 41st Group's later, equally legitimate claim.

Post-invasion pounding of Japanese targets in the Philippines continued, and some eighteen months after Del Monte and other targets of opportunity in Mindanao had been bombed in the first wartime raids by B-25s, the mediums had returned to the islands. The Mitchells of 1944 were much more able to inflict grievous loss on the Japanese than they had been in 1942, and they were heavily escorted by potent fighters – a far cry from the sorry situation early in the Pacific war. B-25 attacks were repeated for several weeks.

On 9 November one flight of the Air Apaches attacked an enemy convoy carrying Imperial Army troops into Ormoc Bay, but despite dropping 1,000lb bombs on the transports, the US aircraft could not prevent the troops landing. However, the Japanese skippers had no desire to hang around, and important equipment remained aboard when the damaged freighters headed back into the open sea. There they became the target for thirty B-25s – the Sun Setters – the following morning, and three ships were sunk. On the down side, seven B-25s were shot down, making 10 November a disastrous day for the group.

On 20 November the Fifth Air Force established itself on Leyte, but it was to be mid-December before a reliable system of control could be created out of the chaos left behind by the Japanese. Driving the enemy out demanded concerted USAAF/USN/USMC air attacks on airfields, bridges, shipping and a range of targets of opportunity as demanded by the fluid tactical situation on the ground. Much able support was provided for further American amphibious landings: a greater part of this entailed the destruction of Japan's air power on the ground by heavies, mediums and fighter bombers.

By mid-December B-25s were ranging over Negros in the central Philippines on virtually a daily basis, and pressure on fast-dwindling enemy forces never slackened during a period when the myriad islands of the Philippines remained crammed with targets. The cream of Japanese Army and Navy air power was decimated in the Philippines, and many serviceable aircraft were simply abandoned where they stood as US ground forces advanced. Numerous aircraft could not be moved: these hulks bore witness to the deadly effect of parafrags and machine-gun rounds, and most airfields that US troops captured were liberally strewn with wrecks, mute testimony to the overwhelming superiority of US ground-attack aircraft.

Winter/Spring 1945

January

The rain of high explosive dropped on Japanese airfields hardly paused as the New Year came in, Fifth Bomber Command B-25s operating what amounted to a bombing and strafing shuttle service. On 7 January Kenney laid on a blitz of Clark Field that all but annihilated any enemy aircraft still capable of operating after previous visitations. Among the participants in this attack were forty B-25s of the 345th BG in company with A-20s, a force that claimed an estimated sixty enemy aircraft shattered by parafrags and bullets. A B-25 and four Havocs went down to AA fire.

With little left to fight with, the JNAF/JAAF commands on Leyte were abandoned on the 8th. The following day Allied ground forces swept ashore in a huge amphibious landing on Luzon, focusing on Lingayen Gulf. Recapturing airfields was a first priority for the ground troops for much of the remainder of January.

The protracted battle for the Philippines saw the medium bombers systematically destroying the ability of the Japanese to hold out in the face of a cripplingly high casualty rate and the loss of supplies and communications, factors which ultimately wrecked any cohesive defence. While the early struggle to retake the Philippines was a joint, tri-service US air operation, the Navy carrier aircraft gradually reduced the scope of their missions when the fighting moved into the interior as the troops fanned out across the islands. The limited range of naval aircraft was one factor, another being that air cover was needed for further US amphibious landings about to take place elsewhere in the Philippines. Marine close support and the Army's

heavy bombers, its mediums and fighters were more than capable of eliminating any hold the Japanese still had on the area.

On 17 January B-25s were over the railway links to the eastern side of the Philippine capital Manila, and for the remainder of January the pounding of airfields, bridges, shipping and port facilities remained the daily bill of fare for most of the Fifth Air Force. Weather now reduced the air effort possible on certain days, but the Japanese were generally unable to exploit any advantage this might have offered. On 23 January sixteen B-25s of the 345th Group, in company with A-20s of the 312th BG, carried out a mass strafing and bombing of Japanese positions around San Jose, San Nicholas and Floridablanca on Luzon.

The morning of 30 January saw B-25s of the 38th complete a seven-hour flight from Morotai to a new home base at Lingayen. An hour after the aircraft landed, an anti-shipping strike was ordered. Fortunately, with the group lacking many essential supplies and personnel who were still en route by sea, this raid was cancelled. But it was on again the next day, and the group duly attacked three destroyers 15 miles (24km) off the southern tip of Formosa: one was sunk and the other two were damaged. Later it was confirmed that the ships had been in the process of evacuating high-ranking officers and other key personnel from the Philippines.

February

The medium bomber missions of early February followed much the same pattern of operations for Fifth Bomber Command as had January; thus B-25s supported the US 6th Army on Luzon using guns, bombs and napalm, the low-level attacks pioneered by Havocs and Mitchells in 1942 continuing to yield results.

On 1 February the 38th Group's 405th and 822nd Squadrons responded to a call by the 6th Army, and strafed and parafragged the village of Umigan on Luzon, which the enemy had fortified well enough to hold up the advance. Using an airstrip at Mangaldan just 27 miles (43km) away, the Green Dragons and Black Panthers took off at 09:38 and checked in with a ground station code-named *Cider* to await instructions. The Mitchell crews watched fighter bombers take the first crack at the target, and when the smoke from these bombs cleared it was their turn. Splitting into two- and three-ship elements with a 20sec interval between each, the Mitchells attacked, smothering the village with parafrags and thoroughly shooting the place up. On the first pass a Green Dragon was hit by flak and shot down; on the second another B-25 was damaged when the parachute of one of the deadly little frag bombs caught in the bomb-bay, swung upwards against the fuselage, and exploded, killing the radio-operator/gunner. The pilot firewalled the throttles to get his aircraft out of the target area and back to Lingayen as fast as possible. The rest of the force circled and watched friendly troops move into Umigan. *Cider* control passed a 'well done'.

Parafrags cascading down over Clark Field as a 13th AF B-25 attack devastates the old US base near Manila on 3 February 1945. IWM

(Below) **By 1945, veteran B-25s of the 38th Bomb Group had well over 100 missions to their credit. 'Tokio Sleeper' was a C model (41-12905) which had completed 135 by February that year, its score including nine enemy fighters and three ships damaged.** F.F. Smith

To deal with major targets, Kenney's commanders would carefully plan and execute a triple punch: this involved B-24s opening an attack with high-altitude bombing, the mediums following up with more bombing and strafing, while the fighters carried out their dual role of escort and ground attack. This pattern was repeated many times with outstanding success. With so large a land mass to contend with, the USAAF was faced with a plethora of Japanese targets; the destruction or neutralization of these would eventually add up to utter defeat – but it was clearly going to take many sorties yet.

On 15 February the 345th Group moved its B-25s from Leyte into San Marcelino on the neighbouring island of Luzon. Fighting centred round Corregidor during February; on the 18th, Fifth BC initiated what it called a 'rolling air barrage', with forty-eight B-25s and sixty fighters supporting an infantry drive to finally clear the enemy from Bataan.

On 25 February Mitchells of the Thirteenth AAF's 42nd BG attacked Jolo-Zetterfield aerodrome, Fort Stotsenburg and other areas on Luzon. In the final phase of enemy occupation, the nature of the war in the Philippines changed as regular ground forces were able to gradually hand over a proportion of the fighting to Filipino guerrillas, whose numbers swelled as the Japanese were pushed out of various areas. Air support to guerrillas became an integral part of Fifth Air Force operations – but otherwise little had changed as far as the aircrews were concerned.

March

American forces continued to reinforce the Philippines, and in March a landing took place at Lubang island in the south. The 42nd Group's B-25s supported this assault, and in preparation hit targets on Mindanao; these included the aerodrome at Jolo, already visited at an earlier date by the medium bomber crews. The 42nd bombed Jolo again on 3 March, the 38th adding its contribution by hitting another aerodrome, that at Batan-Bosco, after weather had diverted the B-25s from their primary targets on Formosa. The latter island remained an important Japanese base, but one that the US had decided not to invade. Consequently, eliminating the air bases from which enemy counter attacks – and especially kamikaze sorties – could be mounted, took on a new urgency.

Before US troops stormed ashore on Mindanao on 10 March, Japanese targets were thoroughly worked over by the air forces, to make it a relatively easy landing. Thirteenth Bomber Command worked with the Fifth to put the maximum possible

number of aircraft over the beach-head, and that same day the troops moved inland to take an early prize, that of Wolfe Field, a former USAAF base near Zamboanga City.

Targets in the Zamboanga area then became the focus for the 42nd BG's Mitchells, the 38th ranging out towards

Formosa to bomb the naval base and fuel stores located at Mako in the Pescadore Islands. However, bad weather during the period continued to hamper the mediums carrying out these attacks.

Panay, Cebu, Lagaspid and Pandanan were just some of the Philippine target

(Right) **So many Japanese ships were sunk or disabled by B-25 attack that this type of photo appeared in the AAF press on an almost daily basis. This attack on Wewak Harbour shows a B-25 climbing at full throttle as one of its bombs falls towards a freighter.** IWM

Dagau, New Guinea being blasted by Fifth Air Force to disable Kawasaki Ki-48 'Lily' and Nakajima Ki-49 'Helen' bombers as well as fighters. B-25s and A-20s effectively grounded many repairable enemy aircraft when their devastating sea blockade also prevented equipment being put ashore. IWM

areas for B-25s, as the spring of 1945 saw the fighting in the region drag on – as it would do until the last days of the war. Even so, the main US focus had shifted once more towards the last bastions of Japanese power in the central Pacific, the islands of Iwo Jima and Okinawa.

By continuing to hold on to many of its former conquested territories, the Japanese Army obliged the US to disperse its resources into numerous target areas. In terms of the medium bomber strength, by the spring of 1945 the AAF had to deploy B-25 squadrons in China, where an Allied victory was by no means a foregone conclusion, in Burma, in the Philippines, against Formosa and in the East Indies.

Further probes out to the fringes of Japan were made by B-25s on 26 March when the 28th Composite Group attempted to attack canneries in the Kurile Islands. On this occasion, enemy fighters thwarted the attack by two flights of Mitchells.

On the 27th, the 38th returned to Formosa with a group-strength attack on Kinsu, and two days later the Sun Setters sent sixteen B-25s to a power plant and oil refinery at Byoritsu. A further attack on the 30th was more ambitious, the 38th's crews bombing various barracks, sugar refineries and railways. On the down side, the Sun Setters lost seven B-25s during the month, with many more sustaining varying degrees of damage, some of which was heavy.

Spring/Summer 1945

April

In the Philippines on the very first day of this month, Fifth AF B-25s supported a US landing on Legaspi Point, Luzon, and then another on the Sulu Archipelago at Tawi Tawi. On the 2nd, attacks were made by B-25s on Cebu, Luzon and Negros, while the 38th returned to Formosa to bomb Kagi aerodrome. Broadening its combat area

(Above) On 29 March 1945 the Air Apaches found several Japanese warships off the Indo-China coast, and made short work of them – but not without cost. This combat camera view shows the tail gunner firing into one of the escort ships, while two other B-25s make their bombing runs. Both vessels went down. USAF

The Bonin Islands witnessed a return to Japan by B-25s on 29 April 1945, three years after the April 1942 Doolittle raid. The 41st Bomb Group took the honour of making the attack, aircraft of the 48th Squadron being seen here on Iwo Jima on 27 June 1945. USAF

Armourers check the guns as the 41st Group's B-25s prepare for the historic Kyushu mission on 29 April.
USAF

(Below) **While the guns are loaded, the armourers prepare their lethal 'calling cards' in the form of parafrag clusters for the B-25s to return to Japan.**
USAF

US aircraft were flying from Clark Field immediately the Japanese had been cleared out, and on 17 May the 38th Group's 823rd Squadron was preparing another B-25 mission from the base. Stanaway

into Indo-China, the 341st BG sent seventeen B-25s to attack bridges at Ninh Binh as well as targets in China, which had occupied the unit almost totally for many months. On the 6 April it was Formosa again for the 38th Group, the B-25s attacking Hokko. Nearer to Japan, the B-25 element of the 28th CG mounted an eight-ship napalm strike on radar stations at three locations in the Kuriles. Army 'ferret' B-24s had located a number of radars on the approaches to the home islands, and although the Japanese early warning and fighter direction system did not compare with that of the Germans in Europe, the US took the precaution of knocking them out. Anything that might impede the planned invasion of the country to finally end the war became a legitimate target.

Also on the 6th, the Air Apaches sent a two-dozen-strong hunting party over the waters of the Western Pacific, and whilst patrolling between Canton and Japan the B-25s found enemy warships. Smothering the ships with bombs and bullets, they sank the IJN escort ships 1 and 134, and the destroyer *Amatukaze* was disabled and beached. Two B-25s were lost.

On 8 April, bad weather caused a change in plans, and an unscheduled B-25

attack on the aerodrome at Chomosui, in the Pescadores. The 38th Group's Mitchells had been briefed for other targets, but as the weather denied the bombardiers good visual conditions at these, Chomosui became the main target, although railyards and urban areas on Formosa were also attacked.

Danger in China

The aerodromes of the Fourteenth Air Force and the Chinese American Composite Wing had been increasingly under threat by a Japanese offensive launched from Paoching; on the 10 April they therefore joined forces to beat it back.

On 13 April a large-scale air operation was launched over China. B-25 attacks were made on shipping in the South China Sea and Bakli Bay, plus points located in the towns of Liuchow and Tenghsien. Six B-25s went after a bridge near Ningming, while four were briefed for targets in the Puchi area; these enjoyed an escort of six P-51s. These and similar attacks not only deprived the enemy of thousands of tons of shipping, but brought CBI and POA medium bomber operations closer – the noose around Japan was reaching strangulation point.

Army Air Force's medium bombers continued to pound all the previous target areas throughout April, an offensive that was maintained with hardly a pause, for weeks on end. On the 27th, the Thirteenth BC extended its reach to Borneo, the 42nd attacking Tarakan Island. In the Philippines the Army medium bomber effort was boosted by 1st Marine Aircraft Wing PBJs, which flew support sorties for ground forces on Mindanao, areas of which were still contested by the Japanese Army. Fifth BC kept up the pressure against enemy targets on Formosa, the crews of the B-25s becoming increasingly familiar with the targets, the terrain and the defences.

Anti-shipping strikes ran as a firm thread through the assault on land targets, and Fifth BC's groups continued their efforts to totally blockade Japan's seaborne lifelines, now decimated by US air, surface and submarine attack. Locations such as Saigon in Indo-China were interspersed with the regular strikes on Formosa and the Philippines.

May

There was little respite for Japanese-held areas or the AAF aircrews, who were flying a spiralling number of sorties aimed at annihilating an enemy who usually refused to surrender territory irrespective of the odds so completely stacked against him. The 42nd BG expended an enormous amount of ordnance on targets on Tarakan Island following landings by Australian troops, who made good progress.

There was little obvious effect on Imperial troops at the news of the surrender of Japan's German ally on 8 May. On Luzon, a final, massive American effort was begun to clear the enemy out once and for all, an objective that was achieved by the 18th.

The blockade of Japan presented medium bomber crews with a range of industrial targets such as canning factories, alcohol distilleries, refineries and sugar mills: these were poorly protected and relatively easy to destroy from low or medium altitude; most of their contents were highly combustible, too. Japanese troops were also attacked as they abandoned areas that had become untenable.

On 20 May the 42nd BG's B-25s went after shipping targets around Balikpapan, which offered a little variety as compared to land objectives in and around the East Indies, repeatedly hit by the group during the month. While Thirteenth Bomber

Command worked over the Indies, the Fifth concentrated on the Philippines, its groups still finding worthwhile targets, primarily on Luzon and Formosa.

June

June 1945 looked much the same as April and May from the cockpit of a B-25, for the target list rarely seemed to get shorter despite the enormous effort of the preceding weeks. In the Philippines the Japanese Army was still holding on to areas of Luzon, and these were pounded much as before; Borneo and Formosa were also proving to be targets of long standing, the medium bombers returning time and again to achieve the maximum disruption, if not outright destruction, over the widest possible area. Few Japanese could have remained confident that their continued resistance could achieve anything of military significance. Allied air reconnaissance was omnipresent, and the almost inevitable bombing and strafing attacks that followed were little short of devastating. The Imperial army was being steadily decimated despite the fanatical bravery of rank and file troops, few of whom even contemplated the shame of surrender.

On 9 June six B-25s of the 28th Composite Group co-operated with US Navy aircraft and surface forces in a sweep of the Kurile Islands. In evading Imperial Navy fighters, one B-25 was shot down by touchy Russian AA gunners while straying over the Kamchatka Peninsula, and a second had to force-land in Soviet territory.

In action again on 10 June, the Crusaders provided a four-plane flight of B-25s for on-call air support as the Australians landed in Borneo at Brunei Bay. This service continued for a week, the 42nd also flying pre-briefed air support missions in the area of the invasion. Borneo was to occupy the group for several more days, the mediums being supplemented by heavy bombers, RAAF strike aircraft and fighter sorties.

The Crusaders then turned their attention to targets in the Balikpapan area. When the area came under Allied pre-invasion bombardment on 28 June, the B-25s based at Sanga Sanga in the Sulu Archipelago operated at the limit of their range. On 17 June the 28th Group sent B-25s against shipping around the Kuriles, while Fifth AF Mitchells continued to support the forces fighting on Luzon.

Summer 1945

July

The penultimate month of World War II began with an historic air attack on Japan, B-25s returning to the home islands for the first time since April 1942. Crews of the 41st Group sent thirty-three aircraft against Chiran aerodrome on Kyushu: escorted by F4Us, the attack was deemed a success, the 41st receiving considerable

Another 'Paper Doll', this time adorning an upgunned B-25G of the 42nd Bomb Group of the 13th Air Force, which fought its way from the Solomons to the Philippines. Crow

(Below) A pilot of the 42nd BG, nicknamed the Crusaders, prepares to touch down, probably at Morotai in a B-25J-25 (44-30551). Crow

publicity for an achievement that seemed to set the seal on Japan's defeat – if mediums and fighters could reach the urban centres, the invasion could not be far off. Concurrently with this B-25 raid, the Australian landings on Balikpapan were what turned out to be the last amphibious operation of the war.

With the conclusion of the Ryukus campaign, the USN could afford to deploy substantial forces in support of operations on Balikpapan while simultaneously completing the last pre-invasion air and sea offensive against Japan.

The 41st Bomb Group returned to Japan on 3 July when thirty-six aircraft in two flights again attacked Chiran aerodrome. This effort was complemented on the 5th when the group sent off twenty-five Mitchells to work over Omura aerodrome and targets in two adjacent towns. Meanwhile, the 341st remained active in Indo-China, the hard-flying Burma Bridge Busters attacking shipping in Haiphong Harbour. Further B-25 sorties were flown in the East Indies to maintain close support for the Australians on Balikpapan and on Luzon: here, enemy troop concentrations were hit on the 11th, although there were now fewer targets. Pockets of Japanese resistance remained, and these could not be ignored: such targets occupied Fifth BC between 13 and 16 July.

Having been joined in the Pacific by the A-26 Invader, Mitchell crews maintained pressure on the enemy, the focus increasingly turning towards China, the only remaining area where the Japanese were on the offensive. Shanghai aerodrome was attacked by a mixed B-25/A-26 force on 17 July while the 341st Group fielded one B-25 and a massive covering force of fighters to hit troops moving through the eastern and southern Chinese provinces as well as northern Indo-China. FEAF B-25s were meanwhile attacking Itu Aba Island.

Ports in China came under Mitchell attack on the 18th, the 341st participating in this and subsequent missions which extended into northern areas of Indo-China. These sorties were flown mainly to curtail enemy troop withdrawals, and to prevent the unpredictable Japanese from attempting any further local offensives. They were notable for their heavy fighter involvement, up to 100 aircraft not being uncommon on a single mission.

Despite hopes to the contrary, on 30 July the Japanese rejected the peace proposals outlined in the Potsdam ultimatum

of the 26th, and the war went on. That day B-25s and A-26s – numbering about sixty aircraft – attacked airfields on Kyushu and Honshu, the home islands having become an American hunting ground with little active defence to prevent scores of bomber and fighter sorties reaching their intended targets. The month rounded out with further bombing and strafing of industrial facilities formerly supporting a dying enemy war economy.

On 25 July the 38th Group's B-25s moved into Yontan airfield on Okinawa, and a raid took place on the 28th: this marked the combat debut of the 38th Group over Japan itself. Leaving some small cargo vessels a little the worse for wear, the B-25s flew inland to Sadohara on Kyushu, where they bombed and strafed railyards. Much the same type of attack was carried out by group aircraft the following day.

The last day of July was made noteworthy by what is believed to have been the first torpedo attack by B-25s during the war, when the 41st Bomb Group launched glide torpedoes against Japanese shipping in Sasebo Harbour, Kyushu. The group's

47th Squadron had pulled out of Makin in the Marshall Islands in November 1944, and returned to Hawaii to convert to B-25Js modified to drop the Mk 13 glide torpedo. The unit had trained for anti-shipping attacks, and had returned to the Pacific on 7 June 1945. Based on Okinawa and led by Maj Herb Gartin, the 47th launched its first raid from Kadena on 31 July, with fourteen B-25Js. Hazy conditions meant that the results obtained were inconclusive, despite the formation launching all the torpedoes. But as the Japanese vessels had been identified as aircraft carriers, they were considered important enough to try out the new weapon. The need for the B-25s to take evasive action in the face of flak negated positive confirmation of hits by twelve Mk 13s – but fires were observed and photographed.

August

Nine B-25Js made a second torpedo attack on shipping in Nagasaki Harbour on 1 August, but again the 47th BS pilots could

Adding to the B-25's already impressive firepower were eight underwing HVAR rockets introduced on final batches of B-25Js. NAA via N. Avery

not verify results due to poor visibility and the distance at which they had launched their weapons. Five Mk 13s were observed to be running 'straight and true' towards three freighters and seven other vessels. No other missions with the glide torpedo were flown, although crews were reportedly quite enthusiastic about using it. Reports were duly written and sent to Washington, where development of the Mk 13 had been given high priority.

The 41st Group returned to conventional bombing and strafing missions from Okinawa, a familiar pattern that changed little for other B-25 groups in the first days of August, as FEAF maintained its schedule of wide-ranging strikes on aerodromes, ports and factories in Japan. From 1–12 August the 38th Group made a succession of attacks on towns, bridges and a single factory on Kyushu. Meanwhile China continued to occupy the 341st Group, the B-25s of which flew against transportation targets at the same time as enemy forces, their extended supply lines increasingly vulnerable to air attack, withdrew from eastern and central areas of the country.

On 6 August the first atom bomb was dropped on Hiroshima – but still no positive moves towards surrender were made by the Japanese. Of more immediate concern to crews of the 38th Group that day was to find a worthwhile target in Beppu Bay. Led by the CO, Lt Col Edwin H. Hawes, the bomber men encountered poor visibility and no target to speak of – until someone peered intently at something large, heavily camouflaged by foliage and moored close-in to the coastline. There was no doubt that it was an aircraft carrier, and Hawes led his B-25s in at low level. Finding himself too far left of the ship, he banked sharply right, clearly opting for a broadside approach. A branch of a tree growing on the water's edge inadvertently helped. It momentarily threw the Mitchell onto an even keel and two 1,000lb bombs left the bay. Both slammed into the side of the carrier *Kaiyo* – but then, as Hawes clawed for altitude, the right wing of his aircraft caught the camouflage netting. The B-25 veered right and cartwheeled into the sea, taking the entire crew to their deaths.

Reconnaissance photos taken later that day showed the Japanese carrier with a dangerous list to starboard. Lt Col Vernon D. Torgerson took over the 38th on 9 August and led it until the end of the war. He was the group's twelfth commanding

officer since January 1942. The day after the atomic strike, FEAF again sent its B-25s to Japan, while Thirteenth Bomber Command mediums remained occupied with clearing the enemy from Luzon.

Such was the strength of the Army Air Forces assigned to the Pacific theatre that, weather permitting, a daily relay of aircraft could be maintained over the most important targets in Japan. The Navy, with occasional diversions away, also pounded targets in the home islands. Nothing short of a miracle could save Japan, and certainly not the 'Divine Wind' – although the Tokyo warlords planned an enormous mass suicide

B-25s making sure that several of the potentially excellent Mitsubishi Ki-46 'Dinah' reconnaissance aircraft do not fly again after an attack on their aerodrome. IWM

bloodbath immediately the first Allied troops set foot on Japanese soil. Most American airmen had no reason to assume that such an invasion would not come about, and the damage they did to Japan's military and industrial base in the last few weeks of the war made that prospect marginally safer. Numerous new military projects, including a number of advanced weapons such as jet fighters, were being rushed through by the Japanese Army and Navy in the face of appalling difficulties and huge disruption of output, supply and transportation.

Even a second atomic bomb on Nagasaki on 9 August failed to convince the Imperial leaders that Japan had no choice but to accept the inevitable: unconditional and immediate surrender. Conventional bombs continued to rain on both pre-briefed and opportunity targets, some of which, having been damaged in earlier raids, were finally stricken. One was the carrier *Kaiyo*, which rolled over and sank on the 10th.

An anti-shipping mission on 12 August brought the war to a close as far as the B-25s of the 41st Group were concerned, the Seventh Air Force having island-hopped

over a huge distance in a remarkably short time. Finally on 14 August it was over: apart from a few final skirmishes with enemy fighters that fell to Navy flyers, the Army Air Forces were stood down. FEAF ordered its final B-25 sorties of the war that day, when attacks were executed against warships located between Kyushu and Korea. When these crews landed, the North American B-25's outstanding contribution was crowned with the victory for which everyone had fought for so long.

CHAPTER SIXTEEN

Marine Mediums

The Marine Corps more or less inherited the B-25, along with a selection of other AAF bombers: the feeling was that as a relatively new force wishing to carve itself an independent role in the US armed forces, it could not afford to turn anything down. Despite having a number of very successful wartime campaigns behind it, the Corps was a young, small service and had yet to prove that its unique concept of close air support to Marine troops with wholly owned Marine airpower should henceforth be an integral part of the US military. New fighters such as the F4U Corsair, and bombers such as the Mitchell could, and would, help prove the case as the US prepared for the final drive on Japan across the Pacific.

In 1941, and again in 1942, requests were made for Army patrol bombers to be transferred to the US Navy, primarily for anti-submarine patrol. By August 1942 the acute need for such aircraft, which would release the AAF from AS duty, was partly met with the diversion of B-24s. The B-25 was among other twin-engined types offered, and although the Navy had no plans to deploy these, the USMC estimated that a patrol type with a useful range could find a role. The entire Navy allocation of 706 Mitchells was therefore diverted to the Corps.

As there was no USMC precedent for operating medium bombers, an air and groundcrew training organization had to be established from scratch, and be manned and ready for combat in the shortest possible time. Fifteen VMB or Marine Medium Bomber squadrons were planned, and on 10 November 1942 a training organization was established, as the Third Marine Aircraft Wing. Operational Training Squadron 8 was formed as part of 3rd MAW at Cherry Point, North Carolina, in February 1943.

First deliveries of Mitchells to the corps were fifty PBJ-1Cs, which were basically equivalent to the B-25C. All PBJ allocations were part of AAF production contracts rather than additional aircraft, and

Photographed during a training flight, PBJ-1C No. 24 shows the typically, plain markings of many Marine Mitchells.

(Below) To avoid casualties occurring when mediums were obliged to fly over ships they were attacking, the AAF developed early 'stand-off' weapons. B-25s of the 41st Group tried the Mk 13 glide torpedo/bomb (GB) without much success, although the crews were quite enthusiastic about these 'safer' weapons. USAF

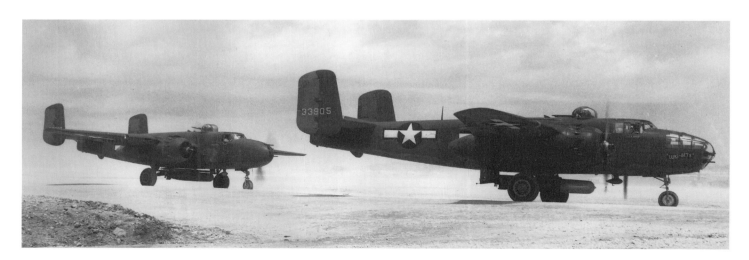

Close to, the Mk 13 GB shows itself to be a relatively crude assembly of flying surfaces attached to a 500lb bomb. By the time it was tested operationally, conventional ordnance had all but completed the job it was designed to improve upon. USAF

The 'hose nose' radome of the APS-3 radar faired into the nose of a Marine Corps PBJ-1C. Much favoured by crews for its 'line of sight' function, the radome still allowed standard equipment to be carried in the bombardier's compartment.
Smithsonian Institution

all examples were given a Bureau of Aeronautics serial number.

It was envisaged that the operational role of the PBJ would be more effective if crews were trained in radar detection of shipping, and, from the earliest examples delivered, all Marine Mitchells carried radar. The main operational set was the ASD (APS-3), developed and produced by Philco and Sperry. An X-band surface search type, intended for installing in smaller patrol and carrier aircraft, it required an 18in (457mm) paraboloidal scanner, and was capable of detecting a ship at 50 nautical miles' range, although in operation 30nm was considered as typical. Radar installation work was carried out at the Consolidated-Vultee Modification Center at Elizabeth, New Jersey.

Radar installations varied in Marine Mitchells, there being three different positions. In the PBJ-1C and D, the set was located in a radome aft of the bomb-bay in the well originally designed for the ventral turret, and was used on both training and operational aircraft. The second type was a nose installation, the scanner being set above the bombardier's position in a prominent fairing in PBJ-1C/Ds and Js. Late production PBJ-1Js were the third instance, having the radar scanner located in a starboard wing-tip radome.

As crew training commenced in June 1943, Marine workshops set about a series of modifications to the B-25C/D which would tailor the Mitchell to the corps' own brand of combat operations. Fixed armament of the B-25C/D was virtually doubled in the Marine equivalent; package guns were added on some machines, and the nose guns were increased to a maximum of five, plus two in the turret and a single such weapon on a flexible mount in the extreme tail. Early PBJs also featured the interim tail gunner's 'cockpit', which was similar to, but not exactly the same as the NAA-designed one fitted to the B-25H and J. Waist-gun positions were either (or in some cases, both) the convex, enclosed perspex type, or the small open hatches set further aft. The wing bomb-racks introduced on the B-25C were also utilized for some missions.

Despite their heavy armament, the Marines were not intending to duplicate the Fifth Air Force's Mitchell strafers. No factory-produced 'solid' gun noses are known to have been used on the Marine mediums, all PBJ-1s retaining the basic medium bomber configuration, even when

That the view over the nose was hardly impaired by the nose radome is evident in this view from the left-hand seat of BuAer 35029, one of the PBJs fitted with torpedo release gear. Smithsonian Institution

(Below) Electronic equipment of the 1940s required heavy duty wiring and a substantial power source, as this interior view of a PBJ-1 radar set clearly demonstrates. Smithsonian Institution

(Below right) Marine radio operators had the dual duty of monitoring radio transmissions and watching the 'scope of the APQ-3 set. Smithsonian Institution

nose radar was fitted and the glazed area was fully or partially painted over, although there were some exceptions to this general rule, particularly in the number of guns that were retained.

These and other modifications made the blue-and-white-painted Mitchells – the aircraft invariably conformed to USN directives on patrol plane paint finishes – used by the USMC distinctly different to any other B-25s. Later in the war the US Navy overall dark blue finish specified for Navy patrol bombers was adopted for some PBJs, particularly those of VMB-612.

Having started out with aircraft that carried a veritable arsenal of guns, the last operational Marine Corps PBJ-1Js had almost all their guns removed. This was certainly true of VMB-612 'Cram's Rams', which flew Mitchells with only a single tail gun, all other positions either being stripped of guns or utilized for other equipment. It was found that guns could be all but dispensed with on many PBJ night missions, which if nothing else offered a considerable saving in weight and an increased performance. Not even the sole remaining tail gun was much used, though just in case an enemy snooper got too close for comfort, a tube of metal slipped over the barrel of a 'fifty' made a convincing enough '20-mm cannon'. This ruse was confined to only a few PBJ-1Js, however.

Surprisingly perhaps, Marine PBJs did not use aerial torpedoes for anti-shipping strikes, although early PBJ-1Ds tested such

installations. This was undoubtedly because not only had the role changed from a daylight to a nocturnal one by the time the first units saw action, but also because by the spring of 1944 the mediums of the Fifth Air Force and Thirteenth Air Forces had sunk or blockaded much of the Japanese sea traffic capable of representing a threat to US operations in the South-West Pacific.

Finding a useful role for the PBJ squadrons had in fact posed a few problems in respect of the primary duty of close air support for Marine troops, because until those troops were in contact with the enemy and within range of airfields from which the Mitchells could fly, little direct support would be possible. But for some months during 1943 and into early 1944 the war in the Pacific was one largely of containment of the Japanese while the Navy geared up for an island-hopping campaign that would bring significant gains on the road to the Empire. Enemy garrisons that were not to be invaded nevertheless needed pounding to ensure that any potentially dangerous build-up of aircraft, ships or troops was prevented. The principle focus of attention in this respect was Rabaul on New Britain, but other pockets of Japanese troops remained in the South-West Pacific as the PBJ squadrons entered their final phase of training. And in general the enemy had not been unduly harassed during the hours of darkness, a situation that the Marine bombers were about to change.

Marine medium bomber training would take one year, on average. By early 1944, OTS-8 had thirty-six PBJs on strength as well as twenty-four SNB-1 Kansan twins to provide basic twin-engined flight experience. With a continual influx of cadets earmarked for PBJ air- and groundcrew training, Cherry Point became a little overcrowded, and on 6 April 1944, MAW-3 shipped out to Edenton, North Carolina. It was from there that VMB-413 and 423, the first PBJ squadrons, had trained before departure for the West Coast of the US and onwards to the Solomons.

Into Action

VMB-413, which took the nickname 'The Flying Nightmares', arrived on Espiritu Santo with thirteen PBJ-1Ds in January 1944, and carried out theatre indoctrination training until March. The squadron occupied Stirling Island in the Treasuries group as its main operating base, and as by then New Zealand forces had secured Green Island which lies midway between Buka and New Ireland, this became the forward base. Coming under the operational control of the Thirteenth Air Force, the PBJs flew their first mission on 14 March. This was a daylight run to Takabar Mission, on New Britain, to bomb a Japanese supply dump. The mission building was small – 500 × 150yd – and it was expected that a squadron new to combat might experience

From being very heavily armed when they first flew in combat, Marine PBJ-1s went to the other extreme late in the war, their armament often being reduced to one tail gun, HVAR rockets and bombs. This example also has a cartridge case collector, despite there being no visible nose guns. via NAA

more than a few near misses. But VMB-413's bombardiers did well to place eighty-two out of eighty-four bombs squarely on the target. This accuracy was no fluke, for the unit did as well on succeeding days, sorties to Takabar and Vunapope equalling the first raid in terms of precision bombing.

Then the target was Rabaul. The PBJ crews joined in a general assault by Fifth Air Force mediums, heavies, Navy dive bombers and fighters as well as RNZAF aircraft, which were succeeding in keeping the Japanese garrison contained. In addition, daylight missions to Kavieng and Bougainville completed the first phase of VMB-413's combat operations before the Marines began flying night sorties.

These 'heckling' missions became a continual irritation to the weary defenders of Rabaul, where there was AA but only limited fighter defence; however, for the American aircrews the weather, if

(Above) Ground- as well as aircrews trained hard to develop a worthwhile role for Marine medium bombers. Night heckling or nuisance raids on enemy targets was the initial role, although this changed. It is believed that 'MB' stood simply for 'Marine Bomber', with a number indicating the 'plane-in-squadron'. Smithsonian Institution

anything, was a more dangerous adversary. Two or three Mitchells were sent out on any night that the forecast indicated reasonable conditions, but it soon came as no surprise to the crews that the weathermen's predictions did not always turn out to be accurate. Storms of awesome intensity, with winds and driving rain, can develop with amazing rapidity over the Pacific, as a significant number of aircrews were to find to their cost.

On the night of 22/23 March VMB-413 lost two aircraft, those flown by Maj James K. Smith and Lt William D. Graul and their entire crews. Both aircraft were believed to have been overwhelmed by a violent storm, although in fact it was established later that Smith fell to the guns of four A6Ms of the 253rd Kokutai. These Japanese fighters were from 'Rabaul's Rebel Air Force', a group of hardy individuals who had been left behind when their comrades largely pulled out to reinforce Truk early in 1944. Acting as rearguard to ensure that Allied air attacks were not totally one-sided, these Navy pilots and mechanics succeeded in repairing a handful

Allied co-operation in the form of Royal New Zealand Air Force PV-1 Venturas and USMC PBJs brought much discomfort to the Japanese defenders of Rabaul. This formation took place in December 1944, the Venturas being from No.1 Sqn RNZAF, although the PBJ unit is unknown. RNZAF

of 'Zekes' and, against daunting odds, flying them in combat. Only long after the war was it revealed that the PBJ-1D flown by Maj 'Ken' Smith and all five members of his crew had been shot down – in fact nobody in VMB-413 was aware that Japanese single-seat fighters were based on Rabaul during the unit's entire time on Stirling Island. This was quite understandable, as the handful of Zekes only flew occasionally, and putting losses down entirely to weather-related causes was natural enough. Usually it was also grimly accurate – as high as 50 per cent of all PBJs that went down, in the view of Bob Millington of VMB-413.

Also operating from Rabaul was a pair of J1N1 Gekko night fighters that tangled inconclusively with the PBJs on two occasions. On 8 April a VMB-413 aircraft flown by Bob Millington was set up for a perfect turret shot at a Gekko, but the turret guns refused to fire. Thus passed this crew's only chance to shoot down an enemy aircraft.

Nightly excursions over enemy targets involved the PBJs carrying a typical bomb load of fourteen 100lb bombs in the fuselage bay and on the wing racks, plus 20lb anti-personnel bombs and magnesium flares. In addition, the crew took along as many Coke and beer bottles as they could, for it was well known that the whistle made by a falling bomb and a bottle was hard to distinguish. Keeping the enemy awake was the object of the exercise, although the Marines could not know that the Japanese garrison had largely retreated into secure underground bunkers.

Strafing also figured in the Marine curriculum, each PBJ-1D packing seven fixed nose guns plus two turret 'fifties' that could fire directly forwards. Attack altitudes varied, some targets requiring a 'maximum effort' of pattern bombing from height, while 'on the deck' skip bombing was also employed against shipping. Nocturnal submarine hunting got the crews' adrenalin pumping, although the radar more often than not failed to show any likely target. On 13 May however, Capt Ed Cornwall did make contact with I-176 north-east of Green Island and managed to damage it. The boat was finished off by surface vessels.

Spring/Summer Offensives 1944

In May, with VMB-413 resting at Espiritu, VMB-423 moved into the line and carried on a similar pattern of operations as pioneered by the Nightmares. The unit's first heckling mission was on 14/15 May, a 6½hr patrol over Rabaul that produced few spectacular results. Skirmishes with Rabaul's skeleton force of Zekes occurred from time to time, the interceptors often being identified as Oscars – which made a change, as throughout the Pacific war the Army fighter usually lost out to the Navy type in combat encounter reports! 'Zeros' were everywhere except over Rabaul, or so it seemed.

An inconclusive clash with the A6Ms took place on 9 June when Lt William J. Hopper's crew traded fire with two pilots who were still under training. Four passes were made by the fighters, culminating in a power dive from 3,000ft (900m) above the lone PBJ. Hopper timed his turn well to ruin the IJN pilots' deflection, whereupon they sped home. By this time Hopper had used plenty of ammunition, and so he, too, headed out of the area. No hits were taken by either side.

In July, VMB-413 moved up to Munda on New Georgia for its second tour. The squadron welcomed some new aircraft as it was becoming increasingly hard to ready six PBJs for certain missions. Operating with Allied air forces in daylight, the night belonged more or less exclusively to the Marine bombers, and wear and tear was heavy. In VMB-413's case the second tour lasted until 18 October 1944 when it moved to Emirau and came under a new command, MAG-16. Meanwhile Lt Col John Winston's VMB-423 carried the war to Rabaul, occasionally in company with RNZAF Venturas and Corsairs.

From 9 June, VMB-423, which later took the name 'Sea Horse Marines', also continued to bomb Japanese airfields and supply points on Kavieng and New Britain, while keeping shipping activity in Simpson Harbour under surveillance, and attacking when necessary. The unit also used Green Island as a staging base. The number of night missions tailed off in mid-1944 in favour of daylight medium bombing interspersed with skip bombing, mainly in the area from Kavieng to the southern tip of New Ireland.

Of all the losses suffered by units during the war, those felt the most acutely were the crews who simply disappeared without trace. This happened to VMB-432's 1st Lt Vernon R. Kistner and crew on 22 June; and two days later Capt Richard A. Edmonds and his crew of five failed to return from a heckling mission to Rabaul.

Unlike its sister unit, VMB-423 was not rotated out of the combat area after its first tour of duty, but stayed in-theatre, with crews being given R&R in Australia. No loss of mission effectiveness occurred, even with crews on leave, for by July VMB-433, the third PBJ squadron, had arrived on Green Island. For maximum-effort daylight missions, particularly against Rabaul, the Marine medium bombers were occasionally flown in company with RNZAF Lockheed Venturas; the American crews were also pleased to be given an escort of Corsairs, with New Zealanders at the controls.

VMB-433 moved back to Emirau in August to fly under MAG-61, by which time VMB-443 had arrived. Four PBJ squadrons represented a useful force, particularly for the difficult bad weather and night sorties for which they were the best equipped in the SWPA. News of the successful combat deployment of the PBJs filtered back to the training establishment in the US, enabling some shift of emphasis in the combat training for crews of VMB-611, 612 and 613, the last three units to reach the combat zone. All were commissioned on 1 October 1944.

New weapons for the PBJs included the 2.75in HVAR on underwing launchers, and the promise of the 11.75in Tiny Tim, the most potent aircraft rocket of the war. Anticipating action in the Philippines, the Marine medium bomber crews were frustrated to have to wait their turn until the Leathernecks were well established ashore. During a stopover in Hawaii in September, part of VMB-611's air and ground echelon innocently embarked on the freighter *Zoella Lykes* which would take them across the Pacific. In a saga akin to the '*Flying Dutchman*', the rusty old transport with its rogue skipper refused to land the Marines in the right place until January 1945, when they were finally reunited with their unit.

Philippines Close Support

By early 1945, direct support for Marine ground troops by the PBJ force in the Philippines was finally realized. Deploying F4U Corsairs, SBD Dauntlesses and PBJs, the advancing Leathernecks came to rely on the fact that Japanese strongpoints, transport and supply dumps could be knocked out from the air within a short time of their being identified, using guns, bombs and napalm.

One of VMB-612's PBJ-1Js converted to carry a pair of Tiny Tim rockets under the belly, seen during operations from Iwo Jima in 1945. US Navy

Help for the flying Marines engaged in the Philippine campaign came from an unexpected quarter on 10 August 1945: on that day a PBJ-1J of VMB-611 carried a passenger in the form of Lt Monoru Wada, a Japanese defector who had once held US citizenship. Deeply disillusioned with the war, Wada had not only surrendered but had offered to pin-point an area on Upian, a new target for the Marine bombers. In fact Wada did more: he guided the US bombs right onto the headquarters of his former unit! This was carried out by Wada using a hand microphone in the waist of a PBJ to guide the pilots in, and the bombing destroyed the position and killed Gen Harada, commanding the 100th Army Division.

To supplement the older PBJ-1s, the Marine bomber force received the PBJ-1J towards the end of the war. Many PBJ-1C/Ds soldiered on until the last days of hostilities in the Pacific, their crews being perfectly satisfied with its performance due to lighter all-up weight and the function of the radar. The early J models were similarly configured with the radar scanner housed in the familiar centreline 'hose nose'. North American meanwhile refined the sea-search radar set-up of the PBJ-1J, and moved the radome of the APS-3 set out to the right wing-tip. Being quite frugal with their aircraft, the corps did not replace the earlier model PBJs with this new version; in fact it was said that old hands preferred to use the more reliable centreline radar set, the wing-tip-mounted unit

exhibiting certain basic malfunctions that distorted the returns and made positive target identification that much more difficult.

For the entire Marine medium bomber force, shipping targets were increasingly scarce as Japan's navy and mercantile marine was sunk at an ever-increasing rate. Army and Navy aircraft were taking a relentless toll of enemy shipping, not only by direct attack, but by extensive mining. In addition, VMB-612 was issued with supplies of the 11.25in Tiny Tim aerial rocket, two of which could be carried externally under the belly of the PBJ-1J. However, the lack of enemy shipping saw the squadron armed with a lethal anti-shipping rocket all ready for use, but with few targets to use it against. For CO Jack Cramm it was a frustrating situation.

Operational deployment of Tiny Tim by the PBJ had been partially delayed by the loss of many rounds stowed aboard USS *Franklin* when the carrier was hit in a Japanese air attack on 19 March 1945. The big rockets added to the carnage aboard the ship when they 'cooked off' in the inferno created by the fires. A second conflagration, this time on Iwo, saw rocket motors and bodies going up in smoke when triggered by blast.

When the rockets were fitted to the PBJ-1Js, Cram and his pilots began an intensive operational training period, flying from Iwo Jima to prove that one Marine Mitchell and two Tiny Tims repre-

sented a lethal combination to any Japanese vessel large enough to warrant attack. But the problem was that not many sizable ships that justified the expending of large and expensive rounds were found on searches by VMB-612 crews. Cram himself flew the first Tiny Tim mission over the South China Sea on the night of 21/22 July, but found only a few fishing boats.

On 29 July PBJ-1Js equipped to use Tiny Tim moved to Chimu Field on Okinawa, these going operational from that base on 11 August. Cram's own crew went hunting that day but found nothing worthwhile. A rock sticking out of the sea off Iwo Jima had previously served as a practice target, and en route back to base Cram acted on the radar return and loosed off one round. Film of this practice run, plus the others, proved that Tiny Tim was quite a weapon, and there remained only one further test.

More activity followed on 14 August when three aircraft took off. A 200ft (60m) vessel was attacked with one Tiny Tim, the resulting explosion leading the crew to report an almost certain sinking. A second PBJ crew missed with its Tims, while the third one fired only its wing rockets.

Over Tsushima Strait that same night one of six patrolling PBJ-1Js found a 250ft (76m) enemy vessel and launched both Tims, though it perceived no visible results. Neither did a second crew, which missed with both missiles. A third crew inconclusively launched one Tim at a 350ft (107m) vessel and reported it as 'seriously damaged'. And that was that; and when these crews returned to Chimu after more than nine hours in the air, the celebrations to mark the end of the war had been going on for hours.

But for the general lack of suitable targets by the time it entered service, Tiny Tim would surely have found greater deployment; as things stood, only VMB-612 had time to use it in action, without much proof of its potential. The pioneering work of the Marine Mitchell crews in the use of the big rocket was followed up in the immediate postwar years with test launchings from Hellcats, Corsairs, Tigercats and several other types. Navy aircraft naturally had priority on a weapon developed for that service, and the PBJ-1H figured in further practice firings involving medium bombers over the range at Inyokern in Japan. What is believed to be the only other combat use of Tiny Tims (probably those originating from Navy stocks in Japan) took place in Korea when USAF F-51s, F-84s and Navy F4Us expended some against ground targets.

Carrier Retrospect

A final series of wartime tests of the PBJ recalled the April 1942 Tokyo raid, but with some 1945 additions, namely the capability for a Mitchell not only to take off from a carrier but to land on one as well. The test took place off Norfolk, Virginia, and involved a single PBJ-1H (BuAer 35277) and a P-51D, the object being to determine whether land-based 'non-naval' aircraft could be catapulted. By the last year of the war, hundreds of medium bombers and fighters had crossed the world's oceans as deck cargo, to be craned and barged ashore at their destinations. Numerous Army fighters had also been launched in the conventional way, and the Navy was curious to determine how practical it was to fly off twin-engined bombers to save docking time and port facilities – and indeed the degree of risk to the carrier if the area was contested.

In order to test the feasibility of launching large aircraft from carriers, NAA co-operated with the Navy in 1945 and ran a series of tests with a PBJ-1H and a P-51. The Marine Mitchell (BuAer 35277) was successfully landed on and launched from the USS *Shangri La*. NAA via N. Avery

(Below) From 'open storage' at NAS Clinton Oklahoma, hundreds of PBJs, including many trainers, were scrapped at the end of the war. A variety of US Navy-derived colour schemes may be discerned in this aerial view. National Archives

CHAPTER SEVENTEEN

Fat Cats and Warbirds

B-25 Transports

When NAA adapted the first production B-25 (40-2165) into a company transport for its executives, word soon got round that in this it was possible to travel across the USA faster than by the average airliner. Thus the company moved into the high-speed military transport business in a small way, filling a gap that existed at that time. Initially more special conversions were made for the top brass, Hap Arnold and Dwight Eisenhower for instance ordering their own personal Mitchell transports.

Arnold's first B-25 (40-2168) was modified in similar fashion to the company's 'Whiskey Express'. Completed in the summer of 1943, this aircraft remains airworthy today, having had a number of owners in the meantime, including Howard Hughes. A second B-25, a J-15 (44-28945), was modified for the AAF chief, and in February 1944 Eisenhower ordered a conversion of B-25J-1 (43-4030). He was most anxious that the work be completed by 1 June, and this caused some speculation over the date of D-Day in Europe. The conversion was completed in time and flown to England for 'Ike' to observe the invasion beaches.

When the first company transport B-25 crashed on 8 January 1945, NAA selected B-25J-25 (44-30047) as its replacement. First flown on 18 October, it lasted until 27 February 1946, when a disastrous fire broke out: as a result the aircraft crashed into the Pacific, killing all aboard including Joe Barton, one of NAA's most experienced B-25 test pilots.

The sixth and last of these conversions was the most lavish. Based on a B-25J-30 (44-30957 alias PBJ-1J BuAer 35848), this became the 'Executive Transport', a company bid to offer the aircraft to a dual military and civilian market. With a completely new nose 2ft (60cm) longer than other Mitchells, and widened to 70in (178cm), it had the pilots' seats moved forwards to make room for four seats ahead of the bomb-bay, with four in the aft com-

Army Air Forces commanding general H.H. 'Hap' Arnold had two personal B-25s, the first being the third example built, 40-2168. via NAA

partment. The centre fuselage bay accommodated a bunk bed and baggage stowage, and amongst the refinements was soundproofing, which made the interior quieter than any previous B-25.

The aircraft first flew on 15 February 1950, and on 1 March embarked on an east

coast sales tour. But on 25 March it broke up in a severe storm with the loss of seven company employees. This was the death knell of a promising project that might have at least secured NAA B-25 conversion contracts from the USAF for pilot and radar fire control trainers; in the event, these went

(Opposite page top) The B-25J transport built for Dwight D. Eisenhower being weighed at Inglewood in May 1944. Soon afterwards it was flown to England for use by the Supreme Allied Commander, although in the event he rarely used it. via NAA

(Opposite page bottom left) Typical of the interior of these well-equipped Mitchells was airliner–type seating, extra fuselage windows with curtains, and a comprehensive communications set-up. via NAA

(Opposite page bottom right) The degree of comfort built into Ike's B-25 was apparently greater than the NAA and Hap Arnold versions. It was sold through surplus aircraft sales after the war. via NAA

(Right) In the days when feeder liners were small, NAA saw the potential for possible commercial sales for an eight-seater transport based on the B-25. via NAA

(Left) An artist's impression of how the 'commercial' B-25 would have looked. via NAA

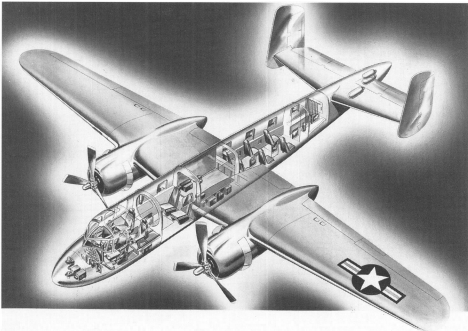

instead to Hayes Aircraft Co. and Hughes Aircraft, respectively.

During the war, numerous front-line combat units acquired the use of one or more B-25s to move supplies from depots to forward airfields. Invariably lacking proper transport aircraft for their own use, many units, particularly those flying nothing larger than fighters, acquired a medium bomber for the purpose. With non-essential military equipment removed, an aircraft such as the B-25 had an interior spacious enough for storage and crew intercommunication,

and was highly prized and invariably well utilized. In typical American style, these aircraft – usually based on operational airfields and maintained by line crews – often made unofficial flights to obtain such sought-after items as liquor, eggs, fruit and other hard-to-obtain foodstuffs and delicacies. As such they picked up the collective nickname of 'Fat Cats'.

That was only part of the story: so remote were some areas in which US combat units were based, particularly in China, that a shuttle service via a B-25 often made

the difference between effective combat missions and a poor showing, when aircraft might be grounded for want of a small replacement part.

These courier B-25s originated from various sources, particularly dumps where industrious groundcrews would rebuild one good machine from parts of numerous write-offs, 'hangar queens' or 'war wearies'; they also anticipated a very long postwar life for individual examples of North American's famous medium. Such second-line duty became very important to aircrews starved of the good things of life. 'Milk runs' by Mitchells naturally brought their own hazards and 'war stories', as one crew operating in North Africa found out: enthusiastically filling up the empty B-25 rear fuselage compartment with supplies, including many eggs, they neglected to allow for the centre of gravity – a few more cartons of eggs put the aircraft heavily back on its tail bumper, with the inevitable result to the cargo!

The 'utility' qualities of the B-25 led it to become a common sight on US air bases around the world in the waning days of the USAAF, the type maintaining a small but important place in the independent United States Air Force, when it was officially established on 26 July 1947. Even in the early jet age, generals, staff officers, air cadets and a host of essential items still

accepted under USAAF contracts; they were instead considered as the contract termination inventory. The 9,889th and last B-25 accepted by the Army was a J-35 (45-8832). The seven suffix letters that identified wartime B-25s were extended in the immediate postwar years, although the J suffix was retained for more than 600 aircraft, which became variously TB-25Js, CB-25Js and VB-25Js. Hughes Tool Co. was responsible for converting 117 TB-25Ks and forty TB-25Ms, primarily to accommodate equipment to operate the company's E-1 and E-5 radar fire-control systems intended for jet interceptors. In addition, Hayes Aircraft Corp converted ninety B-25Js into TB-25Ls, and forty-seven into TB-25Ns for pilot training.

During its wartime service the B-25 designation had been revised for various reasons, that of AT-24A being used to identify training aeroplanes, initially sixty stripped-down conversions of the B-25D. Subsequent conversions to the training role brought about the AT-24B (B-25G), the AT-24C (B-25C) and the AT-24D (B-25J). This system was later changed to a more logical one whereby the prefix and suffix letters were tacked on to a recognizable type number, as 'TB-25J' and so on – probably much to the relief of AAF clerks, whose business it was to keep track of training aircraft inventories. Not only were hundreds of B-24 Liberators being used as trainers, but an A-25 could also have appeared 'on the books' as the AAF equivalent of the Curtiss SB2C Helldiver during the Mitchell's service career!

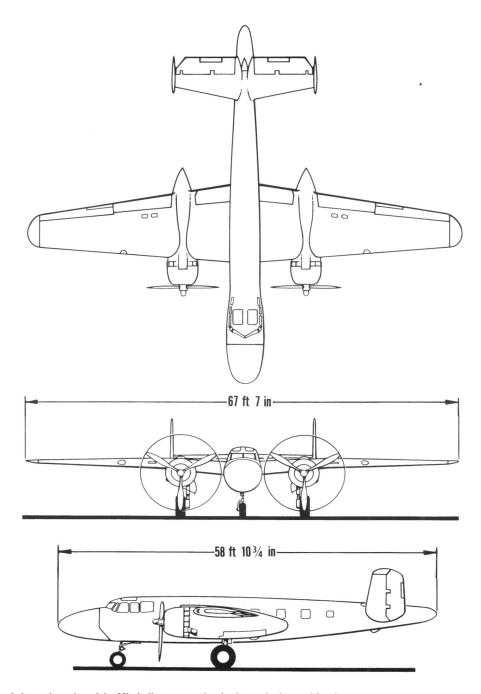

A three-view plan of the Mitchell transport clearly shows the forward fuselage modification compared to the medium bomber. via NAA

Air Guard Mitchells

The air element of the US National Guard, which became the Air National Guard in September 1947 just after the creation of the USAF, acquired examples of the B-25 to serve as support aircraft as the need arose. If, for example, ANG aircrew needed an intensive training course for a specialized duty, then a B-25 proved ideal. If high speed was not essential, the old Mitchell, which had ample interior space to accommodate trainees, proved to be more economical and more docile than jet trainers. One example of this was in the early 1960s when the South Dakota ANG, based at Joe Foss Field in Sioux Falls, needed to train radar fire-control operators for its Northrop F-89 Scorpions. One of the unit's TB-25Ks was utilized, the SDANG then operating three

needed transporting from base to base, and Mitchells therefore remained in second-line USAF service for over a decade, B-25Js predominating. A yardstick of how useful the aircraft became as a transport and trainer is seen by the fact that the USAF's final pilot training course at Reese AFB was not completed until January

1959. Official retirement of the type followed, on 21 May 1960.

North American had closed the B-25 production lines after rolling out the last B-25J (45-8899) completed on 15 October 1945. This latter aircraft was one of seventy-two that were built and flyable, but otherwise lacked equipment and were not

With the commercial Mitchell project having been cancelled, civil customers had largely to convert their own from ex-military bombers. This almost stock B-25J-30 (TB-25N) has carburettor modifications. via NAA

More extensive modifications are apparent on N122B, which has a nose baggage compartment, new fuselage windows and wing-tip fuel tanks. via NAA

Bendix Corporation's converted B-25J (N5548N) had a colour scheme well suited to the Mitchell's lines. MAP

(Above) B-25s were used extensively to train radar operators as well as test the sets themselves. Various radomes were fitted, this example being of H2X type located in the dorsal position. Jarrett

The postwar introduction of military 'buzz numbers' to deter low flying saw the B-25 being allocated the letters 'BD' followed by the last three digits of the serial. This modified J model was probably photographed in 1946.

(Below) Quite extensive use was made of the B-25 in the Air Guard, as this Montana-assigned example shows. The unpainted finish with black engine nacelles on this J model was typical of many such aircraft. R. Burgess via G. Pennick

(Above) Another radar trainer configuration on an 'obsolete' TB-25J which has a relatively unusual dorsal radome.

(Below) The final colour scheme for ANG VB-25s was a white top to the NMF airframe, although the black nacelles remained as always, to hide the worst of the exhaust stains. That this shade was not always the best is obvious! *via NAA*

B-25s – two K models and one TB-25M. Training pilots to operate the Hughes fire-control radar equipment effectively became one of the routine postwar duties of the B-25 flying in Air Guard colours, examples of the TB-25J, K, N and M being utilized by fighter interceptor squadrons equipped with the F-94 Starfire and F-89.

At least twenty-seven ANG squadrons have been identified as having had between one and three TB-25s assigned to them, this total including such units as the 102nd Radar Calibration Flight Test (RDCFT) based at Suffolk City Airport on Long Island, New York, with two N models and one TB-25J; and the 112th RDCFT at Van Nuys Municipal Airport California with a single TB-25N. The 146th Weather Reconnaissance Sqn, also based at Van Nuys, had a single TB-25N on strength during the 1950s.

Veteran Restored – To Vintage

While the long-term survivors of NAA's wartime production were nearly 100 per cent 'low time' B-25Js, not all the early model Mitchells were struck from the USAF. This was particularly fortunate when a B-25D-30 (43-3374) – configured as an F-10 with a number of J model updates including waist windows – was removed from storage at Davis Monthan AFB, and reconfigured to antedate even its own origins, to closely resemble the B-25B flown by Jimmy Doolittle on the Tokyo Raid. The reason the work was carried out on this particular B-25 was to present the aircraft to the Air Force Museum to permanently mark the April 1942 operation against the Japanese capital. Doolittle himself – then aged eighty-three – was pleased to be able to take the controls of a B-25 'one more time', as onlookers at Castle AFB recalled this singular bright spot in the dark days of 1942.

The true vintage of the 'Doolittle raider' conversion was revealed by the Clayton exhaust stacks around each engine cowling, a design innovation brought in after B-25B production had finished. Many 'modern' B-25s masquerading as wartime aircraft also have deeper carburettor air intakes on top of the cowlings; while this may well indicate that a given owner has substituted the original powerplants for those fitted to DC-6s and the like – which had larger air intakes compared to the remarkably narrow ones used on the original Wright Cyclones

– equally it may simply indicate a carburettor change. Most alternative engines that fit the B-25 nacelles also utilize collector ring exhausts, and consequently the separate fairings over the Clayton exhaust stacks are not necessary.

Thousands of routine flying hours were put in by B-25s allocated to Stateside training and second-line duty during World War II, and inevitably such a programme brought a percentage of incidents and accidents, some of them fatal. One of the worst in terms of loss of life occurred on 28 July 1945 when a B-25J lost its way in thick fog over New York City and crashed into the seventy-ninth floor of the Empire State Building. The crew of three, the AAF pilot and co-pilot, and a Navy passenger plus fourteen civilians working in the offices of the 102-storey Manhattan landmark, died in the accident.

Shooting War on Film

Many postwar-generation youngsters may well have had their first sight of the B-25 as a movie star on the silver screen. Some of the earliest productions included the convincing story of the Tokyo raid, with Spencer Tracy taking the part of Jimmy Doolittle in MGM's 1944 production of *Thirty Seconds over Tokyo*. Van Johnson played Capt Ted Lawson, who authored the book that inspired the film. Lawson's aircraft, named 'Ruptured Duck', was one of two B-25Cs towed on to the sound stage and revved up for the cameras in front of a realistic painted backdrop showing the rest of the force on *Hornet*'s flight deck. This pair and other 'real' B-25Cs made a good job of the flying sequences.

Other less-than-memorable epics that used B-25s were filmed for US television and were rarely shown elsewhere – but in 1969 came a highly ambitious adaptation of Joseph Heller's black comedy for Paramount, *Catch 22*. Set against the background of Twelfth Air Force B-25 operations from wartime Italy, the novel was rated as one of the best for turning into an anti-war movie of the type that was so popular at the time. The story centres on one Capt John Yossarian, a B-25 bombardier who endures all manner of indignities en route to giving up on the absurdities and corruption of war, and finally deserting his unit.

Director Mike Nichols had some difficulty in recreating the fictional Italian base of 'Pianosa', as all the authentic loca-

tions had changed so much since the war. After a lengthy search, Mexico yielded the right terrain, a £100,000 strip of tarmac was laid, and the eighteen-strong B-25 fleet moved in to start filming. Taxiing and take-off scenes were particularly well done, reflecting the advantage directors enjoy when a dozen-plus 'real' aircraft are on hand to fill the viewfinder.

Unfortunately, Heller (who had been a wartime bombardier in the 488th BS, 340th Bomb Group) and Nichols either deliberately or incidentally chose to give the impressive squadron of retread B-25Js mustered for the picture exactly the same tail markings as the author's old unit. This naturally did not go down at all well with group veterans, who had to field all kinds of probing questions from their (possibly too easily influenced) children and grandchildren about 'what did they do in the war?'. The film's implication that the 340th sold out to the Germans through mass black market racketeering to the point of standing by while the B-25s destroyed their own airfield, was a little hard for these men to swallow. Many, perhaps understandably, failed to appreciate the humour-laced, anti-war message of it all.

It was, then, doubly ironic that the flying scenes in *Catch 22* were some of the best in Hollywood's chequered history of depicting the air war on the screen: in fact rarely has the B-25 been seen to such advantage. After the completion of filming in Mexico, the Mitchells returned to Orange County, California, where each one was sold off by the studio at prices ranging from $3,000 to $6,000 – these were high in the early 1970s. Furthermore the majority found good homes. Aircraft made flyable for the movie saved would-be private bomber crews thousands of dollars – all they had to do was to keep them that way. To their credit, successive owners of these particular B-25s have made them the core of a healthy medium bomber preservation movement which shows little sign of being grounded. As and when they can no longer be flown, it is virtually certain that the many aviation museums existing nowadays will snap them up.

Other not-so-memorable screen epics featuring Mitchells have included *Hanover Street*, a 1978 movie which depicted five examples of the type operating from England in AAF hands, although this never actually occurred. Harrison Ford and others wrestled with a less-than-worthy script, and critics commented on strange touches

The movie *Catch 22* was an impressive evocation of the Mitchell despite being a black comedy. Most B-25s were saved after the filming although this example looks in need of a little 'tender loving care'. MAP

such as movieland bombs that appeared to float out of the bays. Many of them liked the flak effects, however!

One of the *Catch 22* TB-25Ns (44-30210/N9455Z) became something of a regular on the screen, making the European credits for *Yanks*, *Ike* and *Eye of the Needle* and finally *Hanover Street*. On 28 February 1979 it left the UK to fly back to the US: it got as far as Dublin, and here it languished for two years, the victim of technical problems and lengthy negotiations over its future. In the meantime the Mitchell Flight, headed by John Hawke, was formed and in May 1981 '55Z returned to England.

Mitchell 'fly-on' credits have included *633 Squadron* in which a single B-25J (44-30861) appeared briefly as a clandestine agent-dropping aircraft, although its main duty was carrying out what had become a regular role as the film's camera ship, shooting many of the Mosquito sequences.

Although not, of course, actually seen in Guy Hamilton's *Battle of Britain*, B-25J (N65780) was responsible for many of the dramatic aerial combat sequences. Other movies have benefited from the B-25's spacious interior and multiple gun and obser-

vation positions, which have been adapted to shoot film, rather than .50 calibre bullets, to capture the drama of air combat. This particular aircraft had a modified nose, faired down from the B-25's 'square' fuselage cross-section forward of the cockpit, to a clear circular section that was ideal for camera work. The old gunner's tail position was utilized to mount a camera in an 'open' position in order to obtain ultra-clear footage of aircraft flying behind.

Hollywood stunt pilot Paul Mantz, one of America's best known aeronautical 'movers and shakers', flew his B-25J – named 'The Smasher' – for the air-to-air sequences that helped make the 1949 movie *Twelve O'Clock High* such an enduring success. Hired by 20th Century Fox specifically to shoot the aerial sequences, Mantz had an elongated greenhouse nose fitted to the Mitchell to accommodate Cinerama cameras. He had his work cut out to film all the B-17 flying footage in two days – but more time and the fuel bill for the fleet of twelve USAF Forts would have broken the film's budget. Mantz shot the scenes, flying out of the old Army base at Ozark, Alabama, within the timescale.

B-17 operations by the wartime 8th Air Force were again recalled in footage captured by a B-25J camership conversion piloted by John Hawke for the 1962 production of *The War Lover*. Based on the fine John Hersey novel, this monochrome production captured, via B-25-mounted cameras, many authentic sequences of the Fortress in typical wartime operations from the UK.

Warbirds

Such gainful commercial flying has ensured the survival of a healthy number of B-25s in flying trim – indeed, Mitchells are the most numerous of all the World War II mediums in the world warbird inventory at the start of the twenty-first century. And fortunately, unlike other ex-wartime combat aircraft where only examples from tail-end production batches have survived, the B-25 has both its main versions well represented. It is no surprise to learn that B-25J airframes outnumber those with the earlier B-25C/D configuration: but both examples are flying today, as is one representative B-25H.

Pilots such as Paul Mantz have flown many hours putting mock warfare on film, his N1042B being one of several B-25 camera ships used primarily for this purpose. via NAA

While most flyable B-25s are to be found in the US and Canada, Britain and continental Europe have several excellent examples. A B-25D-30 (43-3318), the RAF's Mitchell II, can be seen to advantage on the current UK airshow circuit. Based at Duxford in Cambridgeshire, the aircraft is an ex-RCAF delivery aircraft (s/n KL156), currently marked as 'KL161'/VO-B 'Grumpy' of No. 98 Squadron. It was still owned by the Fighter Collection at the time of writing, though it may have been sold to a new owner by the time this volume is published.

On the other side of the Channel the Duke of Brabant's Air Force, a private group of enthusiasts, maintains a B-25J in Dutch wartime tricolour flag markings, the aircraft having visited Britain and flown in company with the Mk II to provide Duxford air show visitors with an interesting contrast in marks and markings.

Much rarer on the warbird scene are examples of the short-nosed B-25G and H versions; but in May 1992, B-25H (43-4106 N5548N), named 'Barbie III', took to the air, strikingly decked out in 1st Air Commando Group markings. Owned by the Weary Warriors, an American preservation group, the H model, painted up as '43-4380', represents a fitting tribute to the combat record of the AAF in the

lesser known China-Burma-India theatre – and the machine is as impressive now as aircraft like it were over Burma in 1944. Currently believed to be one of two examples of a flyable, fully restored B-25H in the US, '106 is usually based at Rockford, Illinois.

Being Civil

With the war over, many B-25s in USAAF inventory were simply abandoned on Pacific islands, scrapped in-theatre, or broken up at home to reduce the huge number of now unwanted combat aircraft. To some degree it shared this fate with the majority of A-20s and B-26s, which were in turn replaced by the newer A-26. As the last and most numerous of the piston-engined medium bombers, nothing newer could as economically replace the Mitchell in US service; its adaptable configuration and docile handling therefore helped to ensure for it a useful postwar service life in second-line roles with the AAF, and then the USAF. This meant in turn that well-maintained machines eventually came on to the civilian market at a time when museums were springing up all over the United States, and an early 'warbird movement' existed to help future generations to

appreciate the historic importance of World War II aircraft.

This led to commendable, but often *ad hoc* efforts at preservation – which is not to deny that a substantial number of perfectly airworthy B-25s deteriorated due to inadequate storage and neglect: but the seed was sown. In the last years of the twentieth century, the world warbird community matured into a very substantial 'under restoration', flying and static inventory of historic aeroplanes, still led in the medium bomber category by the B-25, and by a considerable margin.

A 1991 international listing put the world inventory of B-25s at 124 extant examples, ranging from stored airframe parts to fully refurbished and flyable aircraft, the figure including most of the static museum exhibits listed in Chapter 18. This total included at that time one B-25 (40-2168), one B-25B (40-2347), three B-25Cs, seven B-25Ds and five B-25Hs, the remaining 107 being B-25Js.

Warbird inventory figures do tend to fluctuate due to aircraft being lost in accidents, and 'new' ones discovered, albeit only as incomplete hulks, for example. If these latter are suitable for restoration they can legitimately be added to the list. Although the above total of 124 was compiled ten years ago, it is believed to have

If time and care are there in great supply, and a few hundred thousand dollars also happen to be available, maintaining a warbird as large as a B-25 in flyable trim is no problem. S. Howe

remained more or less constant. Even a 10 per cent reduction would still leave over 100 Mitchells in existence in 2001, an impressive enough figure. And even wrecked warbirds usually live on in some form: with the value of veteran aircraft rising, and stocks of original spares dwindling, numerous parts that survive even a bad crash will often be incorporated into others.

A positive factor in the long-term survival of the B-25 was that war-surplus examples found a civilian market. Sold off by the War Assets Administration for around $8,000, these virtually new, low-time aircraft became ideal executive transports for a number of companies. Numerous interior modifications were made to these Mitchells, including airline-quality fixtures and fittings, air-stairs, modern navigational aids – and sound-proofing! This last was an essential item in an aircraft widely renowned for its very high flightdeck noise levels. Such conversion work also tended to alter the exterior appearance of the familiar wartime B-25, when new noses were grafted on, wing-tip fuel tanks were added to boost range, and the redundant observation positions of the military original were plated over or replaced by streamlined fairings.

En route to full restoration, owners often paint World War II aircraft in fanciful colours, as these Confederate Air Force examples show. In most cases the end result is far more authentic in terms of paint schemes and equipment, although items such as gun turrets are becoming rare. Howe

Firefighter Mitchells

Civilian use of surplus military aircraft did not always mean 'cushy' flights, with company presidents and managers riding in the rear seats and enjoying airline-standard comfort. Another postwar duty by B-25s under civil registration was that of water bomber. Converted B-25s were mostly based in the US on this important and usually hazardous flying operation, but they also found their way across the border to serve on similar fire-control operations in Canada. One story related by Stephen Riley of Winnipeg in the *Journal of the American Historical Society* pointed up only too clearly the sometimes primitive 'backwoods' nature of fighting forest fires from the air in 1967. That August a technical problem on a B-25 that was flying fire-control duty in Alberta was solved by quick thinking alone.

The company that undertook the water bombing had two B-25Js and six Stearmans, which were using a gravel strip at Lesser Slave Lake in northern Alberta that consisted of 'a wind sock, a radio shack, an Avgas tank holding about 2,000 gallons and a similar-sized tank of flame retardant, with pumps'. In order to quell the fires the Mitchells had to be kept in the air more or less from dawn until dusk, the crews staying in their cockpits and kept their engines

blue smoke as it caught. This process was repeated on the other engine with equal success, the complete 'priming' task taking about five minutes. Well pleased, the Mitchell pilot took off into the dawn. By dusk that day the fire was under control, thanks to the fire fighters having their full complement of Mitchells on hand. The pilot of the B-25 that had needed help in starting kept his engines running all day.

The B-25 was one of the earliest of the wartime military types pressed into service as a fire bomber, but its rather limited capacity in carrying the large discharge tanks of borate and water meant it was soon replaced by aircraft with heavier lifting

too long, however, it became almost sacrilegious to use ex-World War II military aircraft for any purpose other than entertaining crowds in memorial – preferably flying – to those who had lost their lives in that great conflict.

The degree of restoration work needed to turn a 'basket case' ex-water bomber into a genuine combat aircraft with CAA/FAA airworthiness certification (albeit with restrictions) is sometimes enormous; furthermore, putting such aircraft back together to far more exacting tolerances than wartime factories could afford, by highly specialized engineers, also means that the price has gradually crept

Civilian work for surplus B-25s included that of fighting fires. Demanding and often requiring round-the-clock flying, Mitchell water bombers were operated in Canada and the US for some years. MAP

running while the retardant was pumped into the fuselage tanks. They would take off, dump the load, land and replenish in a continual cycle, staying on the line for about sixteen hours a day during the worst of the fires. But one morning the engines of one of the Mitchells refused to start by any conventional means. Completely unfazed by what was quite an emergency in the circumstances, the pilot hailed the driver of a nearby grader, who promptly backed up to the side of the aircraft. A line from the vehicle's tow hook was wrapped around one propeller hub, the driver gunned the grader's engine and stretched the line taught. Protesting loudly, the prop reluctantly turned, the engine belching

capability. Operating such aircraft on a 'seasonal' basis, however, led to difficult economics for the small companies that contracted to fight fires – it may have been preferable to use a B-17 or a Privateer, but the operating costs could work out that much higher. For some operators that gave the medium bombers the edge.

In 1960 a spate of B-25 water bomber crashes, none of them proven to have been attributable to structural failure, nevertheless led to a blanket grounding order by the US authorities. This ruling, although it was later lifted, all but knocked the bottom out of the B-25's career as a fire fighter – though once again, some survivors soldiered on. Before

up. Inflation affects most things in life, and warbirds are certainly not exempt, leading to the situation where a modern 'old' aircraft such as a Mitchell can cost many times its 1944–45 price, when the US government paid $150,000 for each new B-25J ordered. Today, a flyable B-25 in fully restored condition will cost a truly huge amount of money, and even a wreck is no longer cheap if it has rebuild potential. Fortunately there are also a huge number of highly skilled, well placed individuals who consider warbird restoration work as the only way to spend their days: these fanatics will surely 'keep 'em flying' for as long as airframes with fifty years on the clock can get into the air.

CHAPTER EIGHTEEN

Military Swansong

After the war, 'second-hand' US combat aircraft were in considerable demand, particularly by the smaller air forces around the world, and most especially those of Latin America; this represented quite a substantial market, and led to what might be considered as the third reincarnation of the B-25. With World War II over, many countries were anxious to modernize their air defence forces, for despite the major powers being at peace, this term was relative in many areas of an increasingly dangerous world. Entirely new alignments and nationalistic ambitions had changed the face of the globe out of all recognition as compared to 1939, and to overcome a heightened suspicion of what neighbouring states might do was the desire to re-arm, just in case. This ambition, driven by the ready availability of surplus combat aircraft, frequently came up against prohibitive cost. The US largely overcame this with generous loans and credits, and numerous surplus aircraft were duly delivered.

The down side of this largesse was that certain regimes that appeared to be democratic in the late 1940s subsequently proved to be less stable in that respect. For their part, the poorest recipient nations were able to postpone the financial burden of acquiring turbojet types for more than a decade, yet could still effectively rattle their sabres at their neighbours when armed with relatively modern, combat-proven piston-engined bombers and fighters. By filling the immediate needs of poorer countries, American World War II aircraft therefore found a new lease of life. And although it was not realized at the time, many would later return home to provide the nucleus for a highly prized warbird and museum market.

Not as potent, nor matching the eventual postwar combat record of the more modern A-26 Invader, the B-25 nevertheless saw service with a number of foreign air arms. Relatively few were called upon to fire their guns in anger, but there were instances when Mitchells added to their awesome World War II combat record in the role for which they had been designed.

There follows a brief survey of those countries known to have operated the B-25 in a military role in the postwar years.

Similar data published elsewhere show that several countries acquired individual civil-registered B-25s for a limited military role, rather than procuring them through any recognized channels. These countries have not been included here – but to illustrate this rather confusing issue, both Argentina and Ecuador have B-25s in military configuration on museum display, when neither country operated them: thus B-25J-30 (44-31172) can be seen at Argentina's Santiago del Estro Airport, while Ecuador's example is a B-25J-30 (44-86866) configured as a TB-25J, in the Museo Aereo de la FAE at Quinto Airport. This latter machine was apparently impounded and used briefly by the air force.

Australia

No. 2 Sqn, the RAAF's sole Mitchell unit, did not survive long after World War II ended. It ceased operations at Balikpapan on 14 November 1945, and moved back to Laverton, Victoria, to be disbanded in May 1946. By March 1950, most of its previously stored aircraft had been sold for scrap. In terms of museum preservation, the Darwin Aviation Museum has B-25D-10 (41-30222), which was recovered in 1974 from its 1945 crash site and fully restored for display. The Australian War Memorial in Canberra holds a B-25J-30 44-86791 (VH-XXV), which was flown in No. 2 Sqn markings in the late 1980s before going into long-term storage.

Biafra

In one of the shortest military careers on record, two B-25s, a J-25 (44-29919) and a J-30 (44-31491), were sent to Biafra in October 1967 to fight the Nigerians during the civil war. Complete details of their careers await confirmation, but what is

known is as follows: re-designated before delivery as a TB-25N, '919 flew several ground-attack sorties before a major target presented itself, namely the Nigerian fighters based at Calabar. On the night of 2/3 November, '919 and an A-26, representing two-thirds of the three-bomber Biafran fleet, took off from their base at Port Harcourt to bomb Calabar. This they did, but then both aircraft were lost in crash-landings on return. The second Mitchell, a TB-25J, was always plagued by engine trouble and never flew in combat; it was destroyed when the Nigerian Army attacked the airfield in May 1968.

Bolivia

Four B-25Js were acquired for the Fuerza Aerea Boliviana (FAB) as part of a deal with Venezuela for F-86F Sabres in 1972–73. Three, known to have had the military serial numbers 541 to 543, were subsequently used by the Transportes Aeros Militares (TAM), the Bolivian military air transport service, and were still in service as transports in 1979. B-25J s/n FAB 542 is on display at Cochabamba.

Brazil

The only nation in Latin America to receive B-25s under Lend-Lease during hostilities, Brazil declared war on the European Axis on 22 August 1942. Unlike a single escadron of P-47 Thunderbolts flown by pilots of the Força Aerea Brasileira (FAB), no Mitchells were deployed overseas, the bombers supplied under Lend-Lease being retained in Brazil for basic and advanced operational training. The FAB was allocated fifty B-25s under Lend-Lease, the initial delivery comprising seven B-25Bs, twenty-nine B-25Cs, eleven B-25J-15s and ten B-25J-20s. These equipped the 4 Grupo de Bombardeio Medio based at Foraleza from late 1944, with 6 Regimento de Aviacao's 2

Brazil's air arm was an early wartime recipient of B-25s under Lend-Lease, this J model being one of a number of preserved examples. M. Burton

Rockcliffe, Ottawa, on 14 January 1943). From 15 May 1944 the unit flew Mitchells on an extensive aerial survey of Canada at the behest of the British Air Ministry, using four F-10s (41-29886; 41-29924; 41-30195 and 41-29877, RCAF 891-894 respectively) delivered direct from the US to provide the required tri-metrogen camera coverage. No. 13 Sqn became officially established as an RCAF unit on 15 January 1946 when it was renumbered as No. 413 (P) Sqn.

Much of the Mitchell flying in wartime Canada was for ferrying purposes, aircraft being delivered from the US and flown over both northern and southern routes to England and North Africa, first under civilian pilot contracts and subsequently on behalf of RAF Ferry Command. Numerous such flights originated at Dorval, Quebec, with an en route stop at Gander, Newfoundland, prior to completing the onward legs to Europe.

During the war years the B-25D (Mitchell Mk II) predominated in Canada, with some B-25Js (Mk IIIs) arriving towards the end of hostilities. Numerous B-25Ds survived the rigours of wartime training to serve in a postwar capacity, when two more B-25Ds, four F-10s and eighty-three B-25Js were delivered in 1951. The latter figure may actually have been seventy-five aircraft, there being some doubt as to actual arrivals in the country.

Supporting a strong auxiliary force similar to that of the US Air National Guard, Canada equipped three more squadrons in addition to No. 413, these being Nos 406, 412 and 418. Converting to Mitchells in

Grupo operating a mix of B-25s, PV-1s and A-28s.

Postwar B-25 deliveries began with two in 1946, further quantities of J models bringing the grand total to ninety-six, these serving until the type was declared surplus in 1974. In its latter years of FAB service the B-25 served in second-line PR and transport roles; operating units included 1 Esquadrao of 10 Grupo (GAv) based at Sao Paulo. Brazil follows an admirable policy of preserving its historic military aircraft, this being reflected in the existence of at least three static display B-25s: B-25J-25 (44-30069) Brazilian s/n 5127 is on display in the Museu Aerospacial in Rio de Janeiro; the Air Force Academy in Sao Paulo has a second B-25J (FAB 5133), while a CB-25J (FAB 5097) is held by the Eduardo Andres Matarazzo War Museum in Bededuoro.

Canada

A proportion of British Mitchell allocations under Lend-Lease were diverted to Canada during the war to fulfil a training role, following the retention of a B-25B (FK168) from the initial batch of Mk Is for the RAF. Apart from several additional aircraft that were diverted from British contracts, two batches – twenty-nine Mk IIs (KL133-KL161) and twenty-one Mk IIIs (KP308-KP328), a total of fifty – were the first to be delivered direct to the RCAF. Wartime deliveries of aircraft with

RAF serial allocations to Canada numbered seventy, all B-25Ds.

Canada's early association with the RAF-allocated B-25Bs extended to nine more RAF-allocated examples (seven B-25Bs and two B-25Js) which were flight tested by No. 5 OTU at Boundary Bay and Abbottsford, British Columbia, for a period of one month. Neither of the B-25Js were delivered to the RAF, although six of the B models went to No. 111 OTU in the Bahamas, the seventh aircraft (FK178) being lost in a crash prior to delivery on 12 January 1943.

The Mitchell Mk II entered Canadian service, albeit unofficially, with No. 13 (P) Squadron (originally organized at

Canada's wartime allocation of B-25s helped train crews who would in many cases ply their trade not overseas but at home after the war when the country operated Mitchells extensively. These B-25Cs are from No. 5 OTU at Boundary Bay.

In service long enough to wear a variety of RCAF colour schemes, the B-25 was an important part of Canada's aerial defence during the years of postwar austerity. MAP

(Below) Canadian Mitchells soon relinquished their guns, and VIP and courier flights comprised one important secondary role in RCAF service. MAP

the 1950s, RCAF usually insisted that trainee pilots completed twenty hours on the Harvard and twenty on the Beech Expeditor before transition to the North American medium.

No. 406 'City of Saskatoon' Sqn operated a number of Mk IIIs for a decade, from June 1948 to June 1958. No. 412 'Falcon' Sqn flew Mitchells and other types as part of Air Transport Command, becoming well known as Canada's 'VIP Squadron'. It operated Mitchell Mk IIIs between September 1956 and November 1960.

No. 413 'Tusker' Sqn used Mitchells for survey work between April 1947 and October 1948. At an unknown date it operated three out of the four F-10s taken on charge, these being supplemented by at least one Mk II (KL145).

No. 418 'City of Edmonton' Sqn received its first Mk IIs in January 1947, and these, along with the Mk IIIs subsequently taken on charge, served until March 1958. In 1951, American cartoonist Al Capp gave permission for No. 418 to

recall its wartime Mosquito days by painting his 'Li'l Abner' characters on the noses of its Mitchells. With the exception of No. 412 Sqn, these units undertook a medium/light bomber role in the defence of Canada under NORAD in the immediate postwar period.

The Canadian Mitchells were well maintained, despite some harsh operating conditions during nationwide defence exercises, some of the older Mk IIs particularly serving the country well for over a decade. The attrition rate was augmented by several wheels-up landings, write-offs and accidents, but in the main the type gave good service with a number of training establishments as well as the auxiliary squadrons. Among the former were: No. 1 Advanced Flying School; No. 2 Air Observers School; No. 2 Air Navigation School; No. 3 (AW) OTU; No. 5 OTU; and the CFS at Trenton, Ontario. The Mitchell was not officially stood down until 25 August 1961, the remaining examples being SOC in 1963. RCAF Mitchells remained in service long

enough to wear a variety of national markings and aircraft identification code and number combinations.

Canada is a modern Mecca for warbirds, and several B-25s are numbered among the airworthy examples that are to be seen around the country. The static examples include a B-25J-30 (44-86699; RCAF 5244) in the National Aviation Museum in Ottawa, marked as a No. 98 Sqn RAF aircraft; and B-25J-30 (44-86726; RCAF 5257) at Belmore's Altamont Historical Centre in Alberta.

Chile

Twelve B-25Js (eleven of them being 44-30252; 30272; 30273; 30274; 30392; 30401; 30412; 30413; 30416; 30445 and 30465) originally had the Fuerza Aerea de Chile (FAC) serials 801 to 811, these being subsequently changed to numbers in the 900 range. The Mitchells were delivered under the American Republics Projects (ARP)

China's Nationalist air arm was equipped with Mitchells well past the end of the civil war with the Communists. On or about 22 February 1950, these B-25Js were at Haiku on Hainan Island, which had some old Japanese hangars still awaiting repair. Crow

Two B-25H-1s (43-4120 and 43-4329) with the identification numbers 120 and 329, have been preserved in Beijing.

Colombia

The Fuerza Aerea Colombiana received three B-25J-25s (44-30358, 30397 and 30408); these were given FAC serials 657, 658 and 659 (not necessarily in that sequence) under ARP, and all were reportedly on strength by 5 May 1948. Two remained as of 30 June 1954, their condition apparently being less than pristine at that time. It is said that they remained in Colombia until 1957.

Cuba

After Cuba became a signatory of the 1947 Rio Treaty of Mutual Defence, the country received its first modern combat aircraft via the technically illegal, ex-Dominican Republic invasion force known as the Cayo Confites fleet. Named after an island lying north-east of Cuba, twenty-three of these machines were sent over. They were intended to be used to overthrow the government of Gen Rafael Trujillio Molina of Dominica, but were instead flown to Cuba, where they were in effect interned and absorbed by the air force of the Batista regime.

This fortuitous windfall of US combat aircraft and transports in August 1947 included a B-25H-5 (43-4536) and a B-25C-15 (42-32385), which were given the Cuban serials 300 and 301, respectively. In the meantime the US had initiated ARP, under which Cuba was allocated three B-25J-25s (44-30326, 44-30095 and 44-30348), which were given the Cuban serials 303–305. The intervening s/n '302' was apparently applied to a B-25H, the total of Cuban machines being reliably quoted as six. These Mitchells formed the main equipment of the grandly named Bombardero Ligero Cuatro de Septembre.

They all survived well, apart from the B-25C which was virtually destroyed when a hurricane struck Campo Columbia in October 1948 – a C-46 was blown on top of it, which put it beyond economical repair. In fact the Mitchells equipped the only bomber unit of the Fuerza Aerea del Ejercito Cubano (Cuban Army Air Force). It is understood that four more aircraft were delivered during 1952–54 as

---

assistance programme, which was designed to standardize all tactical and support aircraft serving air forces in the Western hemisphere. They officially arrived on 13 October 1947, although they were reportedly on FAC strength as early as January of that year. The aircraft were operated by the air force's Grupo de Bombardeo No. 8 at Quinterno until 1954 when they were replaced by A-26 Invaders.

China (Nationalist)

Having received 1,378 US combat aircraft under wartime Lend-Lease, including 131 B-25C/Ds, Hs and Js, the Chinese Nationalist Air Force faced an uncertain future as a strong Communist movement had begun to gain ground even before hostilities with Japan had ceased. The Chinese-American Composite Wing's 1st and 2nd Bomber Groups had a nucleus of trained Chinese crews to fly the B-25s remaining after war service, and additional Mitchells, probably less than 100, passed into Nationalist hands when the 391st BG abandoned its aircraft as personnel rotated back to the US. Such 'theatre transfers' made good operational attrition, which was reportedly quite high. In 1946 all B-25s were assigned to the 1st BG, which then had sixty-four aircraft in four squadrons: the 1st, 3rd, 4th and 9th. When the 1st BG generally re-equipped with Mosquitoes, all the Mitchells were grouped in the 9th BS.

Nationalist China was destined not to survive as a political force on the mainland beyond 1950. Exiled to Formosa (Taiwan),

the Nationalist air arm continued to exist and operate US aircraft. The early postwar inventory was built around approximately 160 US aircraft that had reached the offshore island, including an unknown number of Mitchells, most, if not all, being B-25H and J models.

A Chinese Air Force 1st Wing was established in 1953, and the 1st, 3rd and 9th Squadrons of the 1st Group began training on F-84s; second-line types such as the B-25 were transferred to the 4th Squadron, under the Wing's direct control. In July 1953 the 4th Sqn was assigned to the 8th Bomber Group at Hsinchu AFB. Finally, the surviving B-25s were reassigned to the 35th Sqn for target towing and transport duties before being retired from inventory in 1958.

Mutual Assistance Advisory Group (MAAG) support was provided to Nationalist China by the US from May 1951.

China: (People's Republic)

As Sino-Communist forces swept through China in 1945–46, a number of ex-Fourteenth AAF air bases fell into their hands. As Chaing Kai-shek's Nationalists were forced on to the defensive, a substantial quantity of US warplanes – including an unknown number of B-25s – changed hands. CACW-trained bomber crews who had switched their allegiance were almost certainly available to fly the Western aircraft that remained in service before the Air Force of the People's Republic was reorganized on Soviet rather than US lines, with an increasing inventory of Russian aircraft.

attrition replacements, the Cubans finding the maintenance demands of three different B-25 models understandably difficult. The Mitchells nevertheless served until 1955–56, when they were sold and replaced by A-26 Invaders. When Fidel Castro's revolutionary forces took over the island state in 1959, they had little or no organized air support, although a photo exists of Castro and his staff planning air strikes (or learning how to avoid their effects) with the aid of plastic model aircraft, including a B-25H.

Dominica

Four Mitchells were acquired by Dominica: a B-25C-1 (41-13251), a B-25G-10 (42-65168), a B-25H-1 (43-4106) and a B-25J-10 (43-36075); there was also another example (probably a B-25J model) built up from junked parts and possibly identified by the spurious s/n '43-34999'. These were given the Dominican serial numbers 2501 to 2505. They were acquired during a somewhat desperate spending spree by president Gen Trujillo in the late 1940s to early 1950s when he was concentrating on building up the country's air arm, the Fuerza Aerea Dominicana (FAD).

The B-25s had all been purchased privately by Dominican agents, and received

export licences from the US in July 1949; most are believed to have arrived in the country at the same time as the 'composite' example, around April 1950. However, by 1967 apparently only one remained. The air force was given the title Aviacon Militar Dominicana (AMD) in 1952, although this was changed back to the more logical FAD in 1958. Under the Dominican designation system the prefix '25' applied to the B-25 served as a type identification.

France

Greatly depleted in terms of indigenous combat aircraft in 1945, France had little choice but to operate whatever Allied and enemy types could be utilized, in order to rebuild the Armée de l'Air. Thus the postwar French air force held something of a record as regards the very wide variety of aircraft in the inventory. Of the US types that French units had flown in combat, the B-25 would undertake a postwar role as a transport when No. 342 Squadron (with origins in GB.I/20 'Lorraine'), the only wartime AdeA unit to fly Mitchells, reverted to French control on 2 December 1945.

Before that, on 10 June, came a proud demonstration of flying skill over Frankfurt, when French Mitchell crews paid tribute to Soviet general Georgi Zhukov. Part of a 2nd

TAF victory celebration, the aircraft adopted a 'Cross of Lorraine' formation over the shattered German city. The aerial crosses, symbol of French resistance during the war, had grown to four when No. 342 Sqn flew above Paris for a VE-Day parade on 18 June. The squadron's eighteen Mitchells must have stirred every French heart present in the Champs Elysees as they brought up the rear of the flypast at 10:30hr.

No. 342 left Gilze-Rijen in November 1945 and officially ceased to be part of the RAF on 2 December. Most of the Mitchells allocated to No. 342 returned to England to languish before being scrapped, the majority by mid-1947; several, however, remained in French service without being returned to RAF charge. Stripped of armament, these examples were used as staff transports, as were war-surplus B-25s in many other parts of the world.

Mitchells flying in France after the war invariably belonged to GLTA I/60 – the Groupe de Transport et de Liaisons Aeriennes, otherwise known by the acronym GLAM: Air Liaison and Transport Group. Among them was an early B-25D-10 (ex-41-30330) and a Mk III (ex-KJ692). Becoming a military staff transport, '330' flew most frequently carrying General Leclerc, commanding French ground forces in Europe since 1945, who named the aircraft 'Tailly'. This Mitchell made about ten

A familiar sight in those overseas areas such as Morocco and Algeria where France maintained postwar influence, French Air Force B-25s could be seen on VIP duties, on which they flew many thousands of miles. MAP

(Above) Among the last countries to use the B-25 'in anger' was the Netherlands, the country that had first ordered the type in 1941. No. 18 (NEI) Squadron's aircraft finished the war at Batchelor in Northern Australia where some remaining aircraft were seen in 1945. F.F. Smith

(Below) Dutch Navy Mitchells also remained in service long enough to adopt a number of colour schemes. This B-25C/D '2-6' has the 'Kon Marine' branch of service title below the tailplane. Jarrett

Indonesia 'inherited' forty of the best condition ex-Dutch B-25s which then served with the AURI's No. 1 Skadron for many years. Burton

flights to such destinations as Algeria, Oran and Tunis before a fatal crash in a sandstorm on 26 November 1947.

A true globe-trotting machine, KJ692 flew Gen Martial Valin and other officers on numerous visits to French Morocco, Egypt, Germany and England. It was finally retired from French service on 28 July after a landing mishap, in which the left mainwheel oleo collapsed. Struck off charge by the French, it was later sold to a corporate buyer in the US.

The Netherlands

As the original overseas customer for the B-25, the Netherlands maintained its association with the North American medium as the end of World War II did not bring enduring peace to the Netherlands East Indies. The rise of Indonesian nationalism saw Dutch airmen fighting much the same kind of war as they had against the Japanese, and in the same aircraft. As part of the MK-KNIL (Military Aviation of the Royal Netherlands Indies Army), the B-25s of No. 18 (NEI) Sqn had finished the war at Balikpapan, Borneo, where the first months of peace saw the squadron engaged on mercy flights. Food and supplies were dropped to PoW camps, and personnel were repatriated, the Mitchells operating between their home base and Kemajoran, Malang, Soerabaja and Semarang. One aircraft was lost during this period, which lasted until 15 January 1946 when No. 18 Sqn passed from RAAF to Dutch control. Its unit number was retained, and a base move was made to Tjililitan near Bandeng in Java.

With the outbreak of fighting between Dutch troops and Indonesian guerillas, No. 18 Squadron's Mitchells began flying combat missions once again. One of the squadron's aircraft conveyed the Dutch C-in-C, Gen Spoor, to the Hague in August 1946; it repeated this three-day round trip in January 1947.

The squadron was now tasked with a variety of missions, including close support, bombing, reconnaissance and liaison. No. 18's Mitchells were joined by other MK-KNIL machines in the hands of No. 16 Sqdn and a few of No. 20, a transport unit which had inherited some TB-25Ds from No. 220 Sqn, and it remained in the Far East for as long as the Netherlands resisted Indonesian independence. It also remained the premier Mitchell squadron, subsequently operating from bases at Tjililitan and Kemojoram.

In May 1947 the Dutch wartime marking of a red, white and blue flag was replaced by the pre-war segmented roundel in these colours with an orange centre. The exterior finish on Mitchells (B-25C/D and J models) varied from full camouflage to natural aluminium, with partially painted aircraft operating as the need arose. Some reduction of armament was made, there being considerable variation on individual machines; however, the removal of top turrets was fairly standard practice. Eight-gun noses were widely used as they were extremely effective for ground strafing.

Continuing to fight an unpopular war, the Dutch, who relied heavily on US equipment, realized that events had overtaken any colonial ambitions still pursued by the Hague. The country responded positively to an American threat to cut off military aid, and ceasefires were consequently agreed for 11 and 15 August in Java and Sumatra, respectively. When Indonesia gained independence as a republic on 27 December 1949 the Netherlands government no longer maintained a military presence in the region, the MK-KNIL being disbanded on 21 June 1950. No. 18 Sqn was itself disbanded on 26 July 1950. This did not, however, mean the end of service for the Mitchell in the East Indies, as a period of service in Indonesia lay ahead.

Things were more stable in Europe, and No. 320 Sqn returned from Germany to the UK under Dutch naval control (as from 2 August 1945) on the 10th. When No. 320 returned home to Twenthe on 1 April 1946, twenty-eight Mitchells were transferred, these being the remainder of the original sixty-four Mk IIs flown on wartime operations. Despite being Dutch-owned, these Mitchells were identified as RAF aircraft by their serial numbers, and were not officially returned to the Dutch until 22 July 1947. No. 320 Sqn was disbanded, then reformed on Mitchells on 22 March 1949, these being replaced by Neptunes at Valkenburg in 1953–54.

Two B-25s are on static museum display in Holland, while other Mitchells are maintained in flying condition. The National Orlogs en Verzetsmuseum at Overloon has B-25D-20 (41-30792) with a combat record of more than 100 missions with No. 320 Sqn as FR193. The Militaire Luchtvaart Museum at Soesterberg has a B-25J-30 (44-31258; N5-264/ M-464) which was donated to the museum by Indonesia in 1971.

Indonesia

Listed out of alphabetical sequence owing to the fact that all its B-25s originated from Dutch stocks, an air arm of the Republic of Indonesia, the Angkatan Udara Republik Indonesia (AURI), was formally established when the country became independent in December 1949. Muscle for the new air arm was vested in forty-one ex-Dutch B-25C, D and J models operated by the composite No. 1 Skadron, which otherwise flew P-51Ds and PBY Catalinas. The Indonesians selected B-25s in the best condition to equip their first combat unit, thus fostering a loyalty to the North American medium that proved remarkably strong, even to the point of a preference over jet bombers.

With the republic's ten million people scattered across more than 1,000 islands, the AURI's patrol task was vast indeed. Almost inevitably conflict flared between diverse ethnic groups, and the air force was called upon to quell unrest in Ambon in 1950.

By the spring of 1951, Skadron 1 had eighteen B-25Js and six B-25Cs, the latter operating in a dual PR and VIP transport role. Military operations in the southern Celebes in 1953 also involved Sk 1, and although by the mid-1950s the B-25s were overdue for replacement, they soldiered on. In 1957, when A-26s arrived in Indonesia, both types were operated together in Sk 1. Brief air combat operations were undertaken on 21 March 1958 when the AURI bombers knocked out rebel radio stations at Padang and Bukitiinggi in Sumatra, though without causing any casualties. A similar target at Sudawesi was also attacked.

By 1956 the AURI B-25 fleet had shrunk to fourteen aircraft, 1 Sk then being based at Halim Perdanakusuma outside Jakarta. A base change was made at this time, the bombers moving to Adburachman Saleh, near Madang in south-eastern Java. The B-25s continued to be part of Sk 1, and several remained when the unit itself was disbanded on 29 July 1977 – a rare case of a veteran bomber outlasting its parent unit, rather than the other way around!

As with other postwar operators, the AURI converted some of its B-25s for use in the transport and liaison role, and these were, it is believed, flying well into the 1960s.

The Indonesian Air Force Museum at Adisucipto Air Base in central Java holds B-25J-15 (44-29032; M-439) which was ex-Dutch N5-239. A B-25J-25 (44-30399;

M-458), configured as a TB-25M and ex-Dutch N5-258, is on static display in the Armed Force Museum at Jakarta.

Mexico

The other Latin American country to declare war on the Axis and send a fighter squadron to fight on the Allied side during World War II, Mexico received few modern combat aircraft prior to signing the Rio Pact in 1947. Three B-25Js had previously been charged to Mexico's wartime Lend-Lease account, and although these had arrived in the country by December 1945, they were not actually handed over to the Fuerza Aerea Mexicana until 1947. In the meantime the aircraft were held as the property of the US government, assigned to the joint US/Mexican Commission.

The trio of FAM Mitchells were B-25J-30s 44-86712, '717 and '718 – respectively BMM-3501 to '503, the Mexican abbreviation standing for 'Bombardero Mediano Mitchell', or 'Medium Bomber Mitchell'. Originally ordered to replace ageing Douglas A-24s, the US mediums were, according to an order of battle for 31 March 1950, in service with Escuadron Aereo 206, 4/o Grupo Aereo, based at Cozumel. B-25s apparently remained in Mexican air force inventory until the 1960s, and a single example, a B-25J-20 (44-29128) acquired elsewhere, was preserved by being mounted on a pole at the Chaoltepac Park in Mexico City.

Peru

Eight B-25J-25s (44-29912; 30296; 30360; 30361; 30384; 30398; 30403 and 30418) were supplied under ARP on 21 July 1947. CAP three-digit serial numbers included 472 (which had the tailcode 'B'), 473, 474 and 475, the aircraft being assigned to Ecuadron de Caza No. 21 of Grupo de Aviacion No. 2. The Peruvian air arm was then known as the Cuerpo de Aeronautica del Peru (CAP), but in July 1950 it was renamed Fuerza Aerea Peruana (FAP).

Six B-25s remained on strength by June 1954, with five reportedly combat ready. An air force reorganization in 1957 revised unit designations to create four Grupo, the remaining Mitchells, plus A-26s and Canberras, then equipping units within Grupo de Bombardeo No. 21.

Spain

Spain acquired a single USAAF B-25D, which was interned after landing at Medilla, French Morocco in January 1944, and served for many years as an air force staff transport operating out of Metacan AB, Salamanca. It was scrapped in the early 1950s, but a subsequent event affirmed the high esteem in which this aircraft was held – and perpetuated the myth of combat use of the B-25 in Cuba during the revolution.

In November 1987 B-25J-20 (44-29121/N86427) landed in Spain to feature in a film called *Cuba*. Shooting began in Malaga,

with the B-25, painted overall yellow, playing the part of a Batista-era military aircraft flying counter-insurgent sorties against Castro's guerillas. But filming in Spain was cancelled after the Mitchell suffered damage while making a spectacular 180-degree turn at low altitude. The right wing-tip touched the beach and damaged an aileron, although the pilot made a good recovery and landed safely at Malaga airport. The aircraft remained at Malaga under guard until it was eventually restored for display at the Museo del Aire at Cuartro Vientos in Madrid, painted in the colours of the Spanish Air Force, with the same '74-17' coding as applied to the 1944 vintage B-25D.

United Kingdom

Mitchells and other American types sent to Britain during World War II were ostensibly subject to the terms of the 11 March 1941 Lend-Lease bill, which stipulated that surviving aircraft should be returned or destroyed. When the time came in 1945 for this ruling to be complied with, there was such a world glut of largely unwanted military aircraft that the second option of the bill was usually exercised. In the case of the RAF Mitchells, they were scrapped after being struck off charge in 1946–47. This fate was not immediately shared by those that were returned to the US, or transferred to the Netherlands when No. 320 Sqn went home with its own aircraft. But the Mitchell squadrons in 2 Group quickly lost

The longest serving RAF Mitchell was FR209, which arrived in the UK as a B-25G-5 (42-64823). Converted to Mk II standard, it remained in service until September 1951, when it became a maintenance airframe at Dyce, Scotland. MAP

their aircraft even if they were not disbanded. However, a roomy medium bomber still had its uses, and several examples continued to serve after hostilities ceased. They included Mk II (FR209) which had previously flown with A&AEE, the Empire Central Flying School, and the Met Research Flight before becoming one of several Mitchells to end their days as instructional airframes, 6891M in this particular case. Not SOC until 13 October 1951, it was the longest surviving RAF Mitchell.

While the majority of RAF Mitchells had been SOC by June 1947, Mk III (KJ599) ex-Telecommunications Research Establishment, No. 226 Sqn and 2 Group Reconnaissance Flight, survived until 22 October that year, a date on which several other Mitchells, among the last examples in Britain, were retired.

Being expended in the interests of training fire fighters was the lot of another Mk III (KJ590) on 7 October 1947, after service with 13 OTU and the Fighter Command Communications Squadron at Northolt. A little earlier than that, on 11 September, a Mk III (HD373) had been relegated to fire training at RAE Farnborough, this Mitchell also having previously served at A&AEE.

Two Mitchells are currently on static display in the country's two leading aeronautical museums. As part of its Bomber Command exhibit, the RAF Museum at Hendon has a Mk III, alias B-25J-20 (44-29366) – an ex-*Catch 22* Mitchell.

The Imperial War Museum facility at Duxford has a B-25J-30 (44-31171) masquerading as a USMC PBJ-1J in the American Heritage Museum.

Uruguay

The Fuerza Aerea Uruguaya initially received eleven B-25Js, ten J-25s (44-30269; 30273; 30593; 30604; 30641; 30723; 30729; 30735; 30743; 30878) and a single J-30 (44-31190), under ARP in June 1950; FAU serial numbers, preceded by the type designation 'G3' (which was subsequently deleted) were allocated as 150–160. Three more B-25Js (s/n G3-161 to 163) and a single B-25H (G3-164) were delivered under MAP grant aid on 30 June 1954.

By September 1957 these fifteen machines had been reduced to eight on actual strength, but with MAP support the number was reportedly back to twelve by 31 December that year. Ten aircraft

remained active until 30 June 1958. One B-25J serialled G3-158, was preserved at the Museo Nacional de Aviacion.

USSR

Little data has come to light concerning the eventual fate of the survivors of the B-25s supplied to the Soviet Union under wartime Lend-Lease agreements. That some certainly survived into the postwar era was reflected in the fact that the international Air Standards Co-ordinating Committee codewords for Russian aircraft, first drawn up in 1954, saw fit to include the B-25 (on the grounds of blanket coverage of everything that flew with red stars, irrespective of its origins) as a 'Bank'. A reasonable assumption is that several VVS Mitchells saw much the same type of second-line air force service postwar as they did elsewhere. Some may well have been passed on to Warsaw Pact nations, although in common with the US, the USSR was awash with huge numbers of surplus aircraft from its own wartime production, and the obvious drawback of continuing to operate a Western type once the Iron Curtain descended was a dwindling stock of spares.

Venezuela

At least twenty-four surplus RCAF B-25Js were delivered under the ARP during the period 1948–52, fourteen arriving between August 1947 and April 1949 including: B-25J-25s 44-30302; 30411; 30433; 30467; 30614, 30619, 30626, 30627, 30631, 30638, 30678 and 30730 plus one J-30, 44-

31191. These aircraft were used to equip three Escuadrillas of the Fuerza Aereas Venezolana (FAV), namely Escuadrones de Bombardeo Nos 3 and 7, and subsequently No. 40 at Palo Negro. Ten remained flyable in 1952, when ten more were purchased from the US, nine further ex-RCAF aircraft being acquired in December 1963. Another five B-25s (almost certainly all J models) and a B-25H were delivered under the Reimbursable Aid Program prior to December 1957. That year nine Venezuelan B-25s were extensively overhauled by the L.B. Smith Aircraft Corporation at Miami.

Initially the Mitchells, in common with other Venezuelan military aircraft, were given a number-letter-number identity consisting of the 'plane-in-flight number, the Escadrilla letter and the Escadron number. Known B-25 serials are: 5A40, 6A40, 5B40 and 15B40 (B-25J-25 44-30812), all from the first (A) and second (B) Escadrilla of Esc de Bombardeo 40. This simple system, which may have been viewed as compromising security, was substituted by a seemingly random (apparently computer-generated) all-number system during the 1970s. 'New' B-25 identities included 0953, 1480, 3712, 3741, 3898, 4115, 4146, 4173, 5851 and 5880, the last being a B-25J-30 (44-86725). Mitchells survived in FAV service mainly in the transport role, at least until the early 1970s, when Esc 40 was combined with Esc 39 to form Grupo No. 13 and re-equipped with Canberras.

Two Mitchells were preserved: a B-25J-25 (44-30369) carrying FAV s/n 5B40 at Maracay; and a B-25J-5 (43-28096) s/n 4B40 at Teniente Vincentre Landaeta Gil Base at Barquisimeto.

Several smaller South American air arms were recipients of B-25s, among them Venezuela. A B-25J in that country's colours was at Howard AFB in the Canal Zone on 18 November 1966. Crow

Tokyo Raid Pilots and Aircraft

(In Order of Take-off from *Hornet*)

Crew 1: (B-25B 40-2344) 34th BS; Lt Col James H. Doolittle and Lt Richard E. Cole.

Crew 2: (B-25B 40-2292) 37th BS; Lt Travis Hoover and Lt William N. Fitzhugh.

Crew 3: (B-25B 40-2270/'Whiskey Pete') 95th BS; Lt Robert M. Gray and Lt Jacob E. Manch.

Crew 4: (B-25B 40-2282) 95th BS; Lt Everett W. Holstrom and Lt Lucian N. Youngblood.

Crew 5: (B-25B 40-2283) 95th BS; Capt David M. Jones and Lt Ross R. Wilder.

Crew 6: (B-25B 40-2298/'The Green Hornet') 95th BS; Lt Dean E. Hallmark and Lt Robert J. Meder.

Crew 7: (B-25B 40-2261/'The Ruptured Duck') 95th BS; Lt Ted W. Lawson and Lt Dean Davenport.

Crew 8: (B-25B 40-2242) 95th BS; Capt Edward J. York and Lt Robert G. Emmens.

Crew 9: (B-25B 40-2303/'The Whirling Dervish') 34th BS; Lt Harold F. Watson and Lt James N. Parker, Jr.

Crew 10: (B-25B 40-2250) 89th RS; Lt Richard O. Joyce and Lt J. Royden Stork.

Crew 11: (B-25B 40-2249/'Hari Carrier') 34th BS; Capt C. Ross Greening (89th RS) and Lt Kenneth E. Reddy.

Crew 12: (B-25B 40-2278) 37th BS; Lt William M. Bower and Lt Thadd H. Blanton.

Crew 13: (B-25B 40-2247) 37th BS; Lt Edgar E. McElroy and Lt Richard A. Knobloch.

Crew 14: (B-25B 40-2297) 89th RS; Maj John A. Hilger and Lt Jack A. Sims.

Crew 15: (B-25B 40-2267) 89th RS; Lt Donald G. Smith and Lt Griffith P. Williams.

Crew 16: (B-25B 40-2268/'Bat Out of Hell') 34th BS; Lt William G. Farrow and Lt Robert L. Hite.

Of these crews, 1, 2, 3, 4, 5, 6, 7, 8, 9 and 10 had targets in Tokyo, crews 11 and 12 having Yokohama, 13 Yokosuka, and 14, 15 and 16 Nagoya.

B-25 Squadrons

USAAF

Fifth Air Force
3rd Bomb Group 'The Grim Reapers'
    8th BS
    13th BS
    89th BS
    90th BS 'Pair O Dice'
22nd Bomb Group 'Ducimus – We Lead'
    2nd BS
    33rd BS
    408th BS
38th Bomb Group 'Sun Setters'
    69th BS
    71st BS 'The Wolf Pack'
    405th BS 'Green Dragons'
    822nd BS 'Black Panthers'
    823rd BS 'Tigers'
71st Tactical Reconnaissance Group 'Strafin' Saints'
    17th TRS 'Wreckoneers'
345th Bomb Group 'Air Apaches'
    498th BS 'Falcons'
    499th BS 'Bats Outa' Hell'
    500th BS 'Rough Raiders'
    501st BS 'Black Panthers'

Seventh Air Force
41st Bomb Group
    46th BS
    47th BS 'The Crow Flight'
    48th BS
    396th BS
    820th BS

Ninth/Twelfth Air Forces
12th Bomb Group 'The Earthquakers'
    81st BS 'Battering Rams'
    82nd BS 'Bulldogs'
    83rd BS
    434th BS 'Tornado'
310th Bomb Group
    379th BS 'Wetzel's Weasels'
    380th BS
    381st BS
    428th BS
19th Bomb Group 'Holzapple's Circus'
    437th BS
    438th BS
    439th BS
    440th BS
321st Bomb Group
    445th BS
    446th BS
    447th BS
    448th BS
340th Bomb Group
    486th BS
    487th BS
    488th BS
    489th BS

Tenth Air Force
341st Bomb Group 'Burma Bridge Busters'
    11th BS
    22nd BS 'Bombing Bull Dogs'
    490th BS
    491st BS 'Ringer Squadron'

Eleventh Air Force
28th Composite Group
    73rd BS
    77th BS
    406th BS

Thirteenth Air Force
42nd Bomb Group 'The Crusaders'
    69th BS
    70th BS
    100th BS
    390th BS

Fourteenth Air Force
1st Bomb Group, Chinese American Composite Wing
    1st BS
    2nd BS
    3rd BS
    4th BS

NB: The Tenth Air Force had the 12th BG assigned from February 1944 and the Fourteenth AAF had the 341st BG assigned from November 1944

US MARINE CORPS

VMB-413 'The Flying Nightmares'
VMB-423 'The Seahorse Marines'
VMB-433
VMB-443
VMB-611
VMB-612 'Cram's Rams'
VMB-613

ROYAL AIR FORCE

No. 98 Sqn 'Never Failing'
No. 180 Sqn 'Agreeably in manner, forcibly in act'
No. 226 Sqn 'For country not for self'
No. 305 (Ziemia Wielkopolska) Sqn
No. 320 Sqn 'We are guided by the mind of liberty'
No. 342 ('Lorraine' Sqn) 'Here we are'
No. 681 Sqn*
No. 684 Sqn 'Seeing though unseen'

* This unit, the 'parent' of No. 684, had no official badge or motto.

B-25 World War Two Unit Combat Debut Dates

1941

c. June: 17th BG (2nd AAF)*

1942

12 April: 3rd BG (5th AAF)
18 April: 17th BG/89th RS (Tokyo Raid)
5 May: No. 5 PRU (RAF)
3 June: 341st BG (10th AAF)
31 August: 12th BG (MEAF/9th/12th AAF)
15 September: 38th BG (5th AAF)
16 November: 42nd BG (70th BS only) (13th AAF)
2 December: 310th BG (12th AAF)
8 December: No. 180 Sqn RAF

1943

18 January: No. 18 (NEI) Sqn, RAAF
22 January: No. 98 Sqn, RAF
15 March: 321st BG (12th AAF)
19 April: 340th BG (12th AAF)
14 June: 42nd BG (13th AAF)
21 June: 345th BG (5th AAF)
17 August: No. 320 (Dutch) Sqn, RAF
17 August: No. 226 Sqn, RAF
4 November: 2nd BS, CACW (14th AAF)
5 November: No. 305 Sqn, RAF
27 November: 71st TRG (5th AAF)
29 December: 41st BG (7th AAF)

1944

12 February: 5218th Prov (1st ACG) 10th AAF
24 February: 1st BS, CACW (14th AAF)
14 March: VMB-413
16 April: 12 BG (10th AF)
14/15 May: VMB-423
27 June: No. 2 Sqn, RAAF**
13 August: VMB-443
August: VMB-433
4 November: 319th BG (12th AAF)***
13 November: VMB-612
17/18 November: VMB-611

1945

22 January: VMB-613
8 April: No. 342 (French) Sqn RAF****

NB: It should not be assumed that the above dates always represent a combat debut whilst flying the B-25; in particular, some squadrons began combat with other types while other groups were not fully equipped with B-25s. It should also be noted that in some theatres, in particular China, medium bombers were operated in squadron rather than group strength

NOTES
* The 17th was the first B-25 unit and began flying shipping patrols some ten months before the Tokyo raid – shown here as its first major combat mission.
** This was the date of No. 2's first big offensive operation, but it had previously flown some shipping patrols.
*** The 319th had been operational since November 1942 with B-26s.
**** No. 342 converted from Bostons, and had been operational since April 1943.

APPENDIX IV

B-25 Mitchells on British Contracts

LEND-LEASE MITCHELL I (B-25B)   CONTRACT AC-13258   REQUISITION BSC 4617

---

23 AIRCRAFT

21 arrived at destination by air: 1, FK178 for SBA crashed in US. 1 balance by air; 3 to UK: FK161, 162, 165

18 to Nassau (111 OTU) with SBA: FK163, 164, 166, 167, 169–177, 179–183; 1 on special duty, FK168 on loan to 45 Group RAFTC Canada; matching USAAF serials in irregular sequence

---

MITCHELL II (B-25C)   CONTRACT AC-16070, -27390   REQUISITION BSC 4617

---

162 AIRCRAFT

158 arrived at destinations by air: 3 crashed after export, FR368, 369 en route to UK, and FL209 en route to Nassau. 1 crashed in US, FR377 en route to Nassau from Montreal

129 to UK: FL181–183; FL185–186; FL188–198: FL201–207; FL210–218; FL671–696; FL698–701; FL703–709; FR367, 370, 373, 396, 397; FV900–916; FV918–939

1 to 45 Group RAFTC: FV917

10 to Nassau (111 OTU) with SBA: FR375. 376; FR378-384; FR393

18 to Nassau (111 OTU): FL180, 184, 187, 199, 200, 208, 697, 702; FR362-366; FR371, 372, 374, 394, 395

Matching AAF serials in irregular sequence

Mitchell II (B-25D) AC-16070 transferred under MAC (AIR) CASE No. 342; 2 transferred to India: 41-12659 and 41-12666 later became MA957 and MA956 respectively

---

MITCHELL II (B-25D)   CONTRACT AC-19341   REQUISITION BSC 4617

---

285 AIRCRAFT

278 arrived at destinations by air: 7 crashed after export to the UK: FV988, 990; FW138, 159, 165, 177, 243

208 to UK: FV940–945; FV947, 948, 950; FV955–986; FV989; FV991–993; FV995, 996, 998, 999; FW100–103; FW105–122; FW124–131; FW133–137; FW139–144; FW146; FW151–153; FW155–158; FW160–164; FW166–175; FW178; FW180–219; FW221–233; FW235, 236; FW238–242; FW244, 245; FW248–250; FW252–258; FW261–264; FW266, 268, 269, 271; FW275–277; HD302–307; HD316, 321, 328, 329, 336

7 to 45 Group RAFTC: FV987, 994; FW234, 247, 265, 267, 270

41 to 5 OTU, Canada: FW220, 237, 246, 251, 259, 260; FW272–274: FW278–280; HD310–315: HD317–320; HD322–326; HD331–335; HD337*– 345

* HD337 was delivered to Rockliffe by ATC for later delivery to 5 OTU by RCAF

22 to Nassau (111 OTU): FV946, 949; FV951–954; FV997; FW104, 123, 132, 145; FW147–150; FW154, 176, 179; HD308, 309, 327, 330

Matching AAF serials in irregular sequence

MITCHELL II (B-25D)   CONTRACT AC-19341   REQUISITION BSC 4617

---

29 AIRCRAFT

28 arrived in Canada for 5 OTU Vancouver: KL133–156; KL158–161

KL157 crashed in US

These aircraft were released from USAAF service

Matching USAAF serials shown in RCAF records as: 41-30548, -30596, -30637, -30758–30760; 42-30814, -87146, -87288, -87290, -87352, -87379, -87501; 43-3629, -3634, -3647, -3300–3304, -3307, -3308, -3310–3312, -3316, -3318

MITCHELL II (B-25C, D)   CONTRACT AC-27390-19341

---

64 AIRCRAFT FOR THE DUTCH UK PROJECT (NOT ON BRITISH ACCOUNT)

63 aircraft were allotted to Dutch units under RAF control: FR141-152; FR156-207

1 aircraft, FR148 crashed en route

Matching AAF serials in irregular sequence

MITCHELL (B-25G)   CONTRACT AC-27390   REQUISITION BSC 40540

---

2 AIRCRAFT

2 aircraft arrived in UK: FR208 42-64822; FR209 42-64823

Both used for experimental work by A&AEE

MITCHELL (B-25C, G, J)   TRANSFERRED UNDER MAC (AIR) CASE NO. 637

3 TRANSFERRED TO MAAF FROM USAAF STOCKS:
1 Mitchell II (B-25C) off AC-16070:   41-12877
1 Mitchell type (B-25G) off AC-27390:   42-65094
1 Mitchell III (B-25J) off AC-19341:   42-27774

MITCHELL III (B-25J)   CONTRACT AC-19341   REQUISITION BSC 4617

*266 AIRCRAFT
* Reduced by one, KJ686, transferred to USAAF under MAC (Air) Case No.637
8 crashed after export en route to UK: HD352; KJ584, 588, 695, 721, 722, 735, 751. 1 crashed in US, KJ756 for UK: 2 on special duty: KJ764, testing at Rockliffe; KJ771, RAF Del. Communications Flight
*254 ARRIVED AT DESTINATIONS BY AIR:
241 to UK: HD346–351; HD353–400; KJ561–579; KJ585–587; KJ589–640; KJ642–667; KJ672–685; KJ687–694; KJ696–715; KJ720; KJ723–734; KJ736–750; KJ752–763; KJ765–770
1 to RCAF Suffield, Canada: KJ641
12 to Nassau (111 OTU): KJ580–583; KJ668–671; KJ716–719
Matching AAF serials in irregular sequence

MITCHELL III (B-25J)   CONTRACT AC-19341   REQUISITION BSC 43199

*50 AIRCRAFT
*31 only delivered; subsequently transferred to USAAF in US
7 in UK flown back to US by RAF: KJ772, 773, 775, 776, 779, 784, 786
3 en route from US flown back by RAF: KJ774, 781, 783
12 returned to US from Montreal: KJ 777, 778, 780, 782, 785; KJ787–793
9 returned to US from 111 OTU Nassau: KJ795–799: KP308–311

RAF Serials	AAF Serials
KJ772–787	44-31145 to 31160 (16)
KJ788–800	44-31260 to 32172 (13)
KP308–311	44-31273 to 31276 (4)
KP312–328	44-31422 to 31438 (17)

NORTH AMERICAN MITCHELL I (B-25B)   CONTRACT AC-13258   REQUISITION BSC 4617

	RAF Serial	AAF Serial		RAF Serial	AAF Serial		RAF Serial	AAF Serial
1	FK161	40-2341	9	FK169	40-2315	17	FK177	40-2336
2	FK162	40-2340	10	FK170	40-2314	18	FK178	40-2330
3	FK163	40-2313	11	FK171	40-2319	19	FK179	40-2332
4	FK164	40-2288	12	FK172	40-2322	20	FK180	40-2327
5	FK165	40-2339	13	FK173	40-2317	21	FK181	40-2326
6	FK166	40-2328	14	FK174	40-2323	22	FK182	41-2343
7	FK167	40-2289	15	FK175	40-2320	23	FK183	41-2345
8	FK168	40-2338	16	FK176	40-2331			

NORTH AMERICAN MITCHELL II (B-25C)   CONTRACT AC-16070   REQUISITION BSC 4617

	RAF Serial	AAF Serial		RAF Serial	AAF Serial		RAF Serial	AAF Serial
1	FL164	41-12604	14	FL177	41-12660	27	FL190	41-12723
2	FL165	41-12597	15	FL178	41-12654	28	FL191	41-12728
3	FL166	41-12600	16	FL179	41-12727	29	FL192	41-12725
4	FL167	41-12601	17	FL180	41-12651	30	FL193	41-12650
5	FL168	41-12560	18	FL181	41-12645	31	FL194	41-12658
6	FL169	41-12598	19	FL182	41-12575	32	FL195	41-12755
7	FL170	41-12599	20	FL183	41-12570	33	FL196	41-12756
8	FL171	41-12603	21	FL184	41-12652	34	FL197	41-12757
9	FL172	41-12592	22	FL185	41-12653	35	FL198	41-12754
10	FL173	41-12595	23	FL186	41-12726	36	FL199	41-12647
11	FL174	41-12655	24	FL187	41-12722	37	FL200	41-12719
12	FL175	41-12536	25	FL188	41-12669	38	FL201	41-12577
13	FL176	41-12656	26	FL189	41-12724	39	FL202	41-12566

NORTH AMERICAN MITCHELL II (B-25C)   CONTRACT AC-16070   REQUISITION BSC 4617

	RAF Serial	AAF Serial		RAF Serial	AAF Serial		RAF Serial	AAF Serial
40	FL203	41-12581	68	FL683	41-12764	96	FR363	41-13107
41	FL204	41-12624	69	FL684	41-12771	97	FR364	41-13108
42	FL205	41-12641	70	FL685	41-12701	98	FR365	41-13109
43	FL206	41-12648	71	FL686	41-12572	99	FR366	41-13110
44	FL207	41-12649	72	FL687	41-12689	100	FR367	41-13111
45	FL208	41-12665	73	FL688	41-12690	101	FR368	41-13112
46	FL209	41-12667	74	FL689	41-12678	102	FR369	41-13113
47	FL210	41-12718	75	FL690	41-12773	103	FR370	41-13114
48	FL211	41-12716	76	FL691	41-12688	104	FR371	41-13115
49	FL212	41-12717	77	FL692	41-12767	105	FR372	41-13116
50	FL213	41-12720	78	FL693	41-12770	106	FR373	41-13117
51	FL214	41-12721	79	FL694	41-12702	107	FR374	41-13133
52	FL215	41-12802	80	FL695	41-12703	108	FR375	41-13134
53	FL216	41-12803	81	FL696	41-12704	109	FR376	41-13135
54	FL217	41-12804	82	FL697	41-12759	110	FR377	41-13136
55	FL218	41-12806	83	FL698	41-12801	111	FR378	41-13137
56	FL671	41-12758	84	FL699	41-12731	112	FR379	41-13138
57	FL672	41-12761	85	FL700	41-12729	113	FR380	41-13139
58	FL673	41-12762	86	FL701	41-12807	114	FR381	41-13140
59	FL674	41-12763	87	FL702	41-12730	115	FR382	41-13141
60	FL675	41-12587	88	FL703	41-12805	116	FR383	41-13142
61	FL676	41-12657	89	FL704	41-12808	117	FR384	41-13143
62	FL677	41-12766	90	FL705	41-12545	118	FR393	41-13144
63	FL678	41-12765	91	FL706	41-12687	119	FR394	41-12834
64	FL679	41-12760	92	FL707	41-12571	120	FR395	41-12836
65	FL680	41-12772	93	FL708	41-12578	121	FR396	41-12837
66	FL681	41-12769	94	FL709	41-12685	122	FR397	41-12838
67	FL682	41-12768	95	FR362	41-13106			

NORTH AMERICAN MITCHELL II (B-25C)   CONTRACT AC-27390   REQUISITION BSC 4617

RAF Serial	AAF Serial
FV900–919	42-64622–64641
FV920–939	42-64733–64752

NORTH AMERICAN MITCHELL II (B-25D)   CONTRACT AC-19341   REQUISITION BSC 4617

	RAF Serial	AAF Serial		RAF Serial	AAF Serial		RAF Serial	AAF Serial
1	FV940	41-30414	20	FV959	41-30802	39	FV978	41-30845
2	FV941	41-30419	21	FV960	41-30803	40	FV979	42-87113
3	FV942	41-30424	22	FV961	41-30805	41	FV980	42-87114
4	FV943	41-30431	23	FV962	41-30817	42	FV981	42-87115
5	FV944	41-30432	24	FV963	41-30819	43	FV982	42-87116
6	FV945	41-30462	25	FV964	41-30820	44	FV983	42-87117
7	FV946	41-30471	26	FV965	41-30821	45	FV984	42-87118
8	FV947	41-30476	27	FV966	41-30824	46	FV985	41-30660
9	FV948	41-30477	28	FV967	41-30826	47	FV986	42-87140
10	FV949	41-30478	29	FV968	41-30828	48	FV987	42-87149
11	FV950	41-30486	30	FV969	41-30831	49	FV988	42-87150
12	FV951	41-30490	31	FV970	41-30832	50	FV989	42-87154
13	FV952	41-30493	32	FV971	41-30834	51	FV990	42-87155
14	FV953	41-30495	33	FV972	41-30835	52	FV991	42-87156
15	FV954	41-30498	34	FV973	41-30837	53	FV992	42-87206
16	FV955	41-30784	35	FV974	41-30841	54	FV993	42-87207
17	FV956	41-30785	36	FV975	41-30842	55	FV994	42-87208
18	FV957	41-30793	37	FV976	41-30843	56	FV995	42-87209
19	FV958	41-30801	38	FV977	41-30844	57	FV996	42-87210

NORTH AMERICAN MITCHELL II (B-25D) CONTRACT AC-19341 REQUISITION BSC 4617

	RAF Serial	AAF Serial		RAF Serial	AAF Serial		RAF Serial	AAF Serial
58	FV997	42-87211	115	FW154	42-87505	172	FW211	43-3477
59	FV998	42-87212	116	FW155	42-87506	173	FW212	43-3478
60	FV999	42-87213	117	FW156	42-87507	174	FW213	43-3480
61	FW100	42-87214	118	FW157	42-87509	175	FW214	43-3482
62	FW101	42-87215	119	FW158	42-87510	176	FW215	43-3531
63	FW102	42-87216	120	FW159	42-87511	177	FW216	43-3536
64	FW103	42-87217	121	FW160	42-87596	178	FW217	43-3537
65	FW104	42-87218	122	FW161	42-87600	179	FW218	43-3538
66	FW105	42-87219	123	FW162	42-87601	180	FW219	43-3539
67	FW106	42-87220	124	FW163	42-87602	181	FW220	43-3540
68	FW107	42-87221	125	FW164	42-87603	182	FW221	43-3541
69	FW108	42-87223	126	FW165	42-87604	183	FW222	43-3542
70	FW109	42-87224	127	FW166	42-87605	184	FW223	43-3543
71	FW110	42-87225	128	FW167	42-87606	185	FW224	43-3544
72	FW111	42-87226	129	FW168	42-87609	186	FW225	43-3545
73	FW112	42-87227	130	FW169	42-87610	187	FW226	43-3546
74	FW113	42-87228	131	FW170	42-87611	188	FW227	43-3547
75	FW114	42-87229	132	FW171	42-87612	189	FW228	43-3548
76	FW115	42-87325	133	FW172	43-3280	190	FW229	43-3549
77	FW116	42-87326	134	FW173	43-3281	191	FW230	43-3550
78	FW117	42-87328	135	FW174	43-3283	192	FW231	43-3551
79	FW118	42-87329	136	FW175	43-3284	193	FW232	43-3552
80	FW119	42-87331	137	FW176	43-3285	194	FW233	43-3553
81	FW120	42-87334	138	FW177	43-3286	195	FW234	43-3554
82	FW121	42-87340	139	FW178	43-3287	196	FW235	43-3555
83	FW122	42-87342	140	FW179	43-3289	197	FW236	43-3556
84	FW123	42-87344	141	FW180	43-3386	198	FW237	43-3557
85	FW124	42-87345	142	FW181	43-3387	199	FW238	43-3558
86	FW125	42-87346	143	FW182	43-3388	200	FW239	43-3559
87	FW126	42-87347	144	FW183	43-3389	201	FW240	43-3560
88	FW127	42-87348	145	FW184	43-3390	202	FW241	43-3561
89	FW128	42-87410	146	FW185	43-3391	203	FW242	43-3562
90	FW129	42-87411	147	FW186	43-3392	204	FW243	43-3563
91	FW130	42-87412	148	FW187	43-3393	205	FW244	43-3564
92	FW131	42-87415	149	FW188	43-3394	206	FW245	43-3565
93	FW132	42-87417	150	FW189	43-3395	207	FW246	43-3566
94	FW133	42-87420	151	FW190	43-3398	208	FW247	43-3567
95	FW134	42-87421	152	FW191	43-3399	209	FW248	43-3568
96	FW135	42-87422	153	FW192	43-3458	210	FW249	43-3569
97	FW136	42-87423	154	FW193	43-3459	211	FW250	43-3683
98	FW137	42-87425	155	FW194	43-3460	212	FW251	43-3686
99	FW138	42-87427	156	FW195	43-3461	213	FW252	43-3687
100	FW139	42-87428	157	FW196	43-3462	214	FW253	43-3688
101	FW140	42-87431	158	FW197	43-3463	215	FW254	43-3689
102	FW141	42-87432	159	FW198	43-3464	216	FW255	43-3690
103	FW142	42-87433	160	FW199	43-3465	217	FW256	43-3691
104	FW143	42-87436	161	FW200	43-3466	218	FW257	43-3692
105	FW144	42-87453	162	FW201	43-3467	219	FW258	43-3693
106	FW145	42-87471	163	FW202	43-3468	220	FW259	43-3694
107	FW145	42-87472	164	FW203	43-3469	221	FW260	43-3695
108	FW147	42-87473	165	FW204	43-3470	222	FW261	43-3696
109	FW148	42-87474	166	FW205	43-3471	223	FW262	43-3697
110	FW149	42-87476	167	FW206	43-3472	224	FW263	43-3698
111	FW150	42-87477	168	FW207	43-3473	225	FW264	43-3699
112	FW151	42-87495	169	FW208	43-3474	226	FW265	43-3700
113	FW152	42-87503	170	FW209	43-3475	227	FW266	43-3701
114	FW153	42-87504	171	FW210	43-3476	228	FW267	43-3703

NORTH AMERICAN MITCHELL II (B-25D)   CONTRACT AC-19341   REQUISITION BSC 4617

	RAF Serial	AAF Serial		RAF Serial	AAF Serial		RAF Serial	AAF Serial
229	FW268	43-3704	248	HD308	43-3762	267	HD327	43-3798
230	FW269	43-3705	249	HD309	43-3763	268	HD328	43-3799
231	FW270	43-3707	250	HD310	43-3764	269	HD329	43-3800
232	FW271	43-3708	251	HD311	43-3779	270	HD330	43-3801
233	FW272	43-3710	252	HD312	43-3780	271	HD331	43-3844
234	FW273	43-3712	253	HD313	43-3781	272	HD332	43-3845
235	FW274	43-3718	254	HD314	43-3782	273	HD333	43-3846
236	FW275	43-3720	255	HD315	43-3783	274	HD334	43-3847
237	FW276	43-3723	256	HD316	43-3784	275	HD335	43-3848
238	FW277	43-3750	257	HD317	43-3785	276	HD336	43-3849
239	FW278	43-3751	258	HD318	43-3786	277	HD337	43-3850
240	FW279	43-3752	259	HD319	43-3787	278	HD338	43-3851
241	FW280	43-3753	260	HD320	43-3788	279	HD339	43-3852
242	HD302	43-3756	261	HD321	43-3792	280	HD340	43-3853
243	HD303	43-3757	262	HD322	43-3793	281	HD341	43-3854
244	HD304	43-3758	263	HD323	43-3794	282	HD342	43-3855
245	HD305	43-3759	264	HD324	43-3795	283	HD343	43-3856
246	HD306	43-3760	265	HD325	43-3796	284	HD344	43-3857
247	HD307	43-3761	266	HD326	43-3797	285	HD345	43-3858

NORTH AMERICAN MITCHELL II (B-25C, D) FOR DUTCH UK PROJECT (NOT ON BRITISH ACCOUNT)   CONTRACT AC-27390, -19341

	RAF Serial	AAF Serial		RAF Serial	AAF Serial		RAF Serial	AAF Serial
1	FR141	42-32272	23	FR166	42-32352	45	FR188	42-87262
2	FR142	42-33373	24	FR167	42-32353	46	FR189	42-87263
3	FR143	42-32274	25	FR168	42-32513	47	FR190	42-87264
4	FR144	42-32275	26	FR169	42-32514	48	FR191	42-87265
5	FR145	42-32276	27	FR170	42-32515	49	FR192	41-30791
6	FR146	42-32277	28	FR171	42-32516	50	FR193	41-30792
7	FR147	42-32280	29	FR172	42-64688	51	FR194	41-30794
8	FR148	42-32282	30	FR173	42-64689	52	FR195	41-30795
9	FR149	42-32283	31	FR174	42-64690	53	FR196	41-30796
10	FR150	42-32284	32	FR175	42-64691	54	FR197	41-30800
11	FR151	42-32285	33	FR176	42-64786	55	FR198	41-30838
12	FR152	42-32286	34	FR177	42-64787	56	FR199	42-87261
13	FR156	42-32342	35	FR178	42-64788	57	FR200	42-87317
14	FR157	42-32343	36	FR179	42-64789	58	FR201	42-87322
15	FR158	42-32344	37	FR180	41-30720	59	FR202	42-87323
16	FR159	42-32345	38	FR181	41-30721	60	FR203	42-87339
17	FR160	42-32346	39	FR182	41-30724	61	FR204	42-87358
18	FR161	42-32347	40	FR183	41-30725	62	FR205	42-87381
19	FR162	42-32348	41	FR184	41-30804	63	FR206	42-87405
20	FR163	42-32349	42	FR185	41-30812	64	FR207	42-87408
21	FR164	42-32350	43	FR186	42-87132			
22	FR165	42-32351	44	FR187	42-87133			

RAF serials FR153, 154, 155 were wasted

NORTH AMERICAN MITCHELL IIII (B-25J)   CONTRACT AC-19341   REQUISITION BSC 4617

	RAF Serial	AAF Serial		RAF Serial	AAF Serial		RAF Serial	AAF Serial
1	HD346	43-3874	9	HD354	43-27760	17	HD362	43-27990
2	HD347	43-27753	10	HD355	43-27761	18	HD363	43-27991
3	HD348	43-27754	11	HD356	43-27762	19	HD364	43-27992
4	HD349	43-27755	12	HD357	43-27763	20	HD365	43-27993
5	HD350	43-27756	13	HD358	43-27764	21	HD366	43-27994
6	HD351	43-27757	14	HD359	43-27765	22	HD367	43-27995
7	HD352	43-27758	15	HD360	43-27766	23	HD368	43-27996
8	HD353	43-27759	16	HD361	43-27767	24	HD369	43-27997

NORTH AMERICAN MITCHELL IIII (B-25J)   CONTRACT AC-27390, -19341   REQUISITION BSC 4617

	RAF Serial	AAF Serial		RAF Serial	AAF Serial		RAF Serial	AAF Serial
25	HD370	43-27998	82	KJ587	44-28953	139	KJ644	44-29376
26	HD371	43-27999	83	KJ588	44-28954	140	KJ645	44-29377
27	HD372	43-28000	84	KJ589	44-28955	141	KJ646	44-29378
28	HD373	43-28001	85	KJ590	44-28956	142	KJ647	44-29379
29	HD374	43-28002	86	KJ591	44-28957	143	KJ648	44-29380
30	HD375	43-28003	87	KJ592	44-28958	144	KJ649	44-29381
31	HD376	43-28004	88	KJ593	44-28959	145	KJ650	44-29382
32	HD377	43-28005	89	KJ594	44-28963	146	KJ651	44-29383
33	HD378	43-28006	90	KJ595	44-28964	147	KJ652	44-29384
34	HD379	43-28007	91	KJ596	44-28965	148	KJ653	44-29385
35	HD380	43-28008	92	KJ597	44-28966	149	KJ654	44-29386
36	HD381	43-35969	93	KJ598	44-28967	150	KJ655	44-29387
37	HD382	43-35970	94	KJ599	44-28968	151	KJ656	44-29388
38	HD383	43-35971	95	KJ600	44-28969	152	KJ657	44-29389
39	HD384	44-28726	96	KJ601	44-28970	153	KJ658	44-29396
40	HD385	44-28727	97	KJ602	44-28971	154	KJ659	44-29397
41	HD386	44-28728	98	KJ603	44-28972	155	KJ660	44-29398
42	HD387	44-28729	99	KJ604	44-29079	156	KJ661	44-29399
43	HD388	44-28730	100	KJ605	44-29080	157	KJ662	44-29400
44	HD389	44-28731	101	KJ606	44-29081	158	KJ663	44-29401
45	HD390	44-28732	102	KJ607	44-29082	159	KJ664	44-29485
46	HD391	44-28733	103	KJ608	44-29083	160	KJ665	44-29486
47	HD392	44-28734	104	KJ609	44-29084	161	KJ666	44-29487
48	HD393	44-28735	105	KJ610	44-29085	162	KJ667	44-29488
49	HD394	44-28736	106	KJ611	44-29086	163	KJ668	44-29489
50	HD395	44-28740	107	KJ612	44-29087	164	KJ669	44-29490
51	HD396	44-28741	108	KJ613	44-29088	165	KJ670	44-29491
52	HD397	44-28742	109	KJ614	44-29092	166	KJ671	44-29492
53	HD398	44-28743	110	KJ615	44-29093	167	KJ672	44-29630
54	HD399	44-28744	111	KJ616	44-29094	168	KJ673	44-29631
55	HD400	44-28745	112	KJ617	44-29095	169	KJ674	44-29632
56	KJ149	44-28746	113	KJ618	44-29096	170	KJ675	44-29633
57	KJ562	44-28747	114	KJ619	44-29097	171	KJ676	44-29634
58	KJ563	44-28748	115	KJ620	44-29098	172	KJ677	44-29635
59	KJ564	44-28752	116	KJ621	44-29099	173	KJ678	44-29636
60	KJ565	44-28753	117	KJ622	44-29100	174	KJ679	44-29637
61	KJ566	44-28754	118	KJ623	44-29101	175	KJ680	44-29638
62	KJ567	44-28755	119	KJ624	44-29149	176	KJ681	44-29639
63	KJ568	44-28756	120	KJ625	44-29150	177	KJ682	44-29640
64	KJ569	44-28757	121	KJ626	44-29151	178	KJ683	44-29641
65	KJ570	44-28758	122	KJ627	44-29152	179	KJ684	44-29642
66	KJ571	44-28759	123	KJ628	44-29153	180	KJ685	44-29643
67	KJ572	44-28760	124	KJ629	44-29158	181	KJ686	44-29644
68	KJ573	44-28761	125	KJ630	44-29159	182	KJ687	44-29645
69	KJ574	44-28762	126	KJ631	44-29160	183	KJ688	44-29646
70	KJ575	44-28766	127	KJ632	44-29161	184	KJ689	44-29647
71	KJ576	44-28767	128	KJ633	44-29162	185	KJ690	44-29648
72	KJ577	44-28768	129	KJ634	44-29163	186	KJ691	44-29649
73	KJ578	44-28769	130	KJ635	44-29164	187	KJ692	44-29678
74	KJ579	44-28770	131	KJ636	44-29165	188	KJ693	44-29679
75	KJ580	44-28771	132	KJ637	44-29166	189	KJ694	44-29680
76	KJ581	44-28772	133	KJ638	44-29171	190	KJ695	44-29681
77	KJ582	44-28773	134	KJ639	44-29172	191	KJ696	44-29682
78	KJ583	44-28774	135	KJ640	44-29173	192	KJ697	44-29683
79	KJ584	44-28950	136	KJ641	44-29174	193	KJ698	44-29684
80	KJ585	44-28951	137	KJ642	44-29175	194	KJ699	44-29685
81	KJ586	44-28952	138	KJ643	44-29176	195	KJ700	44-29686

NORTH AMERICAN MITCHELL IIII (B-25J)   CONTRACT AC-27390, -19341   REQUISITION BSC 4617

	RAF Serial	AAF Serial		RAF Serial	AAF Serial		RAF Serial	AAF Serial
196	KJ701	44-29687	220	KJ725	44-29851	244	KJ749	44-29982
197	KJ702	44-29688	221	KJ726	44-29852	245	KJ750	44-29983
198	KJ703	44-29689	222	KJ727	44-29853	246	KJ751	44-29984
199	KJ704	44-29690	223	KJ728	44-29854	247	KJ752	44-30193
200	KJ705	44-29691	224	KJ729	44-29855	248	KJ753	44-30194
201	KJ706	44-29692	225	KJ730	44-29856	249	KJ754	44-30195
202	KJ707	44-29693	226	KJ731	44-29857	250	KJ755	44-30196
203	KJ708	44-29694	227	KJ732	44-29954	251	KJ756	44-30197
204	KJ709	44-29695	228	KJ733	44-29955	252	KJ757	44-30198
205	KJ710	44-29696	229	KJ734	44-29956	253	KJ758	44-30199
206	KJ711	44-29697	230	KJ735	44-29957	254	KJ759	44-30200
207	KJ712	44-29826	231	KJ736	44-29958	255	KJ760	44-30201
208	KJ713	44-29827	232	KJ737	44-29959	256	KJ761	44-30214
209	KJ714	44-29828	233	KJ738	44-29960	257	KJ762	44-30215
210	KJ715	44-29829	234	KJ739	44-29961	258	KJ763	44-30216
211	KJ716	44-29830	235	KJ740	44-29962	259	KJ764	44-30217
212	KJ717	44-29831	236	KJ741	44-29963	260	KJ765	44-30218
213	KJ718	44-29832	237	KJ742	44-29964	261	KJ766	44-30219
214	KJ719	44-29833	238	KJ743	44-29965	262	KJ767	44-30220
215	KJ720	44-29846	239	KJ744	44-29966	263	KJ768	44-30221
216	KJ721	44-29847	240	KJ745	44-29967	264	KJ769	44-30222
217	KJ722	44-29848	241	KJ746	44-29979	265	KJ770	44-30223
218	KJ723	44-29849	242	KJ747	44-29980	266	KJ771	44-30224
219	KJ724	44-29850	243	KJ748	44-29981			

Total B-25 allocated British serial numbers: 881

Notes

CHAPTER 1

1. Wright Field report on the NA-40 crash.
2. Correspondence with Norm Avery; copies of letters to Jim Sanders and Rudy Stolz.

CHAPTER 2

1. Avery, Norman L. *The Magnificent Medium.*
2. Reed, Boardman, C. 'North American Bombers I have Known and Flown', *Journal of the American Aviation Historical Society*, winter 1992.

CHAPTER 3

1. *Air Force Combat Units and Combat Squadrons of the Air Force, WWII.*
2. Friedman, N. *US Naval Weapons.*

CHAPTER 4

1. Alcorn, John *The Grim Reapers.*

CHAPTER 5

1. Lawson, Ted W. *Thirty Seconds over Tokyo.*

CHAPTER 6

1. G. J. Casius, letter: *Journal of the American Aviation Historical Society,* winter 1992.

CHAPTER 8

1. Lawson, Ted W. *Thirty Seconds over Tokyo.*
2. Guest, Carl-Fredrik, Kalevi K. and Stenman, K. *Red Stars.*
3. *Red Stars.*

CHAPTER 9

1. Prien, J. *Geschichte des Jagdgeschwaders 77, teil 3.*

CHAPTER 10

1. *2 Group War Diary.*
2. Eyton-Jones, A. *Day Bomber.*

CHAPTER 11

The following sources were used during the preparation of this chapter:
Van Wagner, R.D. *Any Place, Any Time, Any Where.*
Rust, Ken *10th Air Force Story.*
Chinnery, P. D. *Any Place, Any Time.*
Baisdden, C. *Flying Tiger to Air Commando.*
Journal of the American Aviation Historical Society, Vol. 13 No. 3.

Bibliography

Avery, N.L. (1992), *B-25 Mitchell: The Magnificent Medium*, Phalanx Publishing Co.

Barsden, C. (1999), *Flying Tiger to Air Commando*, Schiffer Military History

Birdsall, S. (1977), *Flying Buccaneers*, Doubleday & Co.

Bowyer, M.J.F. (1979), *2 Group RAF 1936–45*, Faber

Bowman, M.W. (1995), *Low Level from Swanton*, Air Research

Bowman, M.W. (1997), *The Reich Intruders*, Patrick Stephens Ltd

Brookes, A.J. (1975), *Photo Reconnaissance*, Ian Allan

Bywater, M. (1993), *B-25s Target Kyushu (41st BG)*, B-25 Press

Chinnery, P.D. (1994), *Any Time, Any Place*, Airlife

Chorley, W.R. (1996), *RAF Bomber Command Losses 1943*, Midland Counties Publications

Cohen, S. (1998), *Destination: Tokyo (Doolittle Raid)*, Pictorial Histories Publishing Co.

Cynk, J.B. (1998), *The Polish Air Force at War 1943–45*, Schiffer Military History

Daniels, K. (1998), *China Bombers (Chinese-American Composite Wing)*, Specialty Press

Drendel, L. (1997), *Walk Around B-25 Mitchell (No 12)*, Squadron/Signal Publications

Eyton-Jones, A. (1998), *Day Bomber*, Sutton Publishing

Ferguson, M.B. (1991), *Bats Outa Hell Over Biak*, Max B. Ferguson

Freeman, R.A. (1973), *North American B-25 1941–45 (Camouflage and Markings 22)*, Ducimus Books

Glines, C.V. (1964), *Doolittle's Tokyo Raiders*, D. Van Nostrand

Hair, C.A. (1987), *The Saga of '54 and More (310th BG)*, Robson Topographics

Hayward, D.K. (1997), *Eagles, Bulldogs and Tigers (22nd BS)*, 22nd BS Association

Hickey, L.J. (1984), *Warpath Across the Pacific (345th BG)*, International Research and Publishing

Honeycutt, T.D. (1989), *Cram's Rams (VMB-612)*, T.D. Honeycutt

Johnsen, F.A. (1997), *B-25 Mitchell (WarbirdTech Srs 12)*, Specialty Press

Kinsey, B. (1999), *B-25 Mitchell in Detail (D & S 60)*, Squadron/Signal Publications

Leaf, E. (1997), *Above All Unseen*, Patrick Stephens Ltd

Mason, T. (1998), *The Secret Years*, Hikoki Publications

McCue, P.M. (1992), *Dunsfold – Surrey's Most Secret Airfield*, Air Research

McDowell, E.R. (1978), *B-25 Mitchell in Action (No 34)*, Squadron/Signal Publications

McDowell, E.R. (1971), *NAA B-25A/J Mitchell (Aircam 22)*, Osprey Publications

Mendenhall, C.A. (1981), *Deadly Duo (B-25 & B-26 in WWII)*, Specialty Press

Middlebrook, G. (1998), *Air Combat at 20 Feet*, Garrett Middlebrook

Mizrahi, J.V. (1965), *North American B-25 Mitchell*, Challenge Publications

Oyster, H.E. & E.M. (1976 & 1987), *The 319th in Action*, H.E. & E.M. Oyster

Pace, S. (1994), *B-25 Mitchell (Warbird History Srs)*, Motorbooks International

Pearcy, A. (1996), *Lend-Lease Aircraft in WWII*, Airlife

Perry, R.S.B. (1987), *The Bombers of MAGSZAM (VMB-611)*, R.S.B. Perry

Pope, S. (1993), *Swanton Morley (Airfield Focus 9)*, GMS Enterprises

Scutts, J.C. (1983), *B-25 Mitchell at War*, Ian Allan

Scutts, J.C. (1993), *Marine Mitchells in WWII*, Phalanx Publishing Co

Shores, C.F. (1970), *2nd Tactical Air Force*, Osprey Publications

Smith, P.T. (1980), *The Pacific Crusaders (42nd BG)*, Mojave Books

Stahura, B. (1998), *Earthquakers: 12th Bomb Group*, Turner Publishers

Thomas, G.J. (1999), *Eyes for the Phoenix (Allied PR in SEAC)*, Hikoki Publications

Thompson, S.A. (1997), *B-25 Mitchell in Civil Service*, Aero Vintage Books

Tornij, G.J. (1999), *Der Nederlandse "Mitchells"*, G.J. Tornij

Van Der Kop, H. (1985), *The Flying Dutchman*, Patrick Stephens Ltd

Van Wagner, R.D. (1998), *Any Place, Any Time, Any Where*, Schiffer Military History

Wagner, R. (1965), *The North American B-25A to G Mitchell (Profile 59)*, Profile Publications Ltd

Whittle, K. (1994), *An Electrician Goes to War*, Air Forces' Publishing Service

Wiley, K.S. (1994), *The Strafin' Saints (71st TRG)*, K.S. Wiley

Wilson, R.E. (1947), *The Earthquakers*, Dammeier Printing Co.

Wilson, S. (1992), *Boston, Mitchell and Liberator in RAAF Service*, Aerospace Publications Pty

Index